Producer & International Distributor
eBookPro Publishing
www.ebook-pro.com

Master of Influence
Kave Shafran

Copyright © 2021 Kave Shafran

All rights reserved; No parts of this book may be reproduced or transmitted in any form or by any means, electronic or mechanical, including photocopying, recording, taping, or by any information retrieval system, without the permission, in writing, of the author.

Cover Photograph by Avi Ohayon, Government Press Office
Translation from the Hebrew by Kaeren Fish

Contact: kaveshafran@gmail.com
ISBN 9798718337815

With all my love to
to Shacharit, Shaked and Ruth

MASTER *OF* INFLUENCE

Benjamin Netanyahu's 10 Secrets of
Power, Rhetoric & Charisma

KAVE SHAFRAN

Contents

Foreword	11
1. Molding the Image: Photo-politics	19
2. His Tongue is His Weapon: Words	49
3. Words That Create Pictures: Imagery	83
4. Mind Games: Neuro-Politics	109
5. Collective Memory: Symbols	141
6. The Leftist Label: Propaganda	169
7. We Are All Riffraff: Covenant	197
8. Controlling the Medium: Communications	231
9. Without Words: Body Language	265
10. Measuring Votes in Centimeters: Bio-Politics	293
The last secret	313
Acknowledgements	321

"In this scorching country, words should be our shade."

— Yehuda Amichai

FOREWORD

There was a moment when Netanyahu was in flames right in front of me, and I stood swatting him. The circumstances surrounding that moment are instructive, revealing some of his covert and sophisticated techniques for influencing the public.

It was a Sunday morning in 2005. I was standing on a small landing on the stairway in the Prime Minister's Office. The perfect spot for an ambush. The government ministers would have to pass by me their way to the cabinet meeting, and the Army Radio microphone would be ready and waiting for them. I had retreated into this narrow corner because of the television crews, who demanded my removal from the top floor since they "needed a clean frame," as they explained to an overly-accommodating official in the Prime Minister's Office. Following an altercation, the official and I reached a compromise: I would take up my position in this corner of the stairwell so that the TV frame would be clear of my microphone, but I would still have access to information. It was from this corner that I observed what followed.

Minister of Finance Benjamin Netanyahu was climbing the stairs. I wanted his response to Prime Minister Ariel Sharon's decision not to extend IDF Chief of Staff Moshe Ya'alon's term in office. I pointed the microphone like a weapon in front of him and asked, "Minister of Finance, Mr. Netanyahu, we are broadcasting live on Army Radio. Is this a political dismissal?"

Netanyahu considered his response, cleared his throat, and

adopted his official tone reserved for speaking on radio and television. "Lieutenant-General Ya'alon is an excellent Chief of Staff ..." he began, thereby aligning himself with the Chief of Staff who was opposed to the Disengagement Plan (and distancing himself politically from the Prime Minister's decision) while still managing to remain somewhat opaque and taking care not to aim his criticism at Sharon directly. Netanyahu was walking a fine line: he was a member of the Disengagement government and had voted in favor of the plan, but left himself room to claim that he was against it. As he conveyed his double message to the public via my microphone, something else was going on that caught my attention; I smelled smoke.

Something was burning. I looked around. Everyone looked calm. Perhaps the antiquated Army Radio tape recorder was burning the white plastic cassette whose wheels were turning as it recorded the Minister of Finance's response? I put my nose closer to it and sniffed; it wasn't the tape. At that moment I noticed Netanyahu's flushed face and realized to my astonishment that the smoke was coming from the Minister of Finance himself. Embarrassed, he was beginning to stammer; his face was turning red. The smoke was emanating from the tiny gap between the collar of his white shirt and his dark suit.

Netanyahu was enveloped in a haze. Another moment went by. The smoke was becoming thicker and darker; it could no longer be ignored. His improvised speech in support of Ya'alon was interrupted when the fire made its appearance. A small, red flame began climbing up his jacket, as though emerging from Netanyahu's heart and threatening to consume him. In another second, his jacket was in flames. Right in front of me, in the Prime Minister's Office, Benjamin Netanyahu stood imprisoned, flustered and flushed in his burning suit.

The microphone was still on. I shouted into it, "Mr. Netanyahu, you're on fire! Mr. Netanyahu, you're burning!" Isaac Herzog, Minister of Welfare in Sharon's government, was making his way up the stairs, also headed for the weekly cabinet meeting. Herzog heard my shouting and leaped up the stairs towards us. As he approached, I held the microphone in one hand while using the other to swat the chest of the Minister of Finance, trying to prevent the fire from spreading. Herzog shouted, "Bibi – throw it away; throw it away!" Together we pulled the jacket off Netanyahu's shoulders. The starched white shirt below was also singed. I blew on it, making sure that it wasn't burning. The expensive jacket, still aflame, was cast in a heap on the floor. The Minister of Welfare and I stomped on it to put out the fire. The smoke seemed to be coming from the pocket. The fire was dying out, but the smell of smoke was still heavy in the air.

The shouting and tumult drew the attention of the General Security Service personnel stationed at the other end of the upper floor. Some guards from the VIP Protection Unit who had been standing at the entrance to the "Aquarium" approached: was this a security-related incident? The Aquarium is where the Prime Minister sits; the most highly secured and most sensitive spot in the entire country. It's called the Aquarium because of the glass doors surrounding it. The GSS men made sure that there was no fire in the secure area. "Everything's fine," Netanyahu reassured them. "Nothing happened." With one hand he waved away the guards; with the other he lifted his charred jacket off the floor. The guards returned to their station at the entrance to the Aquarium, where Prime Minister Sharon would emerge a few minutes later.

The Minister of Finance had headed that morning to the cabinet meeting via a stairway that was usually free of journalists. He had no inkling of the new arrangement in which I had been allocated the recessed corner, and as he walked, he lit up a cigar. When he realized that he was facing the press, he quickly pinched its end and shoved it into the breast pocket of his jacket. He didn't want to be caught enjoying a cigar on his way to a cabinet meeting. His jacket pocket also held the text of the speech he intended to deliver during the meeting. Having disposed of the cigar, Netanyahu stopped in front of me in the hope of earning some points with Right-wing voters who were furious at him for not abandoning the Disengagement government. During the brief interview, a tiny spark from the end of the cigar, which had not been fully extinguished, began to singe the papers in his pocket. The papers began to burn and the spark turned into a flame. Fortunately, there were no photographers on the scene to capture the moment, or the public would have been treated to an endless loop of Netanyahu going up in flames.

"We have a fiery Minister of Finance," quipped his spokesman in response to the many journalists who called in the wake of my broadcast on Army Radio. Netanyahu wisely chose to write off the incident as an inconsequential anecdote.

This scene sheds some light on the secrets of Netanyahu's charisma. The essence of what happened is that he wanted to avoid being seen by the public as someone who was smoking expensive cigars while imposing budgetary cuts. Years later, when Netanyahu later found himself under police interrogation, the investigators claimed that the fact that the boxes of cigars that he received as gifts arrived at his official residence in sealed, opaque packets was proof that he knew that what he was doing wasn't legal. As reported in *Haaretz*, Bibi explained that the rationale was a matter of publicity rather than criminality. He concealed the cigars for fear that they would harm his image. "You're asking me, 'Why did you put the cigars in packets?' Just because! Not because there's something wrong, but because one doesn't want this to get out, see?"

Bibi's behavior raises a question about us, the public, and the way we make our decisions. Everyone knows that he smokes, but he hides his cigars, believing that the sight of them has a negative influence on voters. Do we elect a Prime Minister on the basis of a picture of cigars? Is that how we judge people and leaders? Is a hairstyle really important? Does height really matter? Netanyahu believes that the answer is yes. These details are critical. He may be right.

∎∎∎

At times it seems as though Netanyahu and the Prime Minister's Office have become inseparably and eternally intertwined. When Netanyahu assumed the premiership for the seventh time, he became the longest-serving Prime Minister in Israel's history, surpassing even the legendary Ben-Gurion who occupied the position for 13 years. A survey conducted in 2016 included him among the ten most highly-admired figures in the US. For 17 consecutive years, *Forbes* magazine has rated him as one of the most powerful leaders in the world. Each time he delivers a victory speech after an election, he is hailed incredulously as a "magician"; his adoring fans, invoking the reverent chant traditionally reserved for the biblical King David, cheer in ecstasy (sometimes in tears), "Bibi, King of Israel, lives on forever."

He has sat in the Oval Office more times than most world leaders. No American president can be apathetic towards him, whether in the positive or negative sense. President Biden once signed a picture that he gave him, with the words, "Bibi I don't agree with a damn thing you say but I love you." Former US President Clinton commented, "Never underestimate Netanyahu. He's highly intelligent."

He is a topic of conversation among world leaders. After his summit with Russian president Vladimir Putin, former US President Trump disclosed that "Putin is a great admirer of Netanyahu." At a G20 summit in 2011, in what was meant to be a private exchange, French president Nicolas Sarkozy told US President Barack Obama, "I cannot bear Netanyahu; he's a liar." Obama responded, "You're tired of him; what about me? I have to deal with him every day!" It turned out that their microphones had been turned on and their conversation was overheard by a group of journalists.

You can love him or hate him, but you can't ignore him. And while some call it magic while others insist that it's deception, the consensus amongst the international community, leaders and public alike, is that he is one of the greatest orators of our times. His rhetorical gift is not just an aspect of his leadership, it is its essence. He has been referred to as oozing charisma, a media wizard, Israel's presenter, a genius, a brilliant orator, a public diplomacy machine, an outstanding campaigner, and more. But how did he become what he is? His inordinate success is matched only by the mystery surrounding it. How does he do it? How does keep such a large swath of the Israeli public in thrall to him? What is his recipe? What are the secrets of his charisma? These are the questions that we will seek to address.

∎∎∎

This book is based on systematic research and over twenty years of experience in the media, starting with my military service as the political correspondent for Army Radio. After many years as a radio and television anchor, I founded a company for media production and training which, among other activities, trains leading figures in the public sector and the economy to speak in front of audiences and cameras. I have also trained and prepared IDF General Staff senior commanders for media appearances in routine and emergency situations.

This book took me three years to write, and it turned into a long journey of inquiry, research, and new and surprising revelations about Netanyahu. The journey included background discussions with dozens of people who have worked with Netanyahu as well as picking my way through archives, obtaining classified documents that have never been published, and thousands of pages of drafts prepared for every speech he ever delivered, including comments, deletions, and correspondence between him and his media advisors. Examples drawn from these files – the notes that Netanyahu held during his media interviews and his public appearances – are scattered throughout the book. They offer a peek into Netanyahu's private chambers.

■■■

Over the years, Netanyahu has worked fastidiously and painstakingly to construct a most impressive public image. It is only rarely that one catches a glimpse of the various "cigars" that are concealed underneath – the secrets that he usually manages to keep out of the picture. The reality, devoid of visual processing and perceptual mediation, is hidden from view. We will look at some of these secrets, but our main focus will be the rigorous and meticulous efforts invested by the longest-serving Prime Minister of Israel in creating and maintaining his façade.

In addition to the communication techniques, rhetoric, and body language of Netanyahu himself, we will also look at examples drawn from other charismatic and influential leaders. Our journey will be accompanied by references to contemporary studies drawn from various disciplines which shed light on Netanyahu's techniques from a scientific perspective.

The attempt to understand Netanyahu is at the same time an attempt to understand ourselves: the human mind, the political reality, the history of the State of Israel, Israeli society, and the country's media. It is an attempt to make sense of human beings, human conduct, and our decision-making processes; what influences us, and how overt and covert messages are conveyed to us with a slant toward influencing our consciousness and behavior, both at the polling booth and in everyday life.

1.
MOLDING THE IMAGE
PHOTO-POLITICS

"He's here, he's arrived," one of the photographers reported breathlessly. "Where is he?" his colleagues looked around quickly, afraid of missing the historic picture that they had been sent to capture. "Where's Bibi?" Dozens of journalists were pacing to and fro on the second floor of the Jerusalem District Court building, trying to obtain more information via their phones, or to peep through the windows, but to no avail. Only when they quietened down slightly, did their incredulous ears catch the echo of Netanyahu's voice, floating down from the floor above them. The third floor had been cordoned off as a "sterile area" with no entry, for security reasons. It was from there that Netanyahu addressed the public on this fateful morning.

It was the opening of Netanyahu's trial, in the summer of 2020. The requests by his legal team to exempt him from appearing in person at the opening session had been rejected, and he was required to present himself for a reading of the charges against him, including breach of trust, accepting bribes, and fraud. But the defendant was determined to combat this impression of his status in the public mind. His main objective, on this day, was to forestall a photograph of himself on the defendants' bench.

For security reasons, the Shin Bet's bodyguard unit for public figures had set up a large, opaque tent that the Prime Minister's limousine drove into, so no one could photograph him arriving at the court. Under cover of the tent, his staff had also smuggled in the official wooden podium with its lettering in gold. These were the props that the defendant wanted for the opening of his trial. A week earlier, the Courts Administration had naively agreed to a request, presented as a technical security matter, to assign an empty courtroom on the floor above the one where his trial was to begin, where he could wait with his security detail until the session began. And thus, while the journalists and cameramen awaited Netanyahu on the second floor, members of the private broadcast company that Netanyahu's office had hired entered the heavily-secured court building via the tent, and set up their cameras in the empty courtroom above.

"Step over, join in the frame," Bibi's media advisor urged those present, and they obliged: The Ministers of Finance, Education, and Transport, and even the Minister of Internal Security, responsible for the Israeli Police which had carried out the investigation. Along with additional MKs, they had all arrived, wearing their protective COVID face masks, to stand as a silent backdrop behind the Prime Minister's podium. Once the frame had been created to the satisfaction of the media advisor, and received his approval, the filming company hired by the Prime Minister began its broadcast to all the media channels.

Netanyahu approached the podium, removed his face mask, and began his address, "Citizens of Israel, on trial today is the desire to thwart the will of the people. The attempt to topple me, and the Right-wing camp." While the journalists sat waiting below, Bibi was already speaking in the courtroom that had been set up according to his specifications, in front of cameras that he was controlling, behind the podium that reinforced his status, with a battery of ministers flanking him, and with not a single media correspondent in sight. "I stand here today as Prime Minister, proudly and with my head held high," he continued, and proceeded to attack the left, the police, and the media.

Only after he had created precisely the picture and the impression that he wanted, did Netanyahu go down to the second floor where the journalists and the judges were waiting for him. When he entered the courtroom where his trial was actually going to take place, he took care to keep his back to the cameras and engaged in a whispered consultation with his lawyers, who leaned in, partially obscuring him. At the request of the ushers, all those present took their seats, but Bibi and his lawyers remained standing, careful to avoid any visual record of Netanyahu sitting on the defendants' bench. After the judges were seated, and the frustrated cameramen were forced to leave the courtroom without having captured a picture of the Prime Minister facing the judges, Netanyahu glanced to the back of the hall to make sure that the doors had closed behind the last of them. Only then did he allow himself to sit down on the low bench in front of the three robed justices who would decide whether or not he would be sent to jail.

■■■

"Release the tape!" the Israeli ambassador to the UN raised his voice, speaking into the receiver of the red telephone that connected him to the IDF headquarters in Tel Aviv. "What's going on here is a disaster; a disaster!"

The ambassador was Netanyahu, and the footage that he wanted the IDF to release was hard to watch. He wanted the American public to see it all the same. The "disaster" going on was the public relations beating that Israel was taking on the nightly news broadcasts,

PERMANENT
REPRESENTATIVE OF ISRAEL
TO THE UNITED NATIONS

800 SECOND AVENUE
NEW YORK, N.Y. 10017

21 March 1988

The Honorable
Edward I. Koch
New York, New York 10007

Dear Ed,

    Congratulations on your Newsday article. It is precisely in times like these that Israel discovers who its true friends are.

    I have already tried prying the CNN tape our of our Defense Ministry. The officials there tell me that releasing the tape would create real security problems which outweigh the public relations benefits.

    Given the disaster we see every day on the nightly news, I'm not sure this was a fully informed decision. In any case, I've forwarded your request to Yitzhak Rabin in the hope that he might have second thoughts.

Sincerely,

Benjamin Netanyahu
Ambassador

focusing on IDF activities in Lebanon. The footage showed the cruel execution by Hamas of an Arab youngster accused of collaborating with Israel. The Jewish mayor of New York, Ed Koch, had gotten wind of the tape and was urging Netanyahu, "You get that tape to me. I'll show it. It's the only way people here will understand that there are no human rights on their side."

The security establishment refused to release the tape, for fear of exposing intelligence sources. Koch, who was friendly with Netanyahu, sent him an official letter, "I want to show it to American journalists and news editors. It will force them to change their attitude towards Israel."

Netanyahu wrote back that Israel is not used to explaining itself in pictures. He apologized, "I have already tried prying the CNN tape out of our Defense Ministry. The officials there tell me that releasing the tape would create real security problems which outweigh the public relations benefits.

"Given the disaster we see every day on the nightly news, I'm not sure this was a fully informed decision. In any case, I've forwarded your request to Yitzhak Rabin in the hope that he might have second thoughts."

Rabin, the Minister of Defense, refused Netanyahu's request. The tape was kept under wraps. Thirty years later, Netanyahu ascended the podium at the UN with pictures of Palestinians executed by Hamas, exposing intelligence information painstakingly gathered over time, and used it to turn world opinion against Iran, Hezbollah, and Hamas. For him it has always been clear that when it comes to public diplomacy, a photograph is the heart of the matter.

Bibi's TED Talk

"The Presentation" is the name of a PowerPoint presentation that sits on the Prime Minister's computer. It is classified as highly confidential. One might say that in the Netanyahu era, it is the foundation of Israel's image. Netanyahu himself gives the presentation, and each time he does so, his staff remark to each other that the Prime Minister is "in the middle of his TED Talk." It is indeed a show.

The two people responsible for creating and maintaining the presentation are constantly at war with each other. One is Yarden Vatikai, head of the National Information Directorate for Public Diplomacy in the Prime Minister's Office. The other is a senior Intelligence Corps officer, Col. A., who sits in the Aquarium and enters Netanyahu's office at least twice a day with new military intelligence material.

Condensed within the presentation are Israel's positions on all key diplomacy issues, backed up with high-quality intelligence material. The major part of the presentation relates to Israel's security, and is updated almost on a daily basis. It includes maps, photographs, video clips, and data: maps of Iranian entrenchment in Syria, sketches of weapon-smuggling routes, copies of documents from the Iranian nuclear archive, information about terror organizations' sources of funding and the secret contacts facilitating payments; satellite photos of secret bases in Arab countries, and incriminating footage of Hamas terrorists using civilians in Gaza as human shields. In the days leading up to Netanyahu's meeting with a foreign leader or one of his diplomatic visits abroad, the Mossad is asked for up-to-date materials concerning terror activities in the relevant country.

At Netanyahu's request, every detail is tailored to the leader he will be meeting with, down to units of measurement following the system used in his or her country (miles or kilometers). Netanyahu's instructions for preparing the presentation could be taught in a school for public speaking. One of the rules is defined by Vatikai thusly: A short, clear message, formulated in few words, and if it is expressed visually, it must appear in a single illustration (i.e., one picture, one map).

When the public diplomacy strategist and the intelligence officer meet to update the presentation, the former wants to expose intelligence materials, while the latter wants to keep them secret. The Prime Minister's military secretary and his staff find it greatly beneficial when messages in the presentation are simple, diluted, general, and brief. That way they can "round the corners" of the data in such a way as to maintain the secrecy of intelligence sources. Thus the two sides usually manage, after some haggling, to reach a compromise, although it is not unusual for them to take the conflict to Netanyahu for his decision. He reviews each and every slide, and asks for changes ranging from graphic design to language formulation.

Netanyahu has taken this presentation to meetings with almost every world leader he has met with, including Modi, Trump, and Putin. With certain leaders, he takes care to remove some of the slides for fear of them being leaked.

Of all the subjects addressed in the presentation, it is of special importance to Netanyahu to share information about terror attacks around the world that have been prevented with the help of the Israeli intelligence community. The foreign leaders he meets are constantly amazed by data about attacks that were imminent and would have taken place in their own countries had it not been for Israel's intelligence.

When Col. A. is fearful of possible exposure of agents, Netanyahu reminds him, "We're a state that has intelligence; not an intelligence service with a state." On several occasions Netanyahu concludes preparatory meetings for a foreign visit or visitor with encouragement to Vatikai and Col. A. to continue disagreeing. "It's a healthy argument," he tells them, reminding them how proud he is of this confidential presentation which, in his view, is one of Israel's greatest public diplomacy achievements.

Bibi's advocacy, both inward and outward, revolves around security and threats. He instructed the Intelligence Directorate, the General Security Services, and the Mossad to start sharing classified intelligence with the leaders of Arab countries concerning terror threats against them. At Netanyahu's orders, special emissaries of the National Security Council and of the Mossad have been sent with inside information about threats to leaders in Africa, Jordan, Egypt and the Gulf States, following which, members of terror organizations in those countries were arrested before they could carry out their plans. Mahmoud Abbas, too, owes his continued leadership of the Palestinian Authority to Netanyahu, who passed on information about a Hamas coup that was nearing actualization.

The approach of using intelligence for public diplomacy purposes and to strengthen political ties received a boost when Yossi Cohen, one of Netanyahu's closest confidantes, was appointed director of the Mossad. Since he assumed office in 2016, intelligence information has been used not only for overt diplomatic activity but also – and principally – to develop secret ties with foreign countries, including those that maintain no official contact with Israel.

In recent years, then, Jerusalem's ties with other world capitals are based not only on economic issues, but also on Israel's status as a world leader in espionage and cyberdefense as well as in innovative weaponry, and on Netanyahu's decision to share intelligence with foreign leaders.

Speaking Words, Drawing Pictures

In his youth, Bibi enjoyed sketching and drawing. With his mother's encouragement, he thought about turning his hobby into a profession, and when he completed his military service, he started studying architecture. "I always enjoyed drawing. I always wanted to build a lot of buildings. I even dreamed of planning new cities," he recounts. In his free time – and as the years have gone by, there has been less and less of it – Netanyahu also used to draw portraits.

During government meetings, he often pulls out a pen and paper and starts sketching. Sometimes, especially when Jewish festivals are approaching, he uploads simple line drawings in blue pen onto his Facebook page. Although his occupational focus shifted from architecture to business to politics and statesmanship, it would be fair to say that drawing remains one of his primary means of expression.

For years, Netanyahu has drawn and shown pictures in front of the camera. The climax of his speech before the 67th United Nations General Assembly in 2012, was the moment when he drew a line with a red marker on a cartoon graphic of a bomb, indicating the last possible point at which the Iranian nuclear project could be halted. That unforgettable moment was not a one-time event. Giving his message visual expression is integral to Netanyahu's method of persuasion.

He engages in this method frequently, showing pictures and diagrams. A partial list of the visual aids that he has used in his annual address at the UN include maps of Auschwitz, pictures of Hamas fighters using children as human shields, fragments of a rocket fired towards Israel, books, aerial shots of concealed missile sites in Lebanon, and various text documents. In other appearances he has used maps, diagrams, graphs, coins, posters, Palestinian incitement materials, HAZMAT masks, and more. In front of the camera he is like a magician on stage, drawing the accessory he needs from his bag at exactly the right moment to create the desired optical illusion.

28 | Photo-politics

The timing of the appearance of these accessories during an appearance is determined in advance with great care. In the draft of a speech, we find "stage directions" that he writes for himself in parentheses. Next to the words, "But in another twenty years, this is what they will remember," is his note to himself: (Lift blue book).

This parenthetical instruction comes in the context of an attack on the media for its focus on failures and failings. Netanyahu spends several minutes explaining how in twenty years all these media scandals will be forgotten, while what remains will be his achievements and those of his government, all documented in the blue book that he now "spontaneously" displays.

Netanyahu scripts his appearances with great care. At the press conference that he called a few days before the 2019 elections (later described as "dramatic"), the page he was reading from indicated where he should pause. At that exact moment, his spokesman Jonathan Urich entered, dressed like a stagehand in jeans, t-shirt and sneakers, in stark contrast to the formal backdrop and Israeli flags, and set up a large wooden easel, placing on it a map of the Jordan Valley. Only when this visual aid was in place did Netanyahu continue, "This will be the security belt," pointing at the colored map and promising to annex the Jordan Valley if he was elected for a fifth term.

It was during the Gulf War that Netanyahu first made a stage prop part of a public appearance. He was Deputy Foreign Minister at the time, and was in the middle of an interview with CNN when the siren warning of incoming missiles sounded. The Deputy Foreign Minister promptly donned his HAZMAT mask and continued with the interview. It was a brilliant move. He later recounted that his inspiration for using props came from Chaim Herzog who "made a tremendous impression" when he stood at the UN podium in 1975 and tore up a copy of the infamous resolution equating Zionism with racism.

A journalist who attended closed meetings between the Prime Minister and various media representatives describes Netanyahu doodling: He drew a caricature of himself with a long nose, and explained, 'If you read *Haaretz* or *Yedioth Ahronoth*, that's how I'm portrayed: constantly under pressure, trying to survive. If you watch *Eretz Nehederet*,'[1] he continued, drawing another caricature, 'it's almost the same image: a smooth-talking charlatan, a crook, always looking over his shoulder.' Pointing to the second one he added wryly, 'I prefer this caricature, because I look thinner.'

■■■

On the stage were some large objects covered with black, opaque fabric. As Netanyahu spoke, live, in front of the cameras, he approached the amorphous props, paused from a few seconds, and then theatrically drew back the black fabric, exposing his "rabbit": a bookshelf lined with files, alongside a cupboard whose doors were covered with shiny silver-colored CDs that had been pasted one next to the other. "This is the Iranian nuclear archive …" the Prime Minister declared in his authoritative baritone. The photographers quickly snapped photos capturing this dramatic exposure of Iranian nuclear secrets. What information did the CDs contain? Not a single piece of information. What documents did the files hold? None at all; they were completely empty. The files and CDs had been purchased shortly before the Prime Minister's performance at a nearby office supply store. The aide who had been dispatched to buy them had been instructed to include a few red and green files among the black ones, creating an allusion to the Iranian flag. The image was seen around the world.

The media – both in Israel and abroad – broadcast the moment over and over, at the same time criticizing the misleading nature of the presentation. Why had Netanyahu not sufficed with a display of

---

1   A popular TV satirical sketch comedy show.

a few genuine documents? Why did he insist on his staff purchasing props that he would reveal from behind a dark curtain?

Pictures and actions are two of the most important principles for appearing in public. When a lecturer talks and also performs some action, he makes his message visual and more compelling. It is more persuasive, more illustrative, and more interesting. We generally do not remember words in the long term, but a picture becomes etched in our memory. And this universal principle, applied daily at universities, in classrooms, in TED talks and even in kindergarten settings, applies to politics, too. A picture is worth a thousand words.

Netanyahu's illustrative ability is such that even when no tangible props are available – no files, pictures, or other visual aids – he still manages to turn a verbal message into a visual one. He does so using his hands. He talks, and "draws" his words in the air, in pantomime fashion. His hands perform gestures that illustrate the words he is saying.

"They were so excited, they were in tears. They simply wept. Wept. There's no other word for it," Netanyahu said in one of his speeches, describing the joy of a group of people he had met. As he said this, he raised his hands and placed his index fingers under his eyes, describing a slow trickle of tears down his cheeks.

■■■

When he describes economic growth, his hands always make an upward movement. When he talks about constricting terror activity, his hands draw closer to each other. When the subject is resilience in the economic and security realms, he folds his arms. Increasing budgets – he spreads his arms wide. Palestinians shooting missiles – his hand depicts an arc in the air. The engine driving the economy – his upraised hand moves slowly from right to left, as though pushing the air forward.

A memorable moment took place during his first term in office, when he described the measures he was taking to strengthen the economy as comprising in three stages: halting the decline, turning it around, and takeoff. The great loops his hands made in the air as he described the process from the podium were widely viewed as a dramatic exaggeration, and provided ample fodder for satirical skits.

When one watches Bibi's hand movements as he talks, it looks natural – "That's just how he talks." But this is not so: his gestures are an acquired habit, pre-planned, and deliberate, the outcome of conscientious effort and practice, as demonstrated by Dr. Baruch Leshem in his study of Netanyahu's marketing techniques.

Netanyahu's grooming of his image goes as far as meticulous planning of hand gestures that he will make at certain points in a speech. For one of his early speeches, delivered to the Likud Committee in the early 90s, Netanyahu's notes include the line, "There are five points that were presented to the Committee by my colleague, Arik Sharon…" Next to this line he wrote in parentheses, (Count the items using fingers and fist). When he spoke, Netanyahu lifted his hand and started counting the messages off his fingers one by one. He concluded by closing his hand into a fist, and raised his voice to convey the main message.

When he films clips in his office, too, he repeats the text a few times and plans the appropriate gestures: a hand chopping the air for emphasis; a fist to signify power; spreading hands to show good will and success. When he presents the text and forgets one of the gestures he had planned, he orders the cameramen, "Take two." Netanyahu is his own stage director, and a very demanding one. The erstwhile architect doesn't suffice with what his audience hears from him; he invests meticulous effort in what they see. It is not unusual for a one-minute clip to take more than an hour to film.

Camera-Ready

The Swiss policeman turned off the siren and the revolving light before starting the car. As he climbed the winding mountain road, he clenched the steering with both hands, squinting to see better. The Israeli driver in the car behind him resisted the temptation to glance at the beautiful, snow-covered valley spread out below for fear of plummeting down. The General Security Services bodyguard bringing up the rear in the third car was likewise riveted to the road. It was a very small convoy trying to keep a low profile.

The middle car held Netanyahu and his wife, wearing gloves and ski jackets – his in black, hers in blue. They permitted themselves to take in the view, relying on the concentration of all three drivers snaking their way up the narrow road leading to the Klosters Ski Resort, the starting point for their vertical descent. No one in the Prime Minister's convoy was aware of the van following them. Its driver, Yossi, wearing a peak cap, was keeping a safe distance. When the convoy came to a stop, the van stopped too and photographic and video equipment was unloaded. As the VIP couple reached the skiing site, they found themselves facing a Channel 2 camera team.

Later on, Yossi Mulla, the Channel 2 news producer, recounted, "I was pretty much on my own that day, since most of the media hadn't yet arrived in Davos. I was standing next to the hotel when I saw the bodyguards coming to try on ski clothes. I asked what they had taken, and was told that they had requested gear for six or seven people. It clearly wasn't meant for their personal use. I started looking for the resort where they would be skiing. We had a car, and we drove after the bodyguards. The moment they saw that we were there and were ready to start filming …" That's when the negotiations began.

Netanyahu, who at the time was struggling against the recession and had introduced an economic policy that made life difficult for the weaker sectors of the population, feared the prospect of photos showing him skiing with his wife in the Alps. He was afraid of the decadent image, but even more so, he feared footage of himself trying to ski and falling on his backside, his skis dangling in the air, with the caption, "The Fall of the Prime Minister."

Netanyahu approach Mulla and his team, who were standing near the cable car. "I'm asking you not to film," he begged Mulla, "give us a bit of privacy." "Not a chance," the producer replied. After a moment's thought, Netanyahu said, "Let's agree that you'll film just part of it – the easy slope – and for the rest of the descent you'll allow Sara and me some privacy." Mulla refused once again. He was finding it hard enough to resist documenting the dialogue that he was having with the Prime Minister dressed in his ski suit.

Netanyahu came up with an alternative offer, "Yossi, right? Look, I haven't skied in ages; let me practice a bit, and then you can start filming, okay?" The Prime Minister placed a friendly hand on the producer's shoulder, but Mulla didn't agree to this request either, suspecting that Netanyahu would evade the cameras by skiing to the other side of the mountain. "First let me take some pictures; after I have something, we'll go back to the hotel."

Netanyahu had no choice. He took his skis and squeezed into the cable car with Sara and two bodyguards, heading for the peak. The photographer started snapping, zooming in and zooming out, and then the Prime Minister started skiing. First slow and wobbly, but then, reclaiming the skill he had acquired in his childhood when he visited his relatives in Belgium, with greater speed and confidence, causing his bodyguards to chase after him. Not only did he not fall; he was an expert skier.

But with increased speed came a mistake: on one of his turns, the Prime Minister approached too close to another skier, causing him to fall. Netanyahu himself did not fall. The photographs showed the bodyguards splitting up – some stopping to offer help to the skier who turned out to be unhurt; the others following on the heels of the Israeli Prime Minister who skis better than any of his predecessors – and also knows better than any of them how to control the image and the frame.

Corona-Optics

In his notes for a speech that he delivered three weeks before the national election in 1999 (which he lost),Netanyahu wrote: (Note: Joke about Ehud Barak's election propaganda). When he reached the relevant point in the speech, Netanyahu shifted his posture, leaned towards the audience and changed his tone as though the thought had just occurred to him, and then, with seeming casualness, shared the joke that he had planned with such care, "Sometimes, when I'm driving, I pass by my rival's campaign billboards, showing him in white overalls on the wing of the hijacked plane, holding a gun. I actually took part in that operation too, but I didn't have time to pose for photographs ..."[2]

Inspired by Barak's campaign photo, Bibi later created his own version. At the height of the COVID pandemic in 2020, he had cameras stationed at exactly the same spot at Ben Gurion airport, and was photographed alongside the yellow DHL freightplanethat brought the first batch of vaccines to Israel. Addressing the public as the door of the plane opened, revealing its cargo, he declared it one of his "most moving moments" as Prime Minister, "I worked very hard on it, it's

---

[2] Sabena flight 571, hijacked on May 8, 1972. A rescue operation was mounted by 16 members of the General Staff Reconnaissance Unit, led by Ehud Barak and including Netanyahu. The soldiers were all camouflaged as flight technicians.

a tremendous achievement. It's a great celebration for the State of Israel." He gestured towards the crates of vaccines, giving the cameramen enough time to capture the ideal frame. The hijacking this time involved not a plane, but rather the photograph of him standing on the plane's gangway, which promptly became part of his 2021 election campaign.

One image that was important to Netanyahu to compose in such a way that it would be long remembered was that of Gilad Shalit's return to Israel. There was much that rested on this shot, in view of the thousands of terrorist prisoners who were freed in the exchange, and who were photographed showing a "V" for victory with their hands. Shalit's father, Noam, was asked to wait at a distance of a few dozen meters so that Netanyahu could be the first to welcome Shalit's son. Throughout the flight, the doctor on board had performed physical and cognitive tests on the weakened Shalit, almost to the point of his collapse. "You remember how to salute?" the doctor asked him. Gilad remembered, and demonstrated several times. When the helicopter landed and the door opened, all the photographers were gathered in a fenced-in area. The Prime Minister approached and Gilad marched forward, halted, and saluted Netanyahu. This was followed by a hug, and then Minister of Defense Barak was introduced into the frame, forcing Major-General Orna Barbivai, head of the Manpower Directorate, to shift over to the side.

■■■

The unforgettable, iconic picture of Chief of Staff Yitzhak Rabin, Minister of Defense Moshe Dayan, and Central Region Commander Uzi Narkiss entering the Old City of Jerusalem during the Six-Day War carries a lesson that has been internalized by all Israeli politicians. The photograph was staged by Dayan, deliberately excluding Prime Minister Eshkol. Behind the three victorious generals, another officer is visible, facing away from the camera. That officer is Maj.-Gen. Rehavam Ze'evi ("Gandhi"), who turned for a moment to instruct his soldiers to move out of the frame. No politician wants to make the same mistake and be caught with his back to the camera or out of the picture. In coalition negotiations, ministers haggle over the right to sit next to the Prime Minister so that their faces will appear in the press photographs of government meetings every Sunday. The seat to the right of the Prime Minister is a photographic bonanza.

Every frame of Netanyahu is carefully designed: the flags, the backdrop, the colors (his tie is always either a shade of light blue, or red for a more energetic and powerful look), the bookcase is behind him, the angle is always the same (eye-level with the camera pointed slightly downward, to conceal the double-chin; under no circumstances is Netanyahu to be photographed from below face level); slightly to the right, since that is his more photogenic side (hiding the small scar over his lip); others flank him (he is always at the center of the photograph); the lighting is right (not too bright). At every event that Netanyahu attends, a string is tied around the area where the photographers will be standing. An event at a hotel in Washington was once delayed because Netanyahu demanded that the cameras be relocated, so that he could be photographed from a more flattering angle. When necessary, his spokesman asks that an online photograph be replaced. There are no casual photographs.

Family photographs are likewise part of the photo-politics strategy. Surveys conducted after the "hot tape affair," where he admitted to cheating on Sara (his third wife), indicated a need to work on Netanyahu's family image. He and Sara duly showed themselves in family settings, including their sitting room in the Prime Minister's residence on a quiet evening, or the Prime Minister collecting his children from kindergarten. The press accused them of cynical exploitation of their children for political purposes. Bibi and Sara accused the press in return of invading their privacy.

There are also photos that Netanyahu would like to forget. For example, pictures showing him chumming up to Arafat. Netanyahu wasn't the first Prime Minister to flinch at having his photograph taken with Arafat. A moment before signing the Oslo Accords on the White House lawn, Yitzhak Rabin was seized with panic. He had agreed to a handshake, but with the condition: No hug. President Clinton promised to honor this compromise, and later on he recounted how he stood between Rabin and Arafat, applauding, but ready to step forward in an instant to serve as a physical barrier if necessary and prevent any attempt on Arafat's part to draw close to Rabin.

In his first term as Prime Minister, having promised a "secure peace," Netanyahu was eager to show photos of his successful contacts with the Palestinians, and had not made a point of avoiding physical contact with Arafat. At a White House ceremony, he strode quickly towards the hesitant Arafat, shook his hand energetically, and placed his other hand in a friendly gesture on Arafat's arm. When his hand moved up to the Palestinian Authority President's shoulder, Arafat placed a friendly hand on the Israeli Prime Minister's chest as they stood looking into each other's eyes. Not exactly an embrace, but something very close to it. Later on, Netanyahu's supporters tried to have the photos removed from his Wikipedia entry, while his opponents disseminated the same photos in their campaigns. Pictures can be weapons.

■■■

In 2012, Netanyahu and Putin met in Jerusalem. Shortly before the Russian president's visit, Netanyahu had broken his leg and it was in a cast. Mr. Security was going about on crutches, and that didn't look good next to Iron-Man Putin. Netanyahu had to find a way to receive the Russian president without allowing the photographers to record for all eternity his temporary handicap. The solution: contrary to all rules of protocol, he welcomed Putin from a seated position at a table, and even shook his hand without standing up, so that his broken leg would remain concealed throughout by the tablecloth.

A disturbing example of engineering a picture was the case of Franklin Roosevelt, the US President during the Second World War, who was partially paralyzed as a result of polio. He went about the White House confined to a wheelchair, but the public that had elected him had no idea of his disability. Roosevelt planned every photograph with great care, making sure that his wheelchair would not be displayed. He was a great leader, but one who lived in fear of his handicap being exposed. He feared that his fellow citizens would view it as a weakness. Even the photograph of the victorious Roosevelt with Stalin and Churchill, at the end of the war, shows the three of them sitting.

The historical righting of Roosevelt's misleading of the American people came relatively recently. The Franklin Delano Roosevelt Memorial in Washington was dedicated in 1997 replete with a statue of the president who beat the Nazis. The statue originally depicted him sitting with a cloak obscuring his chair. In the wake of public pressure, the sculptor later added castors to the back of the chair so as to make it a symbolic wheelchair. The National Organization on Disability raised funds and, in January 2001, had an additional statue installed near the entrance to the memorial, showing Roosevelt sitting openly in a wheelchair similar to the one he used, with two large front wheels. History was rewritten to reflect reality as it was.

■■■

Some historical moments are not photographed. An example is the Prime Minister climbing out of the back of a pita delivery truck. Netanyahu needed to undergo a medical procedure just before the 2015 elections. It was a simple procedure with no special risk involved, but the very idea of a photograph of Netanyahu in a hospital was regarded by his media team as something to be avoided at all costs. Physical weakness projects an image of weak leadership. And thus, the Director of the General Security Services received instructions to smuggle Netanyahu to the hospital in a camouflage operation to avoid any publicity. Secret Service Agents hid Netanyahu in the back of the truck and drove to the delivery entrance at the back of the hospital, where he was offloaded and then placed on the operating table.

No Sweat

"Studio Fix powder, Fix Plus moisturizing spray, concealer, eyebrow pencil, translucent mascara for eyebrows," makeup artist Matan Merhav lists the accessories he used to enhance Netanyahu's features in anticipation of an important speech.

It turns out that the public spends quite a sum for Netanyahu to look his best. In 2010, the annual state budget for his makeup and hair styling (not including wardrobe) was close to NIS 100,000. There is a barber visit every week, and makeup and powder are always on hand. Netanyahu is the first politician in Israel to turn makeup into a routine requirement for every public appearance, not just before appearing on television.

The reason that Netanyahu's hair is never tousled is because it is practically welded to his scalp. Without going into the details, suffice it to say that this, too, is the result of planning and effort.

As a young political candidate, while still in his 40s, Netanyahu decided to dye his hair. Most of his contemporaries who chose to color their hair wanted to blacken the parts that were turning white. Netanyahu took the opposite approach, turning himself grey before his time and thereby attaining a more mature, level-headed, responsible look. His hair – recolored grey each time, with a slightly purplish tint - became a perennial joke on satire shows. Netanyahu once responded, in a jovial clip showing him in a grassy, green, bird-watching site in the Galilee:

> "Everything is in bloom, and it's beautiful; everything is green, a bit of brown – and I'm not talking about the color of my hair, right? By the way, they say that brown is the new grey, but I promise – wait a few weeks and the old grey will grow back. The main thing is that you should have a happy holiday. What a beautiful country we have."

In his dress and his persona, Netanyahu introduced an American flavor into Israeli politics. His solution to the problem of keeping up a civilized appearance while campaigning in the summer heat consisted of changing his shirt every couple of hours, thus appearing fresh all day. His suits are custom-made. He is not to be photographed wearing glasses, unless he is reading. A magnifying glass is at the ready on his desk for reading small print.

Fake Bodyguard

"How are we going to make Benny Gantz look like a Prime Minister?" asked Gantz's advisors, gathered in a Tel Aviv office. Different suggestions were made. One suggestion was that he should be shown with a bodyguard behind him in every video interview. The muscular young man appearing in the ads with what looked like a concealed handgun was simply an aide, and he wasn't armed. He stood behind Gantz solely for the sake of the cameras, so that the Blue and White party leader would look like a VIP with a security detail. When

Netanyahu discovered this, he mocked Gantz's "fake bodyguard." But according to a former head of the General Security Services, Carmi Gillon, Netanyahu himself employed the very same tactic as head of the opposition on the eve of the 1996 elections. He, too, had sought to appear important and protected, just like a Prime Minister.

"Look the part," political strategist Arthur Finkelstein had advised him. And thus, long before he was even elected Chairman of the Likud, Netanyahu began dressing like a Prime Minister. For his campaign videos in 1996, he chose a backdrop resembling the Prime Minister's Office, so that the public would become accustomed to the idea that Netanyahu was worthy of occupying it.

Yair Lapid's home has a basement study, and when Lapid decided that he would like to become Prime Minister, he installed a large Israeli flag and started posing for photographs in front of his bookshelf and the flag. (No one is permitted to photograph the red boxing gloves and the pictures on the other wall, including posters of himself in his acting days.) Gantz, too, uses a presidential-looking desk for his media interviews. Anyone seeking to become Prime Minister now follows this protocol, setting up the environment to look like the real thing, and then seating himself comfortably in the midst of it. The branding concept means, first and foremost, creating the proper appearance for the job; the personal caliber and suitability can come later.

The background of a picture or a video has a subconscious influence on viewers. Advertisers pay exorbitant sums to have their logos appear behind a sportsman who is interviewed on the court or in the field. As a director, I made sure to change the backgrounds for online courses that I created for universities in Israel, after reading the results of an experiment conducted at Michigan University. One of their online courses featured a background of a feminine working environment, while another version of exactly the same course featured a background that showed only men working. The students' grades and level of involvement rose when students could see women over the lecturer's shoulder. In academia, in sports, and in politics, the background molds consciousness.

∎∎∎

With each new development in the criminal investigations against him, the Prime Minister's spokesmen activated the fixed "battle routine." Along with a direct response to the criminal charges, they made sure to arrange a security-related trip for the Prime Minister during which, no matter if it was on the northern or southern border, Bibi would release a clip relating in some way to the Iranian threat. The content itself was of lesser importance. A wind jacket, military binoculars, the border fence in the background and the presence of the Minister of Defense and some officers were all calculated to create an image and a feeling that would offset the impression arising from the accusations.

Each time he reached a ceasefire agreement with Hamas, Netanyahu made sure to visit a military base the next day, asking the Regional Commander to stand at his side but not to speak. In the background, viewers saw the base with its IDF and Israeli flags; in the foreground, the Prime Minister stood with the army brass at his side, talking to the public and giving an impression of military strength to counterbalance the image of weakness. When he embarked on his election campaign in 2019 in his capacity as Minister of Defense as well as Prime Minister, he made the most of the opportunity and was photographed daily with soldiers. The heads of the competing parties complained and the Central Elections Committee issued guidelines forbidding it. The Prime Minister's Office responded by calling this "unjustified personal persecution."

The moment that an election date is set, Netanyahu moves into high gear arranging international events whose purpose is to produce photographs. Shimon Peres tried this in 1996, initiating an international conference with Arab leaders and the President of the US, who attended in an attempt to strengthen Peres's candidacy, but it wasn't enough to get him elected. In 2015, Netanyahu's international event took the form of his speech before the US Congress. In 2019, he arranged a meeting with President Trump and a ceremonial signing of US recognition of Israel's sovereignty over the Golan Heights. Another photo-op materialized in April, 2019. Netanyahu attended a unique ceremony at the Russian Defense Ministry in Moscow, where he received the remains of missing IDF soldier Zechariah Baumel.[3] It was an official funeral ceremony, featuring rows of Russian soldiers, led by the Chief of Staff of one of the most powerful armies in the world, with the Prime Minister of Israel at his side. Although the timing of the discovery and the ceremony were apparently unrelated to the elections, political commentators defined the unusual event at the Kremlin as Putin's election gift to Netanyahu. Six months later, just five days before the elections, Netanyahu invited himself to a summit meeting with Putin with the aim of producing an impactful photograph.

Politicians believe that a victory photograph paves the way to victory in elections.

---

[3] One of three IDF soldiers missing since the Battle of Sultan Yacoub in the 1982 Lebanon War. In April 2019, the Russian army, in coordination with the Syrian military, found Baumel's remains, and they were handed over in the official ceremony held in Moscow on April 3rd. The next day Baumel was interred at the Mount Herzl military cemetery in Jerusalem.

Colors and Voters

"A different photograph," Netanyahu ordered, and his advisors set off on their hunt. The next few offerings were likewise deemed unsuitable. Finally, Netanyahu pointed to a photograph and said, "This one." It was a bombshell picture – and not only in the political sense. It showed Iranian civilians hanging in a city square. Netanyahu's decision to display, on his Facebook page, the Iranian regime's execution of its citizens was made after much deliberation, and as part of his strategy for showing the inhumanity of the terrorist mindset.

Once the photograph was selected, a caption was added and it was submitted – like every other piece of information emerging from the office – for the Prime Minister's approval. "Change the colors," Netanyahu ordered. His advisor didn't understand at first, and Netanyahu explained, "Use black and red, not blue." The photograph underwent a few more alterations, including the use of colors calculated to reflect the negative atmosphere prevailing in Iran, and a change of font for the caption, before Netanyahu was satisfied.

The distinction between "good" and "bad" colors has been maintained throughout Netanyahu's campaigns. Even in 2019, Netanyahu and the Likud were presented in blue and white on one side of the poster, while Lapid-Gantz-Barak appeared in a blackened, blurred and stained photograph on the other, with an inscription in red. There are colors that project danger and are associated with the "enemy," while blue and white create a sense of security. Scientists attribute this to evolutionary processes: shades of green and blue are associated with water and vegetation, red makes us think of blood and fire, and black recalls darkness and ashes. Netanyahu is very particular about the use of colors, and the other party heads have learned from him.

In general, Israeli election campaign colors center around the color blue. Studies comparing backgrounds on commercial websites have shown that blue projects reliability. Hence, election posters, with very few exceptions, use different shades of blue or related colors. Benny Gantz, whose party was called Israel Resilience, originally chose a khaki-green color to emphasize his military background. Even the Labor party, historically identified with the color red, has shifted to blue. Red and yellow against a black background, arousing a sense of danger, are usually reserved for negative campaigns that smear the opposing candidate.

The name "Blue and White" was chosen for the unification of the centrist parties led by Gantz and Lapid. On the eve of the launch, Lapid wore a blue tie; Gantz stood at his side with a white tie that had hastily been procured just before their joint appearance. This attention to detail and the symbolic power of color testifies to the professionalism that Netanyahu has bequeathed to the political system in Israel.

∎∎∎

For both rounds of elections in 2019, the Likud produced giant billboards showing Netanyahu shaking hands with President Trump with the slogan, "Netanyahu – a different league." He and Trump were in a different league; his rivals paled in comparison. To produce this image, a photograph of the two men was found that was flattering to Netanyahu: it was at a meeting in Trump Tower in New York, before Trump's election, in a suite bathed in ostentatious gold. The first step in the processing was to remove the gold from the photograph and replace it with a blue and white background, reminiscent of the Israeli flag.

The graphic artists also took care to recolor Netanyahu's shirt. The light-blue shirt that he had been wearing at the meeting was replaced, with the help of graphics software, with a white one. Once all these details had been taken care of, the campaign advisors encountered another problem: Donald Trump was a half a head taller than Bibi. Next to the US President, Netanyahu looked slightly short. This wasn't what they wanted for a billboard overlooking the major Ayalon Highway in Tel Aviv. The whole idea was to display Netanyahu's stature. A solution was soon found: Trump was lowered by a few centimeters, and Netanyahu was shifted a few centimeters upward, so that to drivers on the highway they appeared to stand shoulder to shoulder.

∎∎∎

Secret #1: A Winning Picture Netanyahu takes care to engineer his photographs, approving every frame that is released to the public. He censors and withholds photographs that don't reflect the desired image, and creates backgrounds, colors, and scenery that do. In his meetings with leaders, he uses presentations that turn intelligence materials into pictures, and in his speeches, he uses an array of props, thereby making his messages visual, compelling, and memorable.

2.
HIS TONGUE IS HIS WEAPON
WORDS

"Your Majesty, I would like to say something in conclusion," Netanyahu said. He was wrapping up an historical phone call that had been extremely challenging for the aides of both leaders. The protocol of the call involved no less than five languages: Hebrew, French, Arabic, English, and some expressions in Judeo-Moroccan Arabic. All of these had featured in the exchange between King of Morocco Mohammed VI and the Israeli Prime Minister, following the establishment of formal diplomatic relations between their countries. On this occasion, with a view to winning the king's heart, Netanyahu sought not only a common language but also a cultural symbol to serve as a bridge between Jerusalem and Rabat.

"I want to conclude our historical conversation with the concluding words of a film that I am very fond of," Netanyahu hinted. It was immediately clear to everyone which film he meant, and what his next words would be. The Moroccan king and all the aides listening in smiled in anticipation of the classic line, delivered by Netanyahu in a fair imitation of Humphrey Bogart as Rick Blaine in *Casablanca*, "I think this is the beginning of a beautiful friendship."

I, You, We

Neither content, nor style, not even presentation is key to the success of a speaker or a speech. In my experience as a speechwriter for public figures, only one thing matters, and that is the "meeting point" where speaker meets audience. If a connection is made, the speaker can influence his listeners. How does Netanyahu forge such direct contact with his audience? How does he weld them to himself and his message? How does he create such a sense of solidarity with him?

Analyzing dozens of his speeches, Professor Zohar Livnat of the Hebrew University highlights Netanyahu's frequent use of elementary yet effective linguistic devices. One of them is talking in the first person, addressing the second-person plural. "I want to tell you (plural) …", "Allow me to share with you …", "I will now show you …", "I promise you …" This serves to create dialogue between himself and his listeners. Similarly, he makes use of the first-person plural, "Our soldiers", "We all believe …", "Each of us …", "Our country …"

The proper use of "I, we, and what we share" is the secret of success. Livnat's study is entitled, "Like the rest of the nation, I too was moved" – quoting Netanyahu in reference to Gilad Shalit.[4]

The Prime Minister describes Israel's achievements, and even its covert operations, in a similar manner. A fortnight before the second round of national elections in 2019, he referred to an IDF attack on an Iranian force in Syria:

"We preempted them and foiled this terror attack; we prevented major terror attacks. We will expose any future attempt by Iran to attack us."

The "us" that was almost harmed is the same "us" that is active and

---

[4] The Israeli soldier abducted and held in captivity by Hamas for over 5 years; he was released in a prisoner exchange deal in October, 2011.

attacks; it is "us or them." The entire nation is the army that attacked in Syria. The police investigators are adversaries who oppose "our policy." They want to "bring us down." "I" equals "you" (plural); "you" equals "us." The entire nation equals Netanyahu.

"You are the Vanguard"

Researchers from the Laboratory of Political Psychology at Hebrew University found that Netanyahu uses three main methods to create a connection with his audience. One of them is handy and accessible to anyone, anytime: simply offer praise.

Netanyahu does this no matter who he is talking to. A review of hundreds of his speeches shows that "You are the vanguard" is his favorite compliment, and he has invoked this image with reference to dozens of groups that he has addressed. At the same time, he knows how to tailor his compliments to the situation at hand. For example, tasting some mofletta[5] and waxing poetic about loneliness in the modern world, he declared:

> "This sweetness that we are tasting here isn't the sugar, but rather the love – simply love for every person, regardless of where he comes from. In the modern world, more and more people are secluding themselves behind locked doors, with intercoms and guards at the entrance. A person doesn't know his neighbors from across the way. How lonely the modern world is, and how much it could learn from this Mimouna festival of open doors."

---

5   A thin crepe traditionally eaten by Maghrebi Jews at the Mimouna celebration, the day after the end of Passover

"Hospitality," Netanyahu declared to his hosts, "there's nothing more Jewish than that." But when he met with the Druze community, he paid them a similar compliment and spoke to them "about the values that we Jews learn from you – hospitality …." As Pinchas Sapir, a government minister during the first three decades of Israel's history, once remarked, "No one takes offense at flattery."

The second obvious method is highlighting a common denominator. Netanyahu always does this where foreign leaders are concerned. Every visiting leader is treated to a description of the deep and special connection between the Israeli nation and his own Mongolian/Brazilian/African people. There is no speech that Netanyahu has ever delivered to an overseas visitor that has not emphasized this special connection. Sometimes he enlists the streets of Jerusalem for this purpose:

> "I don't know whether you noticed, Mr. President of Ukraine, that the main road that passes by the Foreign Ministry is named after Yitzhak Ben-Zvi, the second president of Israel. He was from Ukraine."

At the Merkaz HaRav Yeshiva (religious academy), Netanyahu discussed the close relations between his scholarly grandfather, Nathan Mileikowsky, and Rabbi Abraham Isaac HaKohen Kook, the first Ashkenazi Chief Rabbi of British Mandatory Palestine, and mentioned Rabbi Kook's teachings. Speaking to a group of Chabad emissaries, he mentioned how, during his service as a member of Israel's diplomatic mission to the US, he met with Rabbi Menachem Mendel Schneerson, the dynastic leader of this Hassidic movement, and quoted him. Addressing the Prime Minister of Lithuania, he said, "There are many Israelis who are of Lithuanian origin; you are speaking with one of them." He shared with the New Zealand Minister of Defense, "My son, Avner, is backpacking in New Zealand right now. I spoke with him last night, and he told me what a beautiful country it is." He enlisted his older son to create a connection with the President of Brazil: "You know that in Hebrew, President Bolsonaro's first name is 'Yair'. That our son's name, too." He found common ground with the President of Chad: "I discovered today that President Déby is a history aficionado, and I too am a history aficionado … You have suffered for being black; we have suffered for being Jews." After visiting the US aircraft carrier USSGeorge H. W. Bush docked outside Haifa port, he said: "I told the members of this crew a few hours ago that Israel is also an aircraft carrier. It's an aircraft carrier for Western civilization, for the civilization of freedom."

"A Kurd like Me"

A speech delivered at the Saharna festival[6] entailed involved many quotations from religious sources, and was clearly worked and reworked over several days. The speech includes a dialogue that supposedly took place between Netanyahu and his advisors shortly before his arrival at the event:

> "I just left in the middle of a political discussion with the American Secretary of State and members of our security establishment, so that I could come here, to the Saharna. Some of my advisors told me, 'It's too bad; such a busy day, the visit to Sacher Park [where the Saharna festivities are held] will have to be cancelled.'
>
> "But I'm not prepared to miss the Saharna. Do you know

---

6   Traditional Kurdish festival celebrating the arrival of the spring.

why? Because I'm a Kurd. In fact, we're all Kurdish, because our forefather, Abraham, came to the Land of Israel from Ur of the Chaldeans, which is somewhere between northern Iraq and southern Turkey. "And God told him, 'Get yourself out of your country …'"

Netanyahu habitually underlines the most important words in a paragraph. This time, he underlined the words, "Because I'm a Kurd." A reminder to adopt a different tone. He also added vowels to the biblical verse in Hebrew with the punctiliousness of a Hebrew grammar teacher. His definition of Abraham, the first of the Jewish patriarchs, as the first Jewish immigrant to Israel from Kurdistan, was followed by the next section of the speech, in the midst of which he had written himself stage directions in parentheses:

"The Kurdish Jewish immigrants were among the first to start building Jerusalem outside of the Old City walls. Right here, on the hill opposite us (point in the direction of Machane Yehuda market), they built three neighborhoods…"

He reached the relevant line in the speech, and pointed in the direction of Machane Yehuda market. Spontaneously, as it were. Then came a compliment, recalling how "the enemies and terrorists didn't know that they were dealing with stubborn Kurdish Jews", and then a reference to the other enemy: "them." The white Ashkenazi tribe who, in their own way, like the enemies and terrorists, want to eradicate Kurdish Jews:

"There are people and there are movements in Israel who think that we have to be a 'melting pot' that will boil up and grind together all the different ethnicities and all the people, until a uniform Israeli emerges ... In fact, you know what they want? For us all to be Ashkenazi."

Thus, after telling the audience that he preferred their company to the US Secretary of State, and describing in graphic language those seeking to 'grind up' the ethnic identity of Middle Eastern Jews and turn them into Ashkenazi clones, Netanyahu concluded with a traditional Kurdish blessing. To make sure that an Ashkenazi like himself would not mispronounce it, he carefully added vowels, and no doubt rehearsed it over and over until he sounded like a true Kurd.

■■■

A third technique that Netanyahu uses to create rapport with his listeners is a simple but highly effective stylistic device – personal attention. He addresses specific individuals in the audience by name, "I see here ..."

Livnat cites examples from Netanyahu's speech at the cornerstone-laying ceremony for the new National Library of Israel. Recounting how he had gone to and fro in the library to find books requested by his historian father, he addressed the former President of the Supreme Court Dorit Beinisch, who had worked at the library in the past and was among the attendees at the ceremony: "Dorit – I don't know, perhaps you also helped to get something for my father."

The drafts that I was able to obtain show that none of this is extemporaneous. The names of the individuals to be mentioned are duly noted in his handwriting, along with the seemingly ad-lib comments. "Add 'an independent and outstanding governor," he reminded himself in the notes for one of his speeches. For a different occasion he lists the achievements of each of the people he will be speaking to: "Mayor – construction. Minister of Finance – deficit." Prior to memorial ceremonies for fallen soldiers, he obtains information from his military secretary about the families. In one of the documents I obtained, the background supplied for the speech included even the blood pressure issues and diabetes affecting the bereaved mother, and Netanyahu made mention of this in his words. In funeral and memorial speeches, Netanyahu takes pains to write down and mention the names of family members.

■■■

The techniques that Netanyahu uses in reaching out to US audiences include dispensing praise and emphasizing commonalities. He dwells eloquently on how Americans and Israelis share similar values and beliefs and operate in a similar manner as fellow democracies.

"I have to tell you that I started out washing dishes at an American high school, and I ended up becoming Prime Minister …"

Netanyahu tells his story to an audience in the US. The American public likes stories about people who started at the bottom and became Prime Ministers. Netanyahu did not start off as a dishwasher at school; he was born to a family of means with political connections. Even if he did wash dishes at the affluent Jewish high school that he attended in America, he was still the son of the professor from the upscale Rehavia suburb of Jerusalem. But Americans want to hear that anyone can achieve the American dream, so Netanyahu offers his own contribution to the "anyone can do it" narrative. He speaks with his interlocutors in their own language.

"I am just like you," is his covert message. Netanyahu speaks to each audience in codes that hint to the common ground and fundamental identity that they share. What works for an American audience is different from what works for Betar[7] veterans:

---

7   The Zionist Revisionist youth movement that formed the basis for Begin's Herut party, which ultimately became the Likud.

"You know that I often address world leaders. When I speak to world leaders, I am never submissive. I'm not arrogant, but I also don't think that I have to be submissive, because I - just like you – am imbued with the spirit of Betar."

"Even when I meet with dignitaries from around the world," Netanyahu is saying to them, "I'm with you; I'm representing you. I go about it with the same spirit that we share." We are one. The Right is me. When they go after me, they're going after you. When they pick on Sara, they're picking on the Right. We are one.

"I Wanted to Share with You"

Topaz Luk, 22, strode towards Netanyahu's book-lined office and came to a halt in front of the flag and the heavy wooden desk. With great self-assurance, although it was his first day on the job, he asked the Prime Minister to discard his dignified demeanor forthwith and to embrace a syntactical transformation.

Luk, who had served with Netanyahu's son, Yair, in the Army Spokesman's Unit, had been hired by the Prime Minister's Office as social media advisor. From that day onwards Netanyahu was no longer presented on his Facebook page in the third person – "Prime Minister of Israel, Mr. Benjamin Netanyahu, met with/announced/visited …" – in the style of press releases. Netanyahu began communicating with his followers on Facebook in direct language, using the first-person singular and second-person plural: "I wanted to share with you that today I met with …" Since Netanyahu's switch to this style, all Israeli politicians have followed his example.

In 2016, following this syntactical revolution, the word "I" became the second-most commonly used word on the Prime Minister's Facebook page (after "Israel"), with 573 appearances. Along with "I" and "Israel" and their equivalence, another feature of that year's posts was that two-thirds of them related to political and security topics. Leading the list, in third place, was "terror," appearing 163 times, followed by "Jerusalem" (110), "media" (72), "my wife" (67), "Yoni"[8] (45), "Drucker"[9] (16), and "the gloom industry" (4). The word "poverty" made no appearance at all. "In favor" appeared 7 times, while "against" featured in 128 posts.

Aside from the ability to by-pass the generally unfriendly media, the digital platform offered Netanyahu another significant promotional advantage in that it allowed him to tailor his messages to different target audiences. In 2019, his campaign staff divided the public into sectors using detailed databases that Netanyahu obtained, along with the information available from Facebook, and then released video clips or messages suited to each specific category of the citizenry. In the digital age, every online viewer sees and hears what the Prime Minister wants him to see and hear, without knowing what messages are being conveyed to others.

Election campaign messages were accordingly customized on the basis of voter potential. Youngsters who were already identified as Likudniks received a blunt clip targeting Gantz and claiming that he was not in his right mind. Potential supporters from the ultra-Orthodox sector received information about Netanyahu's intention to

---

8 Netanyahu's older brother, Jonathan ("Yoni"), was killed while commanding the elite commando unit that rescued the hijacking hostages held at Entebbe Airport in Uganda in 1976.

9 Raviv Drucker, an Israeli journalist who published a series of investigative reports in 2016 incriminating Netanyahu.

create a coalition with ultra-Orthodox partners. Shas[10] voters were treated to a photograph of Netanyahu with Rabbi Ovadia Yosef[11], while Lieberman's[12] supporters heard about Netanyahu's commitments to advance pensions for immigrants and to support the religious status quo. Internet surfers in every city received a list of what Netanyahu had done for their city. Each group and sector heard from Netanyahu what it wanted to hear.

All this activity focused on "I" and "you (plural)", with no attention to the third person: "them". To avoid wasting the publicity budget, no attempt was made to use social media to create dialogue with those who, according to the data, were not part of the Right-wing block or potential voters.

"We're Not Suckers" in Persian

In anticipation of a speech before an Arab audience, Netanyahu will take up his fountain pen and carefully add vowels to his greetings in Arabic transliterated into Hebrew on the occasion of the Muslim festival of sacrifice (Eid al-Adha). Addressing a group of Guatemalans, he starts off by saying, "Buenos dias – that's all I know how to say." Speaking at the UN, Netanyahu addresses the Iranians directly,

---

10 A party representing ultra-Orthodox voters of Mizrahi (North African or Middle Eastern) origin.

11 World-acclaimed Talmudic scholar, Sephardi Chief Rabbi of Israel from 1973 to 1983, and founder and spiritual leader of the Shas party up until his death in 2013.

12 Avigdor Lieberman, former Defense Minister in Netanyahu's government and head of the secular nationalist Yisrael Beiteinu party representing mainly Russian-speaking immigrantsfrom the formerSoviet Union.

"We're not *sadeh-lowh* (suckers)," and for the benefit of a billion Chinese, following endless rehearsals with the embassy in Beijing, he records a clip in Mandarin Chinese in honor of the Year of the Dragon.

He speaks to every audience in its own language, following the same approach adopted by Clinton whose parting words at Yitzhak Rabin's funeral were "*shalom haver*" (farewell, friend); by Obama who called Israel an "*eretz nehederet*" ('a wonderful country' – also the name of a satirical TV program), and by Kennedy who famously declared, "*Ich bin ein Berliner.*"

Creating rapport between speaker and listeners also requires adjusting the register or levels of usage of language. Netanyahu adapts his choice of words and his arguments to his target audience. In other words, depending on who he is speaking to, he decides whether to appeal to emotion or to the intellect; pathos or logos. Most often – both. He says, "I don't believe in empty rhetoric, but rather in building up well-founded arguments, supported by facts, which appeal to common sense, without neglecting emotion."

Professor Yehoshua Gitay of Haifa University analyzed Netanyahu's speech to the US Congress on the eve of the 2015 elections, slamming Obama's nuclear agreement with Iran. He shows that it was built on logic, not emotion: every assertion was backed up with evidence. Many Americans – including President Obama – were hostile towards the speech and its message, so Netanyahu prepared proofs and support that would leave no room to claim that he was merely fearmongering. Data, past incidents, quotes, the nitty-gritty details of terms – all were enlisted in his appeal to reason. Working day and night with his advisors to prepare the speech and to rehearse every word and every pause, Netanyahu rejected most of the emotional elements that his aides proposed. He delivered to the houses of Congress and the world a systematic and compelling condemnation of the deal in which each point led logically to the next and every assertion was corroborated by facts.

"Here I Have to Take a Breath"

The public relations team huddled around the Prime Minister's heavy wooden desk, adding the final touches. "You have to break up sentences," expounded Netanyahu, red pen in hand. "I told you, no 'ands,'" whispered one aide to another, invoking Netanyahu's long-established rule that every 'and' should be replaced with a period. At one point his spokesman suggested an addendum to a sentence, but Netanyahu replied, "Here I have to take a breath."

"Who talks this way?" one of the younger advisors chipped in, objecting to the expression "heaping ridicule" to describe the media's attitude towards Right-wing positions. "No one talks like that today," he tried to enlighten the 70-year-old Prime Minister as to the accepted language register among the younger generation. But Netanyahu was firm: We'll stay with the 'heaping ridicule'. Since then the expression has recurred several times in his speeches.

Another stylistic revision concerned the avoidance of repetition: "Here you can say 'moving', here it should be changed to 'stirring'; here 'touching'; here 'moved to tears,'" Bibi instructed, illustrating the art of saying the same thing in different ways.

The Prime Minister added another tip, reminding the youngsters of the "sacred trinity" – the way he likes to present any new idea that is somewhat complex by breaking it up into three parts: the three pillars of peace, the three principles of a policy, and so on. For years Netanyahu spoke about Israel's three strengths (economic, military, and ethical) which he had cultivated during his tenure. He later adding a fourth – the diplomatic realm and Israel's improved international standing - but in general he prefers a three-point breakdown.

There have been advisors in the past – whether official or self-appointed – who have prided themselves on their close relations with Netanyahu. Actor and singer Moti Giladi boasted that it was he who gifted Bibi with the key message that he directed to Mahmoud Abbas from the UN podium, "Let's talk 'dugri'"[13] – and since then Netanyahu has kept Giladi at a distance. When entertainer and media personality Didi Harari, who is in fact a close advisor, mentioned on one of his programs that he worked with Netanyahu on body language, too, Bibi responded angrily, "Stop helping me!" – and made sure that Harari would likewise be kept away from him. Netanyahu's loathing of leaks, and the fact that he has been burned in the past by confidants who disclosed too much information to the press, has made him extremely cautious in choosing his people, and has caused him to ostracize any advisor who tries to take credit for his speeches. One might say that whoever is truly close to Netanyahu doesn't talk, and whoever talks isn't truly close to him.

Netanyahu has learned to filter out the background noise and advice that everyone offers, and to make decisions quickly, on his own. "He listens with half an ear, but it's clear to everyone that he's a giant among dwarves," says a member of his bureau staff. Another former staff member offers a more cynical assessment: He surrounds himself with children, so no one will stand up to him.

"You know," he repeated his mantra to the youngsters surrounding him, summing up his theory of speechmaking, "always tell them something new – or at least …?" He dangled the question and the chorus of advisors completed the sentence, "… tell them something old in a new way."

Netanyahu went on marking phrases to be deleted from weaker sections, adding punctuation, and breaking up sentences that were too long. He paid no heed to protests that he was ruining whole paragraphs that had been painstakingly written. "We have to cut the fat," he said, referring to the deleted passages but simultaneously pointing to his own midriff, which had recently grown thicker. When he

---

13 Straight talk; to-the-point.

finished, he handed over the dozens of pages comprising the final version following dozens of drafts, for retyping and reprinting. It was clear to all that while Netanyahu sat at the cabinet table in the Knesset, waiting for his turn to speak, his obsessive reviewing would produce another round of changes before he ascended the podium.

■■■

The deletions that one finds in Netanyahu's drafts often say more about him than what he leaves intact. Much deleting was done in anticipation of his speech at a ceremony marking the changeover of the Chief of Staff, where he was frugal with his praise for the outgoing officeholder in the wake of reports that he might become a political threat in the future. A sentence in the original version read, "He led the IDF during a difficult period for the State of Israel, successfully and wisely." Before getting up to speak, Bibi erased the word "wisely," and later deleted in blue pen another passage that discussed the wisdom of the outgoing IDF Chief of Staff.

Indeed, he prefers not to share prestige and recognition. Ministers in his government complain that they work hard and Bibi takes all the credit. When there are failures, he leaves it to them to explain. The historical agreements with Bahrain, the UAE, Morocco, and Sudan were all developed by Netanyahu without involving – nor even informing – the Foreign Ministry, so that no one else would be able to share the media glory. It was all kept so completely secret that when he flew to Saudi Arabia for a meeting with senior officials in November 2020, it was only when the military radar showed a private jet making its way from Tel Aviv southward to Neom, on Saudi Arabia's Red Sea coast, and then returning a few hours later, that the IDF Chief of Staff and Deputy Prime Minister became aware that the Prime Minister had been outside of Israel's borders.

His unwillingness to share successes led the ministers representing

Blue and White to resign from his unity government, feeling that their contribution was irrelevant and their partnership pointless. They were forced to deal with a public fed up with the government's mismanagement of the COVID crisis and angry with Blue and White for teaming up with a leader indicted on criminal charges, while the Prime Minister was appearing on every possible platform flaunting vaccines and diplomatic agreements. In contrast, with regard to the charges against him, Bibi was eagerly inclusive: "They're persecuting not just me, but all of us," he declared at the start of his trial.

■■■

"Draft, for David Bar-Ilan." This is a pained speech, densely written in Netanyahu's handwriting. "The Israeli government is willing … to give Hebron over to the Palestinian Autonomous Authority." The page is crammed with amendments. Netanyahu is tormented. Benny Begin has just launched a vicious attack on him: "Netanyahu is handing over parts of our homeland. This agreement is worse than Oslo." The harshest political opposition always comes from the closest allies. Benzion Netanyahu, the Prime Minister's venerated father, has spoken to the press, attacking his son without mercy for his relinquishing of Hebron. "Why speak to the press?" the son fumes.

Alone and angry, Netanyahu sits on the first floor of his official residence on Balfour Street and adds more and more reasons why, despite Hebron being handed over to the Palestinians, the Jewish community of the ancient city will not be evacuated: "Just as Arabs live in Jaffa, Haifa, Ramle, and Lod, there's no logical reason why it can't be that way in Hebron, too." Bibi glances at what he has written and strikes through the last sentence with a single, long line. He won't say so, but the comparison is problematic.

Benzion Netanyahu's son chooses a different justification, writing question marks for himself and for his advisors, indicating that they should check the accuracy of the figures:

"In 1929, a pogrom against the Jews led to the deaths of some 60 (?) members of the community. In 1995, Hebron witnessed a massacre of Arabs in which 27 (?) Arabs were killed, in the Cave of the Patriarchs … Let us put an end to the bloodshed in this holy city that is known in Arabic as 'Al-Khalil', recalling our beloved patriarch, Abraham, father of both nations – Israel and Ishmael. Let this place start a process."

"No, not 'process'," Netanyahu decides, and removes the word that alludes to further concessions that he might make as part of the negotiations. The last thing he needs right now is headlines announcing that Hebron is just the beginning of a process of handing over territory. "Let this place start a rapprochement," he corrects himself. Here he arrives at what he considers the key sentence, and he underlines it: "Hebron first, for a firm and lasting peace." Upon reconsideration, he adds an exclamation mark. A decade will pass before he tells Israeli media network Arutz Sheva, "I would re-occupy Hebron. That was a mistake."

He continues working on the speech. "Along comes Netanyahu and says, 'No more. We're not going to sign agreements, we're not going to give up territory, we won't make any further unilateral concessions, so long as our partners are tolerant and supportive of terror."

Then he looks at the sentence again, swipes his finger next to his ear in a characteristic gesture of indecision, and erases the words "we're not going to give up territory," well aware of the pernicious power of the television archive that will remind him of this commitment if he decides, sometime in the future, to give up territory.

He leaves the page with its web of corrections at the edge of the desk for David Bar-Ilan, the media advisor who will have the speech typed up, and leans back in his armchair.

His deletions usually remain secret. After all, when he delivers the speech, everything will follow smoothly, as though nothing had been deleted. Nevertheless, sometimes Bibi allows his listeners a peep at his draft. When the first plane from Abu Dhabi landed at Ben Gurion Airport, in October 2020, bringing a delegation that included the UAE Economy Minister and Minister of State for Financial Affairs, as well as US Treasury Secretary Steven Mnuchin and other American officials, Netanyahu delivered an elated welcoming speech: "My staff wrote me some lines. They started by saying, 'Today we are literally witnessing history in the making.' And I said, absolutely not! Today we are making history! We are making history in a way that will stand for generations."

Lighthearted Moments

"They say thefirst sentencein any speech is always thehardest. Well, that one's behind me, anyway." These words introduced Polish poet Wislawa Szymborska's acceptance speech as winner of the 1996 Nobel Prize in Literature. Speakers are often advised to incorporate some lighthearted moments in their speeches, and Netanyahu does so where appropriate. His jokes are well-executed. He sets aside his notes, tells his joke, and always leaves a moment to take a breath as the audience laughs. The speeches that I obtained from his personal files during the course of my research indicate that everything – absolutely everything – is planned in advance: where to breathe, when to laugh, which direction to point in.

An example is a joke that he jotted in his notes for a speech at the annual INFO Publishers Conference: "I hope that you invited me not as Prime Minister, but also in my capacity as a writer. I'm told that some people wouldn't be too sorry if I went back to writing books – especially if I occupied myself with writing exclusively." The same joke was recycled at an annual meeting of the Israel Editors Association: "Once I dreamed of being a journalist. I imagine that some of you would have liked that ..."

As someone who views himself as being persecuted by the elites, it is not surprising that many of his jokes adopt a martyred or self-deprecating tone concerning the hostility towards him. Concerning his injury in the Sabena rescue operation where he was shot in the arm, he comments: "There are some people who are sorry that the bullet wasn't a few centimeters over to the side," or concerning the fellow soldier who pulled him out of the Suez Canal, "They're still trying to work out who was idiotic enough to save me."

Other jokes use word play to deride his opponents in the media and in politics, as in the reference to Barak's Zionist Union party as the "Anti-Zionist Union." Such quips are among the many effects that he plans and prepares in advance.

The Story is the Message

Messages are conveyed and engraved in the listeners' consciousness by means of stories. Stories are integral to almost every area of our lives, and are also one of the important factors contributing to the charisma of leaders and influencing the behavior of nations.

American psychologist Jerome Bruner defined the "narrative mode of knowing" as a central concept for an understanding of society, and argues that for leaders, stories are a principal device in creating meaning for their peoples.

The narrative that Netanyahu tells the Jewish People repeats itself over and over, depicting reality as an arena where the Jew is persecuted by a savage enemy. This is the super-narrative – "life and death," Right and Left. But aside from this big story there are also "small stories," of the sort that Netanyahu integrates into his speeches as a rhetorical device to illustrate and create identification.

> "I was recently in a flourishing city in the center of the country. I met an elderly woman there, an immigrant from the former Soviet Union, who just sobbed about how she can't manage to buy basic foodstuffs and put bread on the table. I was five minutes away from the center of Tel Aviv, and what I saw there was a family that lives as follows: the father and mother are in one room, their ten children are in the other; there is an eleventh on the way. We cannot resign ourselves to this situation. One cannot simply carry on in the face this sort of reality. And I believe, Members of Knesset, that there are solutions for these problems. We can reduce destitution. We can offer a real future to many people who are living in the State of Israel and who have lost hope."

The wizard of influence on public opinion is well aware of the effect of the "identifiable victim." Studies have shown that we are willing to donate money to a little girl with braids and a first name who loses her leg in an earthquake in Haiti, but are less willing to respond to a campaign to save hundreds of thousands of children who are hurt in that very same earthquake. The workings of the human brain seem to bear out the saying attributed to Stalin: "The death of one man is a tragedy; the death of millions is a statistic."

Among the stories that Netanyahu likes to repeat are those concerning his family: stories about Yoni Netanyahu, about his father, about his military service, and about people he has met. Netanyahu is always able to connect his personal story to the national message, thereby applying the ancient rule: If you have a message to convey, tell a story.

Despite his efforts, Bibi is not a great storyteller. Telling a story requires that one invest emotion in the hero, with whom the listeners are meant to identify. Bibi is not a man who is used to expressing emotion, and he has trouble doing so even in stories. His stories are brief and straightforward, with a clear and pointed message, but they do not inspire emotion, stir compassion, or spark longing. Netanyahu conveys confidence and power rather than inspiration and hope.

Obama, in contrast, knew how to tell a story. In his victory speech following his election, he reviewed the history of the United States through the eyes of an elderly African-American woman who once upon a time had not been permitted to sit on the bus together with white people, and who had just now spent several hours waiting at the polling booth in order to elect an African-American President. With pauses at the appropriate moments, and putting feeling into the story, which he read word-for-word from the teleprompter, Obama brought people to tears. Bibi knows how to impress and enthuse; it is less clear that he knows how to stir emotion.

His favorite story, and one that he has repeated dozens of times, includes several elements reflecting his personal and ideological world:

> "Ladies and gentlemen, on a cold day towards the end of the 19th century, my grandfather Nathan and his younger brother, Yehuda, stood at a train station in the heart of Europe. A group of thugs caught sight of them. They ran towards them with clubs, shouting, 'Death to the Jews!' My grandfather shouted to his brother to run away and save himself, and he stood facing the mob all alone.
>
> "They beat him unconscious and left him for dead. Before passing out, and wallowing in a pool of his own blood,

he told himself, 'What a disgrace! What a disgrace! The descendants of the Maccabees are left lying in the dirt, incapable of defending themselves.' He promised himself that if he survived, he would take his family to the Jewish homeland to build a future for the Jewish People. I stand here today as Prime Minister of Israel because my grandfather kept his promise."

"It's Your Duty, It's Your Job, It's Your Right"

Bibi's speeches are replete with examples of anaphora and epiphora – the repetition of a sequence of words at the beginnings or ends of neighboring clauses, lending emphasis: "Many of the youth know more about Madonna than they do about Moses; more about computer games than about our tradition; more about remote controls than about Israel." This technique has special effect when it comes as a climax and conclusion. Addressing Likudniks and calling upon them to support himself and Israel, Netanyahu declares, "It's your duty, it's your job, it's your right." Uttered with the right intonation, it guarantees applause.

This repetitive device is used for ornamentation and to intensify messages. The effect that it is intended to create among the audience is, "How beautiful; how moving, how powerful, how persuasive." It is the epitome of pathos. It is applicable, of course, in any context:

> "Every time we flick a switch, we are paying an inefficiency tax. Every time we open a tap, we are paying an inefficiency tax. Every time we flush the toilet we are paying an inefficiency tax."

Netanyahu introduced his first speech in the Knesset as Prime Minister in 1996 as follows:

> "Citizens of Israel, friends, comrades. The State of Israel is embarking today on a new path; a path of hope, a path of unity, a path of security, a path of peace. The first and most important peace that has to be made is peace at home, peace among us, peace in our midst … I see as my first task as Prime Minister to mend our fences, to close gaps, to lessen tensions and to strengthen unity among the nation and the sense of partnership … Peace begins at home …"

This was a speech for after elections. The target audience was the entire public and not only Likud voters, and thus Netanyahu could afford to be more conciliatory and inclusive. This would apparently also explain why he included an anecdote aimed at depicting him as the father of the nation, concluding with the rhythmic epiphora:

> "I was in Tamra (an Arab town in Israel) a few days ago, and there was a cute little boy there. I saw him and brought him over, put my hand on his shoulder and said: This boy should have the same opportunities that my son Yair has. There's no difference between the two. Only if he receives a good education will he be able to be part of tomorrow's world, to compete in tomorrow's world, to succeed in tomorrow's world."

■■■

"In my next term we'll reach the moon!" Netanyahu bellowed with enthusiasm in a victory speech before his supporters two days after the Beresheet spacecraft crashed on the moon. Beresheet was, of course, a private initiative that had received next to nothing in terms of state funding. Netanyahu's exuberant declaration was not only an act of taking ownership of the mission, but also a statement to the public: "We will reach the moon." This sense of partnership, playing on the Israeli sense of pride and attributing success to all, is especially effective in creating identity between the leader and his people.

In the same speech that he delivered after the first round of elections in 2019, convinced that he would succeed in creating a fifth coalition government, Netanyahu was still giving everyone a share of accomplishments: "Did you see the heart that Israeli researchers managed to produce using a 3D printer? That's the living heart of all of us. What an achievement; what great hope for Israel." Needless to say, this was not the heart of "all of us"; it was the work of two successful scientists from Tel Aviv University – considered a bastion of the Israeli Left. But appropriating success and triumph and sharing it with the nation as a whole is what creates the ethos of Israeli pride.

At the same time, the speech also made sure to mention "them" – in this case, the media: "The citizens of Israel have placed their full confidence in us, and these commentators are threatening me …" Netanyahu shifts between first, second and third person, and between the political and criminal realms, and continues in a fiery tone as though still at the height of a desperate campaign: "I am not afraid of threats, and I'm not scared of the media. These methods aren't acceptable these days." With that he shifts from the "they" who will not intimidate us, to the crowd, whistling their disdain for the media: "Time and time again you give them a lesson in democracy at the polling booth."

To complete the merging of speaker and audience, most of which is comprised of traditional Jews, Netanyahu invokes biblical sources and ancient history, arousing Jewish sentiment: "Why is this night different?[14] Because tonight is all sweetness; there is no bitterness." The metaphor, borrowed from the Passover Seder, serves to frame the Likud victory as a sort of second Exodus, in which the "sour-faced" Leftists represent the traditional bitter herbs.

This is the moment where the speaker connects with his audience and makes them his active partners. I, you, we. One man with one artificial heart. He shares it, fills it with patriotism and Jewish pride, allows it to feel part of something greater:

"Thank you for mobilizing as one for the Likud's victory … Thank you for choosing our outstanding team. Together we brought about a tremendous victory and an historical achievement."

■■■

The President of Israel was speaking, and Netanyahu, still sitting in his seat in the Knesset plenum, was making final corrections to his speech in memory of Yitzhak Rabin, deleting some of the accusations that he had planned to level at the Left.

He started off by adopting the rhythm he wanted – the three-fold repetition of which he is so fond. He inserted a handwritten note after the words, "There is no place and no justification," adding "no time". And after asserting that there is no place, no justification, and no time for "any sort of violence in the political debate," he charged: "Likewise, there is no place and no justification for maligning an entire community because of the guilt of an individual. That, too, is political violence."

Pensive, apparently influenced by the fact that the speakers before him – the President and the Chairman of the Knesset – had called for moderation, Netanyahu decided to delete the concluding words,

---

14   The traditional question that introduces the Seder – the ceremonial retelling of the story of the Exodus from Egypt - on Passover.

which might appear to draw a parallel between the violence of Yigal Amir[15] and the violence of the Left towards the Right. Instead, he wrote: "Both endanger democracy." Nevertheless, as the draft of the speech indicates, he still wasn't satisfied. He erased this and wrote, "This, too, is a threat to democracy." When he was called upon to ascend the podium, he called "to extinguish the fire of hatred and strife," and reproached the Leftists: "Peace is first and foremost sought among brothers."

A few years previously, on an earlier anniversary of Rabin's death, he had likewise avoided saying what he felt. The deletion of the name of General Security Services Agent Avishai Raviv and other sections of the speech testify to his self-imposed restraint. The draft of the speech which I uncovered shows what he had originally meant to say:

"I have been attacked personally for the abhorrent poster that was displayed at the demonstration held at Zion Square … Today it is clear, from testimonies of journalists and eye-witnesses, that this was a provocation by Avishai Raviv, whose real identity remains unclear, and that in fact the picture was not visible from the speakers' podium … I expect a public and unequivocal apology from them."

Reading over the speech as he sat in the Knesset plenum, he decided at the last moment to delete Avishai Raviv's name, replacing it with the words, "a provocation by one or two individuals," and softened his demand for a "public apology," asking instead that the Left "take a different path." After a second and third reading, Netanyahu usually softens his formulations.

■■■

---

15 The Right-wing assassin (a law student at the time) who shot and killed Prime Minister Yitzhak Rabin at a peace rally in Tel Aviv on Nov. 4, 1995.

Netanyahu is meticulous about every word of his speeches. He edits them over and over. Sometimes, for important speeches, such as those delivered at the UN, the drafts run into the dozens. "Fifty drafts," he once disclosed during an interview with the *New York Times*, with reference to his speech before the US Congress. There is no other politician – and I work with many – who invests such effort in his addresses.

Ron Dermer is his preferred writer for speeches meant for an overseas audience. Even after his appointment as Ambassador to Washington, Dermer was asked to continue writing Netanyahu's speeches for the UN, each requiring many days of preparation. The headings were important, but no less so the accuracy of every detail, and especially historical facts. Despite the precision of every word and clarification of every term, Netanyahu writes himself reminders of where to deliberately abandon his paper and elaborate ad hoc. In a press conference with the British Prime Minister, he placed an asterisk next to the sentence, "Next week we will celebrate [Israel's] Independence Day," and wrote: "*Holocaust. Iran!" adding an exclamation mark. When he delivered the speech, he was ready to elaborate at length on his messages regarding Iran's nuclear program and its desire to annihilate Israel. Sometimes he adds a datum in his handwriting, such as "450 million this year," with reference to investment in the Arab sector.

Netanyahu enjoys editing. In fact, he once thought of making that his profession. "My father started his literary career as a newspaper editor; for a time I wanted to follow in his footsteps, and developed a dream of being an editor. He taught us to think through writing. To edit what we wrote so as to express the idea." He learned from journalists to use superlatives: "the greatest", "more than ever before", "unimaginable", "historical moment". The expression "unprecedented" appears over and over again: "an unprecedented crusade (against …)" and "unprecedented cooperation with the United States" concerning

Trump; "unprecedented security coordination" concerning Obama; "an unprecedented political achievement" concerning his election victory; "unprecedented, record speed" with regard to the Attorney General's decision to indict him; "unprecedented contacts" with Arab states, and many other precedents which his premiership ushered in.

◼◼◼

Conscious of the power of archives, Netanyahu prefers leaving certain statements somewhat opaque and unquantifiable. During his first term in office, he deleted four words from the following statement: "Separate education must be eradicated, and by the year 2000 the relative number of high school and university graduates among Ethiopian youth will be equal to the figures among native-born Israelis. We shall devote the necessary resources to this objective." The potentially damaging words 'by the year 2000' were removed.

In a different speech, addressing the freezing of settlements, he deleted part of his prepared speech referring to the pioneers dispatched by the Labor Party to settle Samaria. He had written, "It's just a pity that in recent years they changed direction and decided to freeze the settlements. But something that is alive cannot be frozen." He erased these words; a short time later he himself would agree to a settlement freeze.

Sometimes he writes dramatic, poetical phrases only to tone down their pathos later on. Drafts of his speeches for the anniversary of Yitzhak Rabin's death are full of deletions and corrections. On one draft he removed the words, "The blood that was spilled was our own blood, and each of us lost something when he died. We were all bereaved." Upon reconsidering the sentence, "I was always impressed by his knowledge in different spheres and his personal modesty," he removed the reference to "personal modesty."

When Netanyahu wants to emphasize something, or when he feels that a sentence lacks the proper intonation, he repeats it. For example, "From now on, Lieberman belongs to the Left. Lieberman belongs to the Left." Such repetition is not spontaneous. In one of the drafts we obtained, the sentence "Jerusalem will never be divided" is followed by parentheses, in which the word "never" appears again with emphasis, as a reminder to repeat it.

Some notations concern the audience. He receives written information in advance about the listeners and the event, and he writes himself reminders in parentheses: (Imams and religious figures in the audience). And indeed, for this particular audience, in 1999, Netanyahu chose to look at the Middle East through rose-tinted glasses, offering the following assessment:

"As Prime Minister of Israel, I believe with certainty that peace with the Palestinians, peace with Syria, and peace with Lebanon are attainable in the short term."

"The Question Is, Who Will Protect and Who Will Part?

Netanyahu makes repeated use of the phrase, "I want to tell you just one thing." These words are a code that Netanyahu employs to focus the audience's attention on his message, on the heading that follows immediately after, on the headline that journalists are meant to convey to their news desks: "I want to say from here just one thing to our enemies …"

He likes the expression, "The question is …", and this too has made repeated appearances over the years. "The question is who will protect and who will part" – who will work to keep Jerusalem and who will give half of it away. He generally notes that the question is very simple – "A Right-wing government, or a Left-wing-Arab government" – and the answer is always the same: Benjamin Netanyahu.

A different technique that he uses is to present a question and then immediately supply the answer: "Which Lieberman? Our Lieberman." Or, adopting a mocking tone in response to his opponents' claims: "What are you talking about? When there's such a long list [of ostensible crimes], there should be a demand that the investigators be investigated." Alternatively, the question can be used to reframe the discourse: "But why weren't they investigated? That's called selective enforcement. It's selective enforcement on steroids, and it's framing. They're setting me up for incrimination."

Sometimes he waits for the audience's response: "Will you allow them to replace the chairman of the Likud?" allowing hundreds of Likudniks to offer a thunderous response to Benny Gantz, or, "If it looks like a duck, walks like a duck, and sounds like a duck, what is it?" and tens of thousands of AIPAC attendees roar in unison, "A duck!" Netanyahu's message: Iran is a nuclear duck.

A more sophisticated approach he uses is to raise questions that allow him to say what he wants to say without taking responsibility for an explicit statement. The following is an example:

"Mr. Rabin – I'm sorry to say – your whole approach comes from you attaching no moral value to this land. For you and many of your friends it's not a homeland, but rather a collection of plots of land that can be traded, bartered, exchanged for something, or relinquished altogether, as though it was some real estate deal … Mr. Rabin, who do you represent? Are you representing the State of Israel, or the PLO?"

Netanyahu couldn't state outright, "Rabin represents the PLO," or "Rabin is a Palestinian," but by means of his question, that is exactly what he was saying.

Questions are considered an especially good means of persuasion, since they lead the listener to arrive at the conclusion himself, and to retain it with greater conviction: "If Gantz couldn't protect his own telephone, how will he protect our country?"

Is this the right question to ask? Is Gantz meant to protect his phone against cyber-attack, or is that the security establishment's responsibility? Is there any connection between a telephone and protecting the security of the state? It doesn't matter anymore. The message was delivered, received, and internalized.

■■■

"Classified. Confidential. Urgency: Immediate. To: Office. Signed: Netanyahu. Re: Schultz and settlements."

The headings, classified status, and urgency might strike one as dramatic: what is Netanyahu writing about? In fact, it is rather boring correspondence quibbling over details. It reflects Bibi's occupation with precise meanings, as though he were a biblical commentator wrestling with the proper interpretation of every word.

The text of the telegram describes how Netanyahu engaged in a series of clarifications and meetings regarding statements by US Secretary of State George Schultz in a media interview. The question at the center of the telegram concerns the choice of the proper description of the settlements: "not conducive," "illegal," or "unacceptable." Netanyahu, a young diplomat at the time, reports to Prime Minister Yitzhak Shamir that Schultz claims that he is adhering to the policy of President Reagan, which remains unchanged: "They make sure that the wording doesn't deviate from the formal framework. Tomorrow I meet with Ambassador Walters and will check further …" Bibi's next telegram is also confidential. He informs the senior American personnel of the "negative connotations" of the word "provocation," which had been used in connection with the settlements. Two days later, in yet another confidential telegram, Netanyahu reports admonishing the State Department for the use of the expression "moderate elements in the PLO."

Netanyahu's telegrams from his period as a diplomat in Washington emphasize his penchant for splitting hairs. He like terms to be precisely defined, attaches importance to every analogy, and is punctilious about the wording of every sentence uttered in public by members of the US administration. The almost pedantic comments are part of his faith in the power of words to change the world.

Netanyahu views his skill with words as a leadership skill of the first order, and language as his main weapon:

"Demosthenes, one of the statesmen of Athens, said: 'Ambassadors possess no warships, nor heavy cavalry, nor fortresses. Their tongue is their weapon.' Even in ancient times they knew that [oratory] is a vital and essential tool for resolving disputes and achieving peace."

Netanyahu doesn't have speechwriters in the conventional sense. Someone who wrote for him once commented bitterly, "There are only collections of materials." Uri Elitzur, who served as his bureau chief during his first term in office, put it this way: "One might say that Netanyahu's speeches are really his own. He speaks with me both before and after [I write], and he adds a thousand corrections. The speechwriter just saves him time." He claims, "It's never happened that I wrote something for him and he read it out just as it was."

Dr. Haggai Harif, a lecturer in political science at Bar Ilan University, has been Netanyahu's main speechwriter in Hebrew since 2013. Time after time, a special committee meets to approve a special financial arrangement with Harif, whom Netanyahu regards as irreplaceable, a "sole service provider owing to special relations of trust." Harif, incidentally, also writes for Chiefs of Staff. Thus, as a civilian employee of the IDF, he has written speeches in the past for Benny Gantz, Netanyahu's rival. Rhetoric is a profession. Influence is a specialized discipline. Oratory skill can serve anyone, for any purpose.

■■■

Secret #2: Weigh Words as Though they were Diamonds
Dozens of drafts, deletions, amended wording, and careful planning precede every one of Netanyahu's speeches. He uses an array of rhetorical and stylistic methods to rally the audience to identify with him. These include use of the first-person singular and plural, compliments, questions, emphasizing the common denominator, personal attention, and stories, along with rational proofs for his claims and logical support for his messages, tailoring each speech and its style to the specific audience.

3.
WORDS THAT CREATE PICTURES
IMAGERY

The woman in the bookstore on Fifth Avenue perusing the shelves for something to read during her summer vacation sensed that something strange was going on. The people standing around the shelves and tables were paging through books, but they were clearly focused less on what they were reading and more on the store employees and customers. Suddenly there was some bustle and hubbub from the direction of the glass doors at the entrance, which slid open to admit a cluster of men in suits surrounding a VIP.

The fake readers promptly abandoned their books and joined the tight circle, at the center of which was Benjamin Netanyahu. Following his meeting with President Trump and his speech at the UN, he had slipped out of the media limelight and into the bookstore, his bodyguards joining the undercover security detail that had been stationed there. Netanyahu stood in front of the shelves, surveying the titles. The woman forgot about her vacation reading and drew closer to the huddle. Netanyahu picked up a heavy 700-page volume and addressed her and the other customers: "Have you read this?"

It was a book about Alexander Hamilton, a founding father of the United States and a key figure in the ratification of the Constitution. Netanyahu had read the book and had also seen the play about him that was running on Broadway at the time, and now he stood in the bookstore delivering a brief history lesson. He insisted that the play had ignored a small but important detail: the woman who had taught Hamilton to read was a Jewess who made him learn the Ten Commandments by heart. "That was actually the basis for the Constitution, and that wasn't part of the play," Netanyahu asserted, enlisting the anecdote (whose historical accuracy is a matter of controversy) as an opportunity to highlight the longstanding bond between the US, Judaism and Israel.

Capturing the Imagination

The book that Netanyahu took home that day with him wasn't prose. In general, he reads only non-fiction, especially history, and he is particularly fond of travelogues written by visitors to Jerusalem in bygone centuries. Churchill's biography is his all-time favorite. But his purchase on this occasion wasn't a heavy, learned biography that might have contributed to his intellectual image, but rather a different genre, which he took pains to hide from the cameras that had surrounded him: *Simply Speaking: How to Communicate Your Ideas with Style, Substance, and Clarity*. The author was Peggy Noonan, primary speechwriter to President Ronald Reagan.

Netanyahu had met Reagan several times during his diplomatic service and had admired him. Now, 35 years later, he was eager to discover the tips that Noonan had to offer.

"With substance and clarity," he would repeat in English, wagging a finger for emphasis, whenever he mentioned the book, sometimes stressing the word "substance," at other times highlighting "clarity." Simplicity, clarity, precision – Bibi makes frequent mention of these concepts when he talks about messages. He put in a large order with Amazon and a number of copies of the book were duly delivered to his office in Jerusalem. "Read it, read it," he would urge whoever he spoke to. "Read it," he ordered his speechwriters and young media advisors.

Noonan's book is about more than just messages and performance in front of a camera. She recommends that a speaker not underrate his or her audience, and take care to base arguments on sound logic. She warns against speaking in language that is overly elaborate or poetical, and emphasizes over and over the need to speak simply and to "paint pictures" – a concept of which Netanyahu is especially enamored.

"[W]hen you stand and speak it is good, if you can, and if it is appropriate to what you're saying, to give people the outlines of a picture that they can fill in with their imaginations as you speak … If you don't, they will probably come up with their own pictures and imaginings, which may not have anything to do with what you're trying to say,"[16] is Noonan's recommendation. Bibi has embraced it fully.

■■■

"Bribery without money is like … an omelet without an egg," Netanyahu wrote on his Instagram account at the beginning of 2019, launching a competition on the social networks that invited submissions of other images that could complete the sentence, "Bribery without money is like …" His followers sent in their own suggestions, all illustrating the absurdity of indicting the Prime Minister for bribery when what he supposedly received was positive media coverage rather than any monetary gift. What was the motivation behind this idea?

---

16 Peggy Noonan, *Simply Speaking: How to Communicate Your Ideas with Style, Substance, and Clarity*, Harper, 1998, p. 57.

Instead of appealing to logical, analytical thought processes, whereby questions are considered in light of the facts (and the facts in this instance were that there *can* be bribery without involving money, but no one had ever yet been accused of bribery for favorable coverage), Netanyahu shifted the discussion to the realm of imagination and intuition, where imagery and impressions reign supreme. Thus, a legal argument turned into a visual image; rules of evidence turned into rules of cuisine. Bribery without money is like an omelet without an egg. It may not convince the judge, but it works for the public.

There are several reasons why images are so important in conveying messages and persuasion. The first has been demonstrated above. Images are "spin." It paves the way to steer the discussion from one field into another; from factual reality to imagery. Images are a way of bypassing cognitive thought.

Prof. Yehoshua Gitay illustrates how US President Obama often employed images to evade difficult questions. For example, when asked about his critics' claims, he made no effort to address their substance, but rather offered the metaphor of a captain needing to ignore background noise in order to steer the ship. Politicians often find it easier to escape into the realms of analogy than to deal with reality.

Netanyahu compared the possibility of his being put on trial to someone accused of stealing and having his hand cut off, only to have his innocence proven later on. "Can anyone give him back his hand? Can anyone give you back your elections?" he demanded, intending by means of the parallel to remind his listeners that those who harmed him were harming the nation. We are one and the same.

The image of amputated limbs was enlisted in the diplomatic realm, too. Netanyahu invoked it to explain why there could be no relinquishing of territory: "Jerusalem is the heart of the nation; we can never cut our heart in two." How could anyone argue? But on a different occasion the image of the land as a living body was employed to convey exactly the opposite message:

"This land is our homeland; blood of our blood, bone of our bones ... For the sake of peace we are willing to cut into living flesh; we are even willing to relinquish limbs of our land. But we are not willing to give up our security."

Upon re-reading, Netanyahu decided to remove this phrase. When pressed to explain why, in contravention of his promises, during his first term in office he signed the agreement for an Israeli redeployment from Hebron, with a handover of territory to the Palestinian Authority, he upgraded this image:

"This painful surgery is removing certain parts of our homeland and the inheritance of our forefathers from us, but it is also cutting us off from the danger of suffocation that was inherent to the agreement that we inherited – the Oslo Accords."

In the wake of Oslo, the body is sick, it needs surgery, and Netanyahu saves it from suffocation.

When attacked for not advancing negotiations towards a political settlement with Mahmoud Abbas, Bibi chose to respond with an image rather than facts: "I'm interested in [achieving] an agreement and implementing it, but it takes two to tango; we're not going to dance alone."

Netanyahu tends towards the realm of imagery, because there he has much greater room for public relations maneuverability. In the world of images, one can say something and its opposite. Comparing the land to a human body can serve as the basis for an argument in favor of giving up territory, or against. With the right image, one can turn the good guys into bad guys, and vice versa.

The Fat, the Thin and the Soldiers

While spearheading major budget cuts and imposing a heavy economic burden on thousands of families, Netanyahu managed, as Minister of Finance, to portray those harmed by his decisions as people who were themselves a burden on the public. He did this by means of the notorious image of "the fat man and the thin man."

Netanyahu called a press conference and described at length a thin man carrying a fat man on his back, with the latter growing continuously fatter and the former gradually wasting away. The fat man, he explained, was the public sector, which had expanded over the previous three years to the point where it now absorbed 55% of the economy's output. The thin man was the productive private sector, which was carrying the public sector on its back. This image of public servants as fat people weighing down the economy was calculated to create the public legitimacy for budget cuts.

In the years that followed he would describe the fat man and the thin man as an "elephant race," embellishing the theory with a story from his days in the General Staff Reconnaissance Unit, recalling how he and his fellow troops had to race each other to the gate of the camp carrying one of their companions on their shoulders. The military realm is an abundant source of metaphors:

> "When I talk to you, the municipal leadership, I feel like I'm talking to soldiers on the battlefield. You are the battalion commanders of the country … the government representatives who are on the frontlines, dealing with the citizen's everyday problems."

The mayors who were his audience basked in the praise and were quick to hush one of their colleagues who pointed out in a whisper that the citizens are not the enemy. The compliment "You are my soldiers" is one that Netanyahu uses often.

Netanyahu likes images, just as he likes rhetorical questions, because they allow him to say things that he cannot permit himself to say directly. More than once he compared Rabin's signing of the Oslo Accords to someone trying to commit suicide ("jumping off the roof"). He elaborated in greater detail on this image in a speech he delivered from the Knesset podium shortly before Rabin's assassination:

> "I want to tell Prime Minister Rabin, who is not present: Come here, listen to the opposition. Go out into the street and listen to the people. They are giving you a simple message: stop.
>
> "The vehicle has veered off the road, you have lost control of the steering, you have lost the trust of the passengers; the people are not with you. And what do you do? Instead of slowing down, you accelerate. Instead of stopping, you press down on the throttle, straight into the abyss … This process has to be halted."

■■■

Another reason why an image is so powerful is its simplicity. The audience identifies with images taken from its everyday reality. The economic debate over the proper relations between the public and private sectors involves many complicated, in-depth questions about welfare and the state's responsibility towards its citizens. When the whole debate is boiled down to a simple picture, not only the relevant professionals but the general public, too, can understand the argument that is being made. Reams of data are replaced with a single image. It makes the message easier to absorb, and this is of critical importance for a leader addressing the public in an attempt to explain a complex situation.

Some of Netanyahu's images stand out for their originality; others are more mundane: the "locomotive of the economy," "growth engines," terror as a "cancer that metastasizes throughout the world"; a "tsunami of police leaks," a comparison of the task of putting together a coalition to a "Rubik's cube." He peppers his speeches with asides about Israel as a "lighthouse," assimilation as "bleeding," the diversity of the nation as an "orchestra."

What is Charisma?

The images are not mere spin, and not just a rhetorical device to simplify messages or embellish a speech. There are those who maintain that they are the key to Netanyahu's charisma.

Researchers in the US looked at a selection of American Presidents who were known for their charisma, and analyzed their speeches in relation to those of other presidents. What they discovered was that image-based rhetoric is actually an indicator of the speaker's charisma. Leaders who engage our experiential senses, using words that conjure up images, smells, sounds, and tastes and not just our intellect, make their message more real and more compelling.

It is no wonder that the most memorable speeches in Israeli history are identified by the images they painted. In 2017, Netanyahu referred to the opposition as "sourpusses" (literally, "pickles"), continually griping about everything in the country. (Then-) Chief of Staff Gantz came to regret his "anemones speech" in August 2014, calling upon the residents of the South who had left their homes during the Gaza war to return home, waxing poetic about the seasonal beauty of nature awaiting them. The "whales speech" by Minister of Health

Haim Ramon, in 1994, compared the Labor Party to a whale that had lost its sense of direction and kept grounding itself on the beach while he was desperately trying to head it back to the open sea. We have already mentioned Netanyahu's "duck" speech at the AIPAC conference in 2012, calling for the Iranian nuclear program to be recognized for what it was. A few days after the withdrawal of Israeli troops from Lebanon in 2000, Hezbollah chief Hassan Nasrallah asserted that Israel was "feebler than a spider's web."

Images are integral to Netanyahu's charisma and influence. He aims them at his opponents: "Who would put himself in the hands of a doctor who messed up an operation? Who would get on a bus whose driver had been involved in a huge collision?" Netanyahu asked with reference to Olmert, following the Second Lebanon War. Addressing Rabin from the Knesset podium, he said: "We know that you are joined to Arafat like Siamese twins."

∎∎∎

Over the course of 2020, Netanyahu called dozens of prime-time press conferences to convey COVID-related information, instructions, and recommendations to the public. In his efforts to make his explanations accessible and relatable, he invoked a series of different metaphors.

After the first peak of the disease was receding and he had already encouraged the public to get back to living, he was forced to warn: "COVID is still here with us and among us. We have extinguished the big blaze, but the embers of the disease are still smoldering and every gust of wind stirs up new flames." In a leaked recording of a cabinet meeting a month later, one hears clearly his hand banging down on the table as he berates his ministers, using another metaphor, for refusing to impose additional limitations on public movement: "The warships are approaching, one after the other, yet still we refuse to believe. We say, 'Nothing's going to happen.' It's our responsibility to halt this epidemic; the disease is returning." He compared the need for quarantine to the story of Jonah the prophet, "who encountered a violent storm at sea … and spent three days in quarantine, swallowed up by the great fish." When criticism arose over his handling of the crisis, he used yet another metaphor: "It's easy to look in the rear-view mirror, but a leader's job is to look forwards." He summed up the policy for dealing with the economy during an epidemic with a metaphor of one word and great flexibility: "We open up when the numbers go down, and tighten and constrict when the numbers go up. Like an accordion."

■■■

For foreign audiences, too, Netanyahu creates imaginative and memorable images to illustrate his leadership. "The Israeli economy might be compared to a small, easily maneuverable speedboat among tankers. I will steer the boat out of the crisis." On a different occasion, he said: "Making changes to the economy is complicated, hard work. Like turning a big ship around. Do you know what it is to turn a big ship around?"

In his secret conversations with publisher of the *Yedioth Ahronoth* daily newspaper Noni Mozes, too, Netanyahu spoke of his desire to turn a ship in a different direction – this time referring to the paper and its coverage of him. In 2019, he described the distribution of voters in Israel as the body of a submarine divided into Right and Left, and the balance between them. He described the government's faulty leadership in the Second Lebanon War by invoking the greatest naval disaster in history: "Olmert and his people say … we dare not replace the captain. But that's like saying, after the disaster of the Titanic, that if the captain had survived, he should have been given another ship."

A review of his early speeches shows that even while serving as Deputy Minister of Foreign Affairs in the 80s, Netanyahu employed images. Discussing the danger to Jews in South Africa, he said: "Jews have to understand that wherever glaciers start moving, cracks suddenly form, and a jet of gas bursts out of the ground. Generally this jet includes anti-Semitic gasses, too."

The animal kingdom is likewise an unending source of images. *The Israeli Tiger* was the name of a book about the Israeli economy that Netanyahu wrote over the course of more than a year. It was meant to promote his own image as the Minister of Finance who had turned the economic "pussycat" into a tiger. "We need a tiger economy. The Israeli tiger economy. We need it … because that the only way we can finance our security needs," he explained. Despite all the work he had invested, Netanyahu was forced to shelve the manuscript when it was rendered irrelevant by the economic crisis of 2008. The recession hit Israel hard, and pulverized the Irish economy known as the "Celtic tiger" – the model upon which Netanyahu had based his book.

■■■

Over the years, Netanyahu has always found new and creative ways to convey his messages in a manner that simplifies complex arguments so that most of the public can follow them. Here is an example from one of his speeches:

> "A tsunami of extremist Islam is washing over the entire region. Just two days ago, close to 100 people were killed in the heart of Ankara, Turkey, and the flames are reaching us, too. All our neighbors, over an enormous radius, are fighting the Islamist volcano; hundreds of thousands are being slaughtered beyond our borders; millions of refugees are fleeing the sword of zealotry. I promise you, they

understand very well. Ask them. They understand well the abyss that the zealots of extremist Islam have driven them into."

The covert message here is threatening: falling into the abyss, being pierced with a sword or burned by volcanic lava, drowning in a tsunami. Combatting all of these looming disasters is the one and only chairman of the Likud, offering an "island of security."

The Answer: Israel's Security

Ambassador Netanyahu gazed despairingly at the pile of correspondence on his desk. It was growing higher by the day. Every appearance that he made and every mention of Israel in the American media generated another flurry of letters. Most were from Jews from all over the US. Many were from important figures and communal leaders who Netanyahu could not afford to ignore. After a year during which he had tried to respond to each letter personally, he had to find a solution that would save him time. "Let's hope that no one will notice," he said to his assistant, John Kingsley, and instructed him to divide the correspondence into two piles: letters of support and letters of criticism. The heap of correspondence from critics of Israel's policies in Judea and Samaria, and of the IDF's conduct in Lebanon, was higher than the pile of letters in support.

Netanyahu dictated two responses to his assistant. His supporters received a brief "thank you for the warm words," followed by another sentence about how importance their encouragement was in these difficult times. The others received a response that began, "Thank you for your letter. I was sorry to read your words and your sentiments." What followed were two full pages explaining how every country is obligated, first and foremost, to establish law and order and to protect its security, and that this was the aim of Israel's actions. It concluded with a paragraph about Israel's aspirations for peace. "Sincerely, Benjamin Netanyahu, Israel Ambassador to the United Nations." One of these two versions was sent in response to every letter that arrived. Only the name at the top of the page was changed. Dozens of people who wrote to complain or criticize, no matter what the subject, received exactly the same generic reply, designed to apply to the war in Lebanon just as it applied to Israeli policy in the West Bank.

In this manner, the Israeli Ambassador to the UN managed to gain control over the correspondence. Two public relations principles would accompany him from this post all the way to the Prime Minister's Office: to customize responses to target audiences, and to repeat a message over and over. No matter the question, the answer was Israel's security. Beneath the "Israel's security" heading there lay a third principle, which has made Netanyahu such a great spokesman on Israel's behalf. He has employed it ever since his very earliest days in the political arena:

"Don't be quick to judge. You are seeing only a few minutes out of a full-length film," he wrote to anyone who wrote in with criticism. "You're watching the moment when the police jump out onto the road and they start shooting. But you don't see what preceded the police's arrival. You're ignoring the whole film, which shows a rioting gang of criminals who are shooting in all directions and killing civilians. The police are only acting in response …"

Netanyahu explains by means of visual images. The American public is fond of images borrowed from Westerns. Netanyahu replaced the verbal argument that Israel is merely responding to attacks by terrorists with an argument that was visual. This image was stronger than any words – even coming from a fluent English speaker.

■■■

As a high-school student in Philadelphia, Netanyahu would send his brother Yoni, who was serving in the Joint Staff Reconnaissance Unit, the assignments that he prepared for his teachers. Yoni responded with admiration tinged with fraternal jealousy: "You have an amazing ability to express yourself," he wrote, after reading an assignment about Thomas Jefferson. "If only I knew English half as well as you. It seems you know how to utilize the entire range of language at your disposal. If you continue this way, you'll achieve great things. If you can write an assignment like this in 10th grade, who knows what you'll write later on."

Netanyahu's level of English wasn't a God-given gift, but rather the result of very hard work. In fact, Israel's public diplomacy owes a great deal to a little girl named Judy. Netanyahu would like to thank her personally, but he hasn't managed to find her. It was she who sat next to him in class in his early days in the US, which he describes as traumatic. He describes his family's move to the US from his perspective as a young boy: "It was awful; a real upheaval. Really hard. I was eight or nine, and I didn't know a word of English. Not a word."

Judy, his classmate, had a set of cards, each showing a different sentence. She would show him one card at a time and patiently teach him the words. Netanyahu still remembers the sentences ("Spot is a dog") and his mother Zila's instructions for pronouncing the "th" sound: "Push your tongue forward, let it press up against your front teeth, shape your lips like this."

And so thanks to Judy, the immigrant boy who knew no English learned the language that would help him become the most eloquent spokesman Israel ever had.

Did Netanyahu learn how to appear in public? Yes and no; in truth, he's still learning, each time anew. He prepares for every interview, plans the route he will take to the podium, rewrites, rehearses aloud, makes improvements, practices. Now in his fifth term in office, he still buys books on the art of rhetoric. Before important speeches, like those at the UN or before the US Congress, he frees up his calendar so he can spend hours upon hours preparing.

Does it come to him easily and naturally? Yes and no. It becomes natural with time because he lives in a glass cage, exposed to merciless cameras and leaks of every word he utters, and he's become used to the spotlight, but he still works very hard on maintaining his image. There is no media activity that is casual or offhand. His media advisor enters his office more times during the day than his military secretary does.

Creating a Virtual Reality

The "bottles" gimmick was a turning point. He used this image, on the eve of the 2015 elections, to snatch the votes of the religious sector. It happened during a visit to the pre-military religious academy in Eli, a bastion of Religious Zionism. There were two bottles of water on the table in front of him, and he used them to explain why it was dangerous to vote for Right-wing parties other than the Likud: "This is the Likud, and this is the Left – Labor, or whatever they call themselves now," he said, pointing to each of the bottles in turn. "Forming a government will be the task of the party that has the highest water level. Having a large Right-wing bloc isn't what will make the difference."

As he continued speaking, some of the water in the bottle that had been designated the "Right" spilled onto the table. At the polls, there were no accidents; Netanyahu slurped up the votes of the Religious Zionists, and won the election.

It is not just that Netanyahu creates pictures that illustrate his message (drawing a bomb or holding up a bottle). His message itself is a picture (a fat man, a jet of gas). He presents concrete images and explains them by means of verbal images. He steers the audience towards the realm of the imagination, creating a virtual reality in which feeling replaces cognition. This was exactly the accusation that he once levelled at Shimon Peres:

> "I don't know if Mr. Peres knows it, but there's a game that kids like to play today, a very advanced game, called Virtual Reality. They wear a sort of helmet, a kind of a mask, and imagine reality in all sorts of ways. They are transported to the realms of imagination, to other lands, to distant places. It's fine as a game in a closed room, but it's very dangerous for a leader to wear this sort of helmet, this mask, and simply cut himself off from reality. Because the vision of a 'new Middle East' assumes that this is Europe, not the Middle East."

∎∎∎

In the digital age, it makes sense not to appeal to logic. There's no need to waste so many words, which take up valuable screen time.

Technology companies are constantly measuring the average speed at which people scroll down through the advertisements on a news website or social network site. A second or two and we move on.

Most of the information we receive about politics is absorbed in fractions of seconds. No one takes the time to read in-depth analysis, and no one is interested in really paying attention to the political discourse and listening to the arguments offered by the different parties. We just keep scrolling. In the face of this overload of information, there is no benefit to be had in adding even more information and even more words. Visual and emotional arguments are the basis for persuasion in the high-speed, digital mass media.

"An image is more compelling than writing. It imposes its meaning all at once, with no analysis and no dispersion," writes Roland Barthes in *Photography and Electoral Appeal*, to explain how in our times leaders force images on us in order to be elected.

In Front of the Mirror

"Mr. Prime Minister, the speech is very important – I needed to give it more time and thought. Unfortunately, the job 'landed' on me today. It's completely crazy. The result you see requires some improving and rounding out. I hope it will be of help to you all the same," writes one of Netanyahu's aides, hinting to work procedures in the Prime Minister's Office.

Netanyahu scribbles over the aide's message and starts making improvements. He deletes a lot of the content, removing almost all the biblical verses, and adds balloons in the margins with notes to himself: "Here – maintaining security and protecting Jerusalem," or "The opposition shoots its arrows at us instead of at the Palestinians." After every few sentences he adds a capital "P" – pause.

He writes instructions to the typist on the front page: "Please print in a large font. Pay attention to paragraphing." His speeches are printed out in short paragraphs and in a huge font so that he can look up at the camera.

Fellow students from the Cheltenham High School in Pennsylvania recall Netanyahu as a somewhat snooty boy who looked down on their frivolous American games, but was very active in the school's debating team, where he excelled. At the age of 33, when he joined Israel's diplomatic mission in the US, debating became his profession. Other embassy workers would sometimes observe him standing in front of a mirror, practicing before interviews. One of them recounts how Netanyahu would work on his voice, practice his stance, try out facial expressions that would serve his verbal messages, and sometimes perform a chopping motion in the air with his arms to energize himself.

He also took private lessons with Lilyan Wilder, a Jewish actress who became an internationally-acclaimed communication and media consultant with a clientele including George Bush and Oprah Winfrey. Together they would analyze US President Ronald Reagan's appearances and his utilization of the skills that he brought with him as a Hollywood actor to the White House. It was Reagan who coined the memorable "Evil Empire" moniker for the Soviet Union. More than three decades later, Netanyahu would apply the same label to *Yedioth Ahronoth*.

To improve and enhance his media appearances, the young diplomat purchased a video camera and stationed it in the living room of his apartment. His American wife, Fleur, played the role of interviewer. They would film the simulations and then analyze them to learn lessons, polish hand movements, and fine tune messages.

In her books about acting techniques in front of the camera, Wilder offers a great many practical tips. She also developed a seven-stage method for persuasive appearances. Along with instructions pertaining to body language, short and catchy sentences, and the importance of connecting to emotions, Wilder emphasizes the need for the speaker to "be real," or at least to appear to mean every word, rather than just reciting the text: "You have to speak as though you're saying something really important that you really mean," students are taught in Wilder's communications courses. The advice she offers in her books includes not relying on speech alone to convey messages but to involve all the senses.

■■■

Netanyahu uses words that have real impact. We can listen to the argument about the relative sizes of the public and private sectors, backed up with numbers and percentages, but the "fat man and thin man" analogy is something we can both see and hear. We absorb the message via both senses. We can all understand the statement, "Iran is a threat to Israel." But when the Prime Minister asserts that Iran is a "tiger unleashed from its cage," the message has tangible, visual and emotional impact.

As Minister of Finance, Netanyahu described even a topic as dry and technical as planning and construction processes in a manner that included humor, emotion and imagery, all accompanied by body language and hand gestures that reinforced his message:

> "Via Dolorosa! Pain ... suffering ... it's terrible ... You start off with the national committee, then you go on to the regional committee, and then on to the local committee, and then back to the regional committee, and so on in circles, in an unending loop, like a snake coiled on itself. It coils around and around and in the end, eventually, after years of suffering, you might get the permits. There's nothing like it anywhere else in the world. This bureaucracy is suffocating everything."

When the brain receives a message from more than one of our senses, it experiences it more powerfully. The information is more "solid," as it were, and thus we remember it for longer. Hence the importance of using of words that describe pictures, arouse feelings, and recall tastes and smells. The more senses are acted upon, the greater the impact on the listener. The challenge facing anyone who addresses an audience is getting them to not only "see things in their mind's eye," but also tasting, smelling, and feeling.

Great speeches are often described as "giving one goosebumps."

Indeed, great rhetoric produces physical sensations, the words transcending the boundaries of auditory intake and touch the imagination, memories, and experience. One of the most memorable examples of Netanyahu succeeding in arousing physical sensations was his "pickles speech" in the Knesset.

A Smile Slanting to the Left

The Knesset correspondents of all the TV channels were standing in a row and reporting animatedly on his speech and the commotion that it had produced when Netanyahu appeared, coming down the stairs behind them, surrounded by bodyguards. "Mr. Prime Minister …" the correspondents tried to shout their questions, but Netanyahu, experienced enough to avoid answering, kept walking until he was inside his office and the door closed behind his entourage.

Inside the office, the group of aides broke into enthusiastic applause. They were celebrating a victory – the success of a speech in which they had invested dozens of hours of preparation. "That was good," Netanyahu beamed. An aide was already showing him a selection of online reactions and his spokeswoman reported that all the channels had broadcast "everything, live." Topaz Luk, his new media advisor, suddenly announced, "I just had a great idea," and ran out of the office.

The speech started with Netanyahu adopting an "I have a dream" tone and introducing the words that would repeat themselves throughout: "A hundred years ago …" One hundred years ago, Lord Balfour issued his declaration; today, Israel's diplomatic relations are flourishing; next week I am flying to London. A hundred years ago, Australian troops captured Beersheba; next week, the Australian Prime Minister will be coming to Israel for a visit. And if we're already talking about Beersheba – a few words about how it has become a cyber powerhouse in our time. A hundred years ago Allenby liberated Jerusalem; look at how it is flourishing today, under our government. A hundred years ago Sara Aaronsohn, heroine of the Nili underground,[17] committed suicide; look at Israel's security today. Of course – we are working to commemorate Aaronsohn and her companions."

The historian's son surrounded himself with the country's achievements, attributed them to himself, and wove them together as part of the historical continuity of the overall Jewish awakening. It was a masterful creation that had developed over more than 20 different drafts and versions, because Netanyahu attaches great importance to speeches delivered at the opening of a Knesset session, which are broadcast in their entirety on all the TV networks. On this occasion, the speech was memorable mostly because of one word, by which the speech has become known, and the copywriter was Netanyahu himself.

"Oh, it's good; it's really good," Netanyahu had laughed, hitting the desk with his open hand as he always does when he jokes (or when he is angry), every time he read the line from his paper. "It's going to be amazing. I can just imagine what Tzipi and Herzog's faces are going to look like."

"Mr. Prime Minister, you will likely have a lot of interruptions," opined one of his aides. "Very good," Netanyahu replied. He thrives on being heckled when he is at the podium. He requested that the speech be retyped with the new corrections.

This is what Netanyahu said at the opening of the session:

---

17   A Jewish espionage network which assisted the United Kingdom against the Ottoman Empire duringWorld War I. Aaronsohn was intercepted by the Ottomans and tortured, but she gave no information and ultimately shot herself.

"The gloom industry still exists, and it has some respected representatives in the Knesset and in the media. Recently, this gloom industry has opened a new branch: pickles … Today they say, 'There's a sense of sourness amongst the public,' or, alternatively, 'Netanyahu is going around with a sour face.' They can't decide whether I'm sour, or arrogant, or both …

"Things are slow right now, so the pickles do something else: When we're in power, they will always – but always – describe the situation in the country as 'treading water,' 'a freeze,' 'walking in place.' As they see it, if we aren't evacuating Jewish communities, that's 'treading water'; they think nothing of all our achievements … I want to correct what I said before, about them only saying negative things all the time; it's not true. Sometimes these pickles give a half-baked compliment: 'Okay, he knows how to talk, but what is he doing?'

"So the blossoming diplomacy, the economic growth, the shrinking unemployment and lower poverty level, the powerful security situation, the cyber activity, the halting of the illegal migrants, the transportation revolution, the blooming of the Negev and the Galilee – all of this may as well not exist. Why? Because if you haven't evacuated anyone, you haven't done anything! It's a simple formula.

"… In reality, of course, it's all exactly the opposite: not treading water, but moving forwards. Not withdrawal but progress. Not sourness, but smiles."

Topaz returned, carrying a large jar of pickles. He had gone off to the cafeteria and asked for a jar of pickled cucumbers. Now he persuaded the Prime Minister to have his photo taken with the jar, with the Israeli flag and a document shredder in the background. "Words aren't enough; you need a picture to make sure the message stays with them," he insisted, offering the jar. Netanyahu, having learned to go along with his young advisors when it came to social media, agreed. The smile captured by the camera is lop-sided. An arrogant smile.

People Choose an Image

Sheena Iyengar is a blind researcher who, as in the ancient fable, sees further and better than most seeing people. She is a professor at Columbia Business School, and her research focuses on the many facets of human choice and decision making. Her blindness is relevant to a study that is helpful for an understanding of Netanyahu's charisma.

Iyengar, an expert in the art of choice, is unable to choose the color of her nail polish; she has to rely on others. Once, on a visit to the beauty parlor, she was offered two shades of pink: one was called "Ballet Slippers," the other "Magic." Iyengar asked some of the other clients to advise her. They were all firm in their opinions – but divided.

One woman said that the professor should definitely go with "Ballet Shoes." "What does it look like?" Iyengar asked. She was told, "It's a very elegant shade of pink." But a different woman interrupted, declaring that "Magic" was a much better choice. She, too, was asked to describe the color, and her reply was, "It's a shiny shade of pink." Each woman was very sure of her choice, and the blind professor's deliberation led to a heated debate. To try to reach a conclusion, Iyengar asked, "So how would I tell them apart? What's the difference between them?" They explained over and over again that the one shade was more "elegant," the other "shinier." It's not easy to describe a color. Iyengar recalls with a big smile that the only thing that the two sides agree on was, "If you could just see 'Ballet Shoes' and 'Magic,' you would understand right away what we mean."

Which nail polish did the professor end up choosing? She took both bottles to her research lab and removed their labels so she could conduct an experiment to see whether the women arguing in the beauty parlor had been influenced by the name on the bottle or by its contents. Iyengar brought a number of women to the lab, presented the two colors of pink, and asked, "Which would you choose?" Half of the women accused her of trying to trick them: "It's obvious that you've filled both bottles with exactly the same color," they retorted.

Sheena hadn't tricked them. The people who had actually tried to "mess with their minds" were those who had created the labels branding the products. The argument in the beauty parlor, while heated, was actually based not on the difference in color, but rather on the different emotional effects produced by the labels. The next stage of Iyengar's experiment involved exchanging the labels "Ballet Shoes" and "Magic," and the results were unequivocal. We make choices on the basis of the label, the wrapping, and not the product itself. The vast majority of the women tested preferred the "Ballet Shoes" label, even when the labels were exchanged. When the labels were removed and the choice was made solely on the basis of the color, there was a slight preference for "Magic."

People don't choose substance, leaders, and positions. They choose an image.

■■■

Netanyahu relies on the results of Iyengar's research, and many other studies focusing on branding, sales, and politics, when he meets with his campaign teams to decide on the image to be associated with each of his rivals. After he defines the image, his team starts disseminating it in the media.

Tzipi Livni was portrayed as a cardboard cutout, Gantz was a puppet controlled by media consultants; Isaac ("Bougie") Herzog was "Pizza Bougie"; the leaders of Blue and White were depicted as squabbling dolls; Bennet and Shaked were portrayed as children in kindergarten, playing with Lego. The images were aimed at turning these rivals into one-dimensional caricatures. In unofficial advertisements funded by the Likud, Livni was portrayed as a political harlot, and Gantz as schizophrenic. Lapid was consistently portrayed as a newsreader and presenter. In another clip, Gantz was presented as down-and-out, looking for work, lacking answers and experience.

Considerable resources were devoted to developing these images and identifying them with Netanyahu's rivals, including experienced actors, polished scripts, professional directors, focus groups to offer comments, and so on. With their hefty production budgets, each of these clips received over a million views.

The State Attorney's office was portrayed as a sewing workshop, with tailors working on criminal "suits"; Noni Mozes, publisher of *Yedioth Ahronoth* (which Netanyahu views as a menacing media threat) was compared to Lord Voldemort.

Netanyahu reduces himself to an image, too. In clips released just prior to the elections he allowed himself to play different imaginary roles. In one clip he is a lifeguard on the beach, tossing back tennis balls, rackets, and any other threats that approach Israel's shores. "I'll be starting a new shift on Election Day, if you give me your trust," he explains to two voters who have come to swim in the choppy waters of the Middle East. In a different clip he plays a tour guide in a forest full of dangerous threats; Lapid and Gantz are inexperienced tour guides who have lost their way. Bibi gathers the frightened youngsters around him between the trees so he can show them how to make their way through life and politics. In another clip, which received international responses, parents try to book a babysitter for the children, but end up with "Bibi-sitter" instead.

Netanyahu is the "responsible adult," the guardian of Israel, the children's last defense. Beneath everything lies the image of the father – the father of the nation. No matter which image he chooses, he takes pains to maintain the status of the guardian and protector.

∎∎∎

Secret #3: Synesthesia By making use of images that arouses our senses, imagination, and emotions, Netanyahu simplifies his messages and makes them compelling and real. Sometimes this also helps him to bypass critical thinking that is based on facts and data, shifting the discourse to the emotional realm that allows his listeners to identify with him. In his election campaigns he attaches negative images to his rivals, while presenting himself as the guardian of Israel.

4.
MIND GAMES
NEURO-POLITICS

Two correspondents for *Time* magazine accompanied Netanyahu over the course of two intensive days of activity in July, 2019. They were surprised to discover the extent of his preparations for their encounter.

In the spacious living room of his official residence in Jerusalem, Netanyahu took out a file crammed with laminated documents. A detailed explanation accompanied each as it was drawn from the file. The coffee and cookies were moved aside to make room for diagrams and infographics that were spread all over the glass table. Many of them showed rows of blue columns indicating Israel's economic growth over the years under Netanyahu's leadership. Following this presentation, Netanyahu asked his aides to bring out "the other file."

The other file was full of diplomatic and security maps, and satellite and other intelligence photographs. One map was marked with black and red blotches, showing the areas gobbled up by ISIS. Another showed the range of Iranian missiles, including over Europe and the East Coast of the US. There were also photographs of terrorists in Gaza using civilians as human shields, and residential homes serving as arms depots in Lebanon. One picture was shown to the *Time* journalists in an attempt to convey a message to the Arab countries. The map showed a plane making its way from Ben Gurion Airport to

India. It was meant to illustrate the potential economic benefits to be gained if the Al Saud royal family would allow El Al pilots to shorten their flights eastward and to fly over Saudi Arabia – as indeed happened, within the framework of the peace agreements signed in 2020.

After a lengthy exposition, there was time for questions. Brian Bennett, *Time's* senior White House correspondent, tried to coax a headline out of the Prime Minister: "If Iran starts stockpiling nuclear material, beyond JCPOA[18] and other agreements, what kind of action are you willing to take?" he asked. Netanyahu replied, "We will take whatever action is necessary to prevent Iran from acquiring nuclear weapons." Bennett tried again: "Does that include an open strike on Iranian nuclear facilities?" and got the same response: "Whatever action is necessary, will be taken." Bennet asked, "Are those facilities too far in the ground to be impacted by strikes?" and Netanyahu replied, "Let's consider what an intelligent journalist like you would consider an intelligent response to that, if I say yes, or if I say no. Neither one is satisfactory, so I'm just going to say: we will take whatever action is necessary."

This was the fourth time that *Time* magazine had chosen to profile Netanyahu. One of the previous cover stories had been entitled "King Bibi." This time he was photographed sitting on a simple wooden chair under the large map in his office, with a play of light and shadow over his face and a determined look in his eyes. The heading this time was, "The Strong Survive."

■■■

---

18 The Joint Comprehensive Plan of Action, more commonly known as the Iran nuclear agreement or Iran deal, signed in 2015 between Iran and China, France, Russia, UK, US (the fivepermanent members of the United Nations Security Council), Germany, and theEuropean Union.

Election campaign slogans in Israel make heavy use any word derived from the Hebrew root *h-z-k* (strong). "Strong" is the holy grail of campaigns. This assertion is supported by data on the most commonly used word in campaigns since the 1980s.

Netanyahu repeats the word "strong" more vigorously than any other party leader. In 1999, Likud campaigns touted "a strong leader for a strong nation," and "Likud – strong leadership." Later on, the party boasted that it was "strong against Hamas" and promised "a strong Likud – a safe Israel" that would be "strong on security, strong on economy." Other slogans included "A strong Prime Minister – a strong Israel," "Bibi and Lieberman – a strong combination for Israel," and so on over the years. In the 2019 elections the "strong" theme became even more pronounced. The Likud slogan was "Netanyahu. Right. Strong."

In every public appearance that Netanyahu made during the 2019 campaigns, the background behind him included the slogan, "A Strong Right,", and the contrasting message – "Lapid-Gantz – a Weak Left." Netanyahu wanted to frame the election as a choice between strength and weakness.

Gantz's campaign staff understood his intention and were ready to thwart it. Benny Gantz launched his political campaign with the slogan "Only the strong win," showing the numbers of terrorists killed in Gaza in the military campaigns that he had led.

Gantz named his party "Israel Resilience," and when he joined forces with Lapid's Yesh Atid to form Blue and White, the new party's all-male leadership with its lineup of former generals in effect embraced Netanyahu's view that whoever the voters regarded as being strong would win the political war.

"So we're a 'weak Left'? Netanyahu is ignoring the facts. In the meantime, it was I, and not the Prime Minister, who destroyed a nuclear reactor," declared Gabi Ashkenazi. Ashkenazi was also quoted as saying, "We're living in a reality that has no place for weaklings," in the context of the possibility of concessions to the Palestinians. It is virtually identical to an earlier post from Netanyahu's Twitter account:

> "In the Middle East, and in many parts of the world, there is a simple truth: There is no place for the weak. The weak crumble, are slaughtered and are erased from history while the strong, for good or for ill, survive. The strong are respected, and alliances are made with the strong, and in the end peace is made with the strong."

Declaring War

"To beat Netanyahu you have to have dead-set on winning. It's not for the faint-hearted," said Yair Lapid. "I put a 'bullet between Netanyahu's eyes,'" boasted Naftali Bennet when he managed to thwart a political decision. The Attorney General's decision to investigate and indict Netanyahu was referred to by the Prime Minister as an "attempt at political assassination," and he claimed that his "blood was being spilled." At one point there were reports that "knives were being drawn" in the Labor party. Gantz has been described as lacking the "killer instinct," and Right-wing voters are called upon to "do their share carrying the stretcher."

The political realm is a battlefield. From the moment that the opening shot of the election campaign is fired, it becomes a battle of political survival in which every side charges forward and fights ferociously for every vote. The contenders attack each other and tear apart each other's arguments, knowing that in the end there is only either victory or defeat. Each party adopts a strategy and tactics of political assassination. They mobilize support, present the situation as critical, line up attractive candidates, evade political landmines and explosive topics, plan painful blows (or, where necessary, shoot from the hip), and drop political bombshells. The fray often includes friendly fire.

A study of images used in election campaigns shows that every society has its own "supreme metaphors" and it is these that shape the public consciousness and, by extension, the vote. In Israel, war is a supreme metaphor in political life.

Immediately upon Netanyahu's victory in the first round of elections in 2019, before becoming bogged down in his efforts to form a government, journalist Amit Segal wrote a column entitled "Political Genius", in which he enumerated Netanyahu's achievements: "He shattered the Left, got rid of Bennet and Shaked, gained five mandates, slaughtered Kahlon and Lieberman, and obstructed Feiglin." Shelly Yachimovich, who claimed during the election campaign that Gantz had "declared war" on her party, lamented afterwards, "Blue and White massacred us." The defeated candidates from Blue and White likewise hurried to assure the public following the first election, "We lost the battle, but not the war. We are preparing for the next round." Lapid promised, "We will turn the Knesset into a battleground." Following Netanyahu's failure to form a government, the Prime Minister's spokesman instructed all Likud MKs and ministers: "No holding back – free fire in Lieberman's direction." And following the second round of elections, Blue and White boasted, "We won the war for democracy," while Netanyahu accused the police, who was investigating his advisors, of committing "a terror attack against democracy." He referred to Gantz's effort to create a minority government with the Arab parties as a "national terror attack."

At the swearing-in of the new Knesset, President Reuven Rivlin pleaded, "Now it's over. Enough. We have to start climbing back up. To put aside the swords that were drawn in the elections, and to clean up the mess." His words recalled the opening lines of Szymborska's poem *The End and The Beginning*: "After every war / someone has to clean up. / Things won't / straighten themselves up, after all."

The war metaphor influences the voter subconsciously. It is interwoven in every news report and it hovers perpetually in the background, shaping a consciousness that leads to a vote for "strength."

The feeling among the public during election season – the sense that "there is a war on" – serves Netanyahu well, in view of the fact that he brands himself as Mr. Security and is perceived as strong. If a war is going on, it makes sense to stand behind the current, strong leader and to maintain stability. Now is not the time to make changes; one can't afford the privilege of voting for someone else or being open to other possibilities. Since the elections are not a discussion over the country's future but rather a war of survival, Bibi is the preferred leader among voters on the Right. At the negotiating table, the smarter side wins; in court, the winner is the party with justice on its side. On the battlefield, strength is what counts.

First and Foremost – Security

HaPortzim Street is closed to traffic. At its far end, near Yoni Netanyahu Square, the VIP Protection Unit has put up a blue awning to provide shade for the X-ray security scanner and magnetometer. A very long line of visitors is waiting outside the house where the Prime Minister is sitting "Shiva"[19] for his father, Benzion. My visit has been coordinated with Edna Halbani, who has served as director of international visits at the Prime Minister's Office for more than four decades. The metal detector raises no objection to my arrival, and I head for the stone steps.

---

19   Traditional Jewish 7-day mourning period.

I think about what to say when I shake his hand and offer my condolences. Perhaps I should mention that I have had the opportunity of meeting three generations of the family: I knew the late Benzion Netanyahu as my neighbor from HaPortzim Street; I have met Netanyahu himself, and I know Yair, his son, from my years of service as commander of the School for Communications in the IDF Spokesman's Unit. There is also a message that I want to convey about the chain of generations and a father's pride in his son. I presume that it is more important to me to convey this message than is to him to hear it.

The living room is packed and the line snakes around in circles until the visitors reach Netanyahu, who is seated at the far end. Before me in line are authors Eyal Megged and Zeruya Shalev. Netanyahu's face lights up when he sees them. He holds writers in great esteem, all the more so when they are counted among his supporters. I approach to shake hands with the Prime Minister who, judging by his facial expression, doesn't remember my name. I remind him and he nods, "Yes, yes, of course," but just as I start telling him about my acquaintance with the three generations, I feel a domineering hand on my shoulder.

"Excuse me, Mr. Prime Minister, now, please." The voice is authoritative. It is National Security Advisor Yaakov Amidror. "Now, please, Mr. Prime Minister."

Amidror lifts one hand, the other is holding a folder full of documents. He announces, loudly and clearly, "Ladies and gentlemen, the Prime Minister is now entering a meeting. It is a matter that cannot be delayed. Thank you very much, thank you." Netanyahu shakes my hand, "I appreciate your coming," but Amidror is already urging him in the direction of the adjoining room, and the door closes behind them.

The door opens again for a moment when another man in uniform joins the political advisor and the military secretary who are now sitting with the Prime Minister at the wooden table where history books used to be written. Now it is covered with documents from the confidential folder. "Security comes first," Edna politely explains to the visitors.

The next morning I am up at five thirty. At exactly seven o' clock I turn on the microphone. The technician on the other side of the glass partition plays the jingle – "Israel this morning; two hours of current events with Kave Shafran." The red light in front of me blinks on and I report, "It's seven o'clock on Galei Israel radio, and here is the news. According to foreign sources, Israeli air force planes attacked last night …"

"Security comes first" isn't meant only in the sense of how the Prime Minister prioritizes visitors, meetings, discussions and daily agenda. Security dictates whether or not he will be elected. Security is uppermost in the voter's mind.

What Goes on in the Brain

Neuropolitics is a relatively new field of research that seeks to discern voting choices based on brain activity. It uses neuroscience to explore which area of the brain is responsible for the decision to vote for a particular candidate. That becomes the part of the brain that is targeted in campaigns – and thus we arrive at the neurology of politics.

Two parts of the voter's brain are relevant to politicians and their advisors. One is the "feeling brain," known in professional language as the limbic system, which deals with emotions, memories, and intuition. The feeling brain makes quick, automatic decisions based on sensory input.

The other region of interest is the "thinking brain," known as the prefrontal cortex, responsible for executive functioning including verbal expression and abstract thought. This type of thinking is slower than the activity of the feeling brain. It delves into details, examines arguments, and engages in reasoning.

We generally assume that voters are rational – in other words, that they make their decisions using the thinking brain. This, it seems, is simply not true. A rational citizen who wants to make a sound political decision using his analytic, thinking brain should study the competing parties' platforms and compare each parameter (e.g., economic, social, diplomatic, security, etc.,) on the basis of past experience and different indices. Then he should weigh all the information and decide which party best represents his position.

In reality, surveys conducted in every country show that most voters don't even know what the various parties' positions are on the different issues. Researchers have compared positions, parties and votes and found that many people vote for parties that don't stand for many of the values and policies that they themselves believe in. The reason why extremist parties grow stronger is because people who are not extremists vote for them. At the same time, a growing body of data indicates that voting patterns are largely identity-based (i.e., residential area, type of household), rather than position-based. The decision to vote for a particular party or candidate is not made by the thinking brain. Rather, it originates in the feeling brain, in the limbic system, the seat of images and representations, where decisions are made in an associative, intuitive manner. Intuitive judgment is feeling-based and rife with stigmas, which is exactly what political propaganda wants. This is the foundation for the claim that politicians play with voters' minds. Indeed, they do. They adapt their messages to specific areas of the brain.

Useful Illusions

How can people come to believe something that they know is incorrect? They have to hear it repeated over and over again. Ultimately, we believe that which is familiar to us. This was discovered when participants in a study were asked once a week to gauge the reliability of different statements presented as facts, and it turned out that the reliability of "facts" that appeared frequently, rose with each passing month. Even people with broad general knowledge, who originally awarded the statement "A sari is a Scottish skirt" a low level of reliability, raised the ranking week by week. This is the "illusion of truth effect"(, also known as the reiteration effect).

Marketing professionals are familiar with this effect, which explains why advertisements are broadcast again and again, sometimes within an interval of only half a minute. Netanyahu repeats an argument again and again for the same reason, until his voters adopt it.

Aside from the illusion of truth effect, the brain has other tendencies that affect our voting. For example, there is the confirmation bias whereby we unconsciously seek out and favor information that confirms or supports our prior beliefs or values, while ignoring information that contradicts them. What this means is that we don't really listen to political rivals. Then there is herd behavior: the probability that we will embrace some statement or another grows with the number of people who profess it. The result is that surveys that predict victory for a certain party actually cause people to vote for the "winner." Anchoring, or cognitive bias, leads us to place undue reliance on an initial piece of information that we are given, and to deal with whatever information follows in relation to that initial anchor. For instance, in negotiations, the first offer becomes the yardstick for assessing all subsequent ones, and thus determines the outcome. What this means is that whoever sets the media tone in fact molds the agenda that everyone thereafter subscribes to.

According to Netanyahu, one of the reasons that many Likud voters did not bother to turn up and vote in the 2019 elections was a false belief that victory was assured. They were certain that he would be elected "as always" and hence felt no need to make any effort to make this happen. Netanyahu tried to arouse them from this false sense of security by warning of impending defeat in battle. He failed. The reason for their nonchalance was the human tendency to believe that what has been up until now will continue.

There are other psychological tendencies that work to Netanyahu's benefit. One is the choice-supportive bias, which causes us to justify our choices retroactively even when they turn out to have been detrimental. In other words, there is a good chance that we will vote again for whoever we voted for in the past. Then there is the ostrich effect, which causes us to bury our head in the sand when it comes to negative information. Other effects cause us to think along stereotypical lines even when we think that we are unbiased. This tendency awards elements such as race and gender an inordinate political importance. Our brains cause us to judge leaders by their external appearance, their height, their voice, and their facial features, rather than by their views and values.

In keeping with all of the above, Netanyahu uses images and non-verbal messages, prefers feelings to facts, tells stories and describes characters, uses first and second person and speaks of "us and them," and frames the elections as a war in which the strong are victorious. These are just some of the tactics that are based in neuropolitics. In coming chapters, we will analyze some more cognitive and political biases by means of which Netanyahu gains votes.

Magnetometer for the Brain

Netanyahu, more than most other leaders, makes use of another part of the voter's brain – the amygdala, a cluster of nuclei located deep in the brain's medial temporal lobe that is responsible for our survival. Any information or stimulation that reaches the brain passes via the amygdala and is classified as a threat, an opportunity, or irrelevant. The amygdala is the brain's magnetometer.

In prehistoric times the amygdala had the important role of protecting man from animals of prey, and it continues to function despite the processes of urbanization that mankind has undergone. It is continually monitoring the environment for any danger. Since the amygdala is programmed to identify threats to our survival, it is constantly scanning for negative messages.

More than two million people follow Netanyahu's Facebook page. This is the message that they received on the eve of the 2019 elections:

> "On Tuesday you can determine the future of our state. Prime Minister Netanyahu brings with him a Right-wing policy of a Jewish state, security, and a strong Israel. A dangerous Left-wing government with Lapid, Ouda, Gantz and Lieberman must not arise next week. A Left-wing, secular, weak government that relies on the Arabs who want to eradicate all of us – women, children and men – and will allow a nuclear Iran to destroy us. We cannot let that happen!"

The sound of glass shattering on a campaign broadcast on TV as Arafat walks next to Shimon Peres; the sound of wailing sirens and the sights of terror attacks; enraged, masked men shouting "blood and fire" in Arabic – these are some of the non-verbal elements from the Likud election broadcasts from 1996 that were calculated to activate the alarm in the brains of Israeli citizens. Almost 25 years later, Netanyahu is still using the same tactics.

The words "catastrophe," "exploding buses," "a thousand casualties" that repeat themselves in Netanyahu's speeches to describe what was and what will be if the Left come into power, along with the mainstays – "blood and fire," "Iran," "Holocaust," "terror," "danger of annihilation," "existential threat" – are all meant to activate the amygdala and warn of impending danger.

Netanyahu's messages are powerful and have an impact because they deal with questions of survival, and therefore, when it comes to processing information in the brain, they are the first to be absorbed. Immediate threats activate primal evolutionary mechanisms. Netanyahu proceeds not from politics, but from evolution. When he accused of Gantz of trying to create a minority government with the Arab parties, he presented this as an act of terrorism and a deliberate blurring of the difference between Blue and White, and Gaza and Teheran:

> "We understand that we have to come together for emergency action in the face of an emergency situation … If such a minority government arises, they will be celebrating in Teheran, in Ramallah and in Gaza just as they have celebrated after every terror attack, but this will be an historical national terror attack on the State of Israel; it must not happen."

Life-and-Death Voting

> "When dealing with matters of life and death, and matters of the State's existence, there is no room for politics and personal considerations."

This was Netanyahu's statement in 2019 when he wanted to avoid bringing forward the elections. And when he ended up calling for elections, he immediately defined them as "a battle for our home." Every election campaign that Netanyahu leads is, from his point of view, a matter of "life and death," and thus the decision of who to vote for is transferred to the voter's amygdala. In the run-up to the 2015 elections, too, Netanyahu said, "When it's a question of life and death, I'm not prepared to play political games."

During a visit to the Bergen-Belsen death camp, Netanyahu appealed to the "Jewish brain" programmed by history to recognize threats to survival:

> "Nowadays people say, there won't be another Holocaust. Never again. The world won't allow it; Israel won't allow it. But we dare not ignore the dangers that exist … The danger of mass destruction has not passed and we have no reason to think that the world will prevent the armament of those who seek our annihilation."

For more than twenty years, Netanyahu has been warning, with clear allusions to the Holocaust, that the danger of mass destruction hovers over Israel. Year after year he warns that in another moment Iran will have a nuclear bomb, year after year he claims that we are dealing with new security threats. Sometimes he claims that they are quite unprecedented:

> "I'm not exaggerating when I say that the threats are greater than ever. They may perhaps be greater than they have been since the establishment of the State, or since the difficult periods that we experienced in the first decades of our independence."

The above is a quote from 2013; both previously, in 2009, and later, in 2019, Netanyahu similarly defined the threats at the time as "greater than ever." Therefore, went the foregone conclusion, vote only for a strong Right-wing. But when Netanyahu chose, in October 2019, to advance a unity government with Benny Gantz, he again used the survival argument, invoking life and death. A strong Right-wing was no longer enough:

> "A tremendous security challenge is approaching us at enormous speed; it is already here. In order to deal with it, we have to join forces, since the nation needs to be unified and it needs to be ready. We have to prepare the nation with a broad front …"

Bibi's messages are directed at the amygdala and the primal human defense mechanisms. It is not a mere political trick to convince our minds. He seems to really believe it. He is convinced that history has appointed him, Benjamin Netanyahu, to save the Jewish nation from another holocaust. Thus, it is not a question of politics, but rather of life and death and the continuation of history: "The results of our struggle will determine not only our fate, but the fate of the Jews and of Judaism itself." Netanyahu's campaign always perceives the questions as existential ones, and hence his rivals are not just a political threat but an existential threat.

As part of its survival management, the amygdala dictates the fight-flight-freeze response. In prehistoric times, this was of critical importance. If an animal of prey approached, a human could remain absolutely still, making no movement that would attract the animal's attention. This could save his life. Freezing is certainly an option in the political context, too. Change requires an investment of energy. According to researchers in the field of decision making, such as Prof. Yossi Yassour, when we are tired or threatened, we tend to choose to maintain the status quo, without moving or changing anything.

At a time of danger we close ranks behind whoever the leader is. Fear paralyzes our adventurousness and the daring needed to make changes. Netanyahu is the status quo. His wife, Sara, once expressed this way of thinking as follows:

> "Sometimes there are issues of personal squabbles and getting back at each other, but there's one thing they don't understand: that the country is on fire, that there are terror attacks, that beyond all the political squabbles there is one person who can save the country. And when I hear all the complaints of some of the Likud members, I say: To hell with it; if that's what they're interested in, to hell with it.
>
> "Bibi is a leader who is really too big for this country. He is truly a leader on a national scale. If everyone in this country wants to be slaughtered and burned, then fine; why does he need to work so hard? We'll move overseas. Let the country burn down. This country won't survive without Bibi. People here will be slaughtered."

■■■

John Hibbing, a professor of political science at the University of Nebraska and a pioneer in the field of neuropolitics, studied neural responses among voters of various parties and discovered differences in brain activity between conservatives and liberals. Hibbing found that conservatives (Right-wing voters in the Israeli context) experience actual physical discomfort (as evidenced by their squirming in their chairs and increased sweating) when they hear about foreign influences or are exposed to new ideas that will lead to change in the existing situation.

"I don't agree with the assertion that threats influence everyone to the same extent. Conservatives are sensitive to threats of any sort, including sensitivity to threats towards their groups of supporters and towards their leader," argues Prof. Hibbing, whose co-authored book about the genetics of politics examines the attitude towards Trump as well as some nationalist Right-wing leaders in Europe. The book stirred up a storm among political psychologists in the US owing to its assertion that genetic and hereditary predisposition could explain about a third of the difference in political views in most countries of the world.

According to this neuropolitical approach, it is no wonder that Netanyahu's threats are especially effective specifically among Right-wingers in Israel. The constant undertone of danger and fear of change and loss is particularly well suited to his audience of conservative voters, and it is for this reason that he is always appealing to the amygdala.

Emergency is routine, and hope can turn out to be a dangerous illusion. "Even when 'the wolf shall dwell with the lamb', we will keep our swords at the ready," Netanyahu once explained. On a different occasion he said, "Even then, we won't agree to be the lamb." It's important to Netanyahu that the public know that the political struggle is a battle of survival:

> "We cannot and may not get caught up in daydreams, which are an attempt to escape the grim battle imposed on

us by the very fact of our existence as a nation among the Arab nations. Even if we manage to establish formal peace with the Arab countries, the dangers of war and future conflicts won't disappear … We can't escape the battle for survival without relinquishing life itself."

Holocaust, Corona, and Politics

"Unlike the Holocaust, this time we identified the threat in time," Netanyahu declared at a memorial ceremony for the six million Jews slaughtered in Europe during WWII, with reference to COVID. The surprising comparison raised quite a few eyebrows. There's no apparent connection between the Holocaust and the COVID pandemic, but Bibi is a master at linking different threats and fears – especially where there's political advantage to be gained.

In a similar way, while conducting intensive efforts to court the Left and coax them into a unity government, Bibi managed the following feat of rhetorical acrobatics, linking COVID to the destruction of Jerusalem:

"Two thousand years ago, while a foreign enemy was besieging Jerusalem, Jews were at war among themselves, and disaster wasn't long in coming. Therefore I say, today specifically: We have to join forces. We have to establish a unity government. We have to form a national emergency government. I say to the members of Blue and White: take your place under the stretcher, we will carry it together, we will lead it together, and together we will save the people and the country."

After the unity government fell apart, Netanyahu embarked on another election campaign promising to save the people and the country, once again enlisting COVID for his political purposes. This time he blamed his Left-wing rivals for the continued spread of the disease. He referred to the Left-wing demonstrations outside his official residence as "COVID incubators" and accused the opposition of putting people's lives at risk:

"There has been a gradual weakening of adherence to the Health Ministry guidelines: people are neglecting to wear masks, neglecting to maintain social distance, and holding numerous, dangerous gatherings. Unfortunately, this is being spearheaded by populist politicians ... They said this disease 'isn't a disease', that there's no need to obey guidelines. This evening I heard Yair Lapid, head of the opposition, at a time of national emergency, when he should be uniting everyone and consolidating support for the government's decisions – he's eroding it instead, and thereby endangering the lives of Israel's citizens."

Bibi is the guardian of the people. The Left is the enemy of the people. Netanyahu, who finds ways to connect different and disparate dangers, also knows how to link external enemies with internal ones. For instance, when Gideon Sa'ar, a long-standing member of the Likud and former minister, announced that he was leaving to form a new party and would be running for Prime Minister, Netanyahu was quick to assert that his new adversary had joined the Left bloc, while reasserting his own status as saving Israel from the dangers of Iran and COVID:

"While I'm busy bringing vaccines and healing to the citizens of Israel, there are others who are busy saving their political careers. I think the citizens of Israel know very well who is bringing vaccines, who is saving them from COVID, and who is constantly struggling against Iran's efforts to arm itself with nuclear weapons."

There is no logical connection between the COVID threat and a nuclear Iran, but Bibi takes pains to create a link through his use of words. One threat follows another. One day it's the Holocaust, the next it's COVID. The covert message is: I am protecting you from a holocaust; I am protecting you from Iran; I am protecting you from COVID; I am protecting you from terror. The contest between Netanyahu and his rivals is a matter of life or death.

Shortly before the 2021 elections, after Facebook closed fictitious Instagram accounts critical of Netanyahu, some of which were operating from Muslim countries including Iran, the Likud put out a public statement connecting the Israeli Left to those seeking Israel's destruction:

> "Iran used social networks to fuel demonstrations by the Left against Prime Minister Netanyahu, and to generate criticism of his fight against COVID. Iran, which pursues the aim of annihilating Israel through its efforts to attain nuclear weaponry and to arm the enemies surrounding us, is investing efforts in bringing down Netanyahu because it knows that Netanyahu has stood firmly for years against these efforts. The leftist demonstrators will not be able to obscure the fact that they are supported by one of the most repressive regimes in the world, and they both share the same aim: to bring down Prime Minister Netanyahu. We shall not allow Iran to prevail."

Netanyahu's propaganda brew includes his leftist foes along with his enemies in Iran, all seasoned with references to the Holocaust, fear of COVID, and distant memories of the destruction of Jerusalem. Both the nuclear threat and the biological threat have only one correct answer, and it is Netanyahu.

Let Cortisol Decide

Within a fraction of a second after a possible threat is identified and the amygdala activates the survival mechanism, there is a release of the hormone cortisol, also known as the "stress hormone." Cortisol, no less than Netanyahu himself, has emerged as a hero of Israeli election campaigns. It is present especially at the climatic moments in politics where all the campaigns and messages converge: Election Day. Cortisol, as Netanyahu's emissary, enters the voting booth along with the voter.

When Endocrinology and Democracy Collide is the title that researchers from Haifa University and the Soroka Medical Center chose for a study which used saliva samples as indicators of the cortisol levels in the bloodstream of voters arriving at voting booths. What they found was that the level of anxiety on Election Day was very high. The cortisol level jumped considerably higher at voting time than its usual level, especially among those who were voting for parties for which the polls predicted defeat.

Negative polls have the effect of raising cortisol levels. Netanyahu knows that cortisol and the survival instinct serve him well, and he works to increase the amount of this stress hormone – not only by means of a slew of security threats, but also by means of what has come to be known as his "gevalt!" (Yiddish; a cry of shock or impending doom) tactics.

The warning of impending loss starts about a week before Election Day with a blitz of public appearances: "It's important for me to be interviewed so that everyone can hear me and understand that we dare not be complacent." Netanyahu conveys exactly the same message on every local radio show and on every sectorial website: "We're going to lose."

Three days before the elections, when the media is prohibited from publishing polling figures so as not to sway public opinion, the Prime Minister speaks from every available platform, citing the least favorable of all published polling results, and warns that the Likud is headed for defeat. He took this approach in the 2015 elections, when he was up against Livni and Herzog, and again in 2019 when his rivals were Gantz and Lapid.

"Right now what we're seeing in the surveys, including internal surveys, is that Lapid and Gantz are leading by a number of mandates," Netanyahu intoned, his expression deliberately somber. "It's not a shoo-in. Right now, if we don't wake up, what will happen is that Lapid and Gantz will put together a Left-wing government," he exhorted the public, and quickly called a meeting of Likud-affiliated local government heads. "If you don't come to the polling stations, we won't be able to close the gap," he told them. He also put in an appearance, cameras in tow, on the beach, using a megaphone to address the complacent bathers: "If you stay here at the sea and don't go and vote, we're going to lose to the Left!" He went to the outdoor markets and warned, "We're going to wake up tomorrow morning with Yair Lapid as the Prime Minister of a Left-wing government!" He told them, "Lapid is starting to write his victory speech."

Six hours before the polling booths were due to close, an announcement was released to the media that had presumably been prepared by the campaign team a week earlier: "Netanyahu has cancelled the rest of his itinerary for today in view of the low voting turnout at Likud strongholds; he is holding an emergency discussion at the Prime Minister's residence." Politicians aren't interviewed on Election Day. Netanyahu seized the opportunity to pose in front of his tablet camera and start a live broadcast on Facebook. The headline for the broadcast was formulated along the lines of a news broadcast after a terror attack:

"Emergency for the Right. Lapid and Gantz are leading by four mandates. Go out and vote for Likud right now!!! Live broadcast, ongoing." For over an hour, Netanyahu broadcast panic. Almost half a million people watched. Netanyahu won the first round of elections in 2019 because he forecast impending disaster. The threat of defeat is what brought him glory. Cortisol was on his side, both because of the security threat and because of the threat of defeat.

"This psychological state has a decisive impact on the elections," claim the authors of *When Endocrinology and Democracy Collide*. They explain that the psychological stress reflected in the bloodstream may adversely affect people's judgment. They point to several studies showing that when cortisol is released, people make decisions that are based more on gut feeling than on rational thought.

■■■

On Election Day, while Netanyahu was trying to fan the fears of his defeat, the Left was trying to project hope that Netanyahu would finally be replaced. "To put a stop to the regime of fear, we are today putting up a wall of hope," declared Lapid and Gantz when they united against Netanyahu. But evolution has taught man that fear comes before hope. People are easily startled or frightened with a shout or a loud boom. Sowing the seeds of hope requires much more effort. Thus, despite Livni's campaign promise in 2013, later echoed by Avi Gabbay, that "Hope will vanquish fear," the opposite is the case, physiologically speaking: fear wins.

If the Left talks about the chance of peace and the Right talks about the chance of war, who will the voter listen to? Which message will be absorbed in his brain and dictate his vote? War or peace?

It was this very question that occupied a group of brain researchers who performed MRI scans on volunteers while showing them different words with positive and negative associations. When words like "crime" or "war" were displayed, the brain responded faster than when positive words like "love," "hope," or "peace" appeared.

The discrepancy was only a few hundredths of a second, but the conclusion was that negative, threatening messages make a quicker impression.

Shelly Yachimovich tried to lead the Labor party with a sense of hope for society as encapsulated in her campaign slogan: "Things could be better here." Gantz proposed a different, more inclusive and bipartisan discourse; Kahlon promised justice; Gabbay presented a different leadership model; Peretz offered a social platform. All of them focused on more advanced stages of human thinking. Netanyahu appeals to the most fundamental survival instinct.

It may be that in the second round of elections in 2019, specifically because they came so close on the heels of the previous round, the warning bells that Netanyahu sounded no longer made an impression on the voters, who had simply become apathetic. An exceptional and unprecedented emergency loses its urgency when one hears "Emergency, emergency!" as a matter of routine.

Threats of Peace

"Extremely confidential." The panic between the lines is discernible. A significant threat that has arisen prompts Netanyahu, in Washington, to dispatch a secret telegram to Prime Minister Begin and a small circle of ministers. "Urgent for tomorrow morning," he emphasizes, hoping that Begin will see his recommendation the moment he wakes up, before Israel suffers grave harm.

He dispatches the telegram to the Minister of Defense and to the Intelligence Branch of the IDF, too, choosing to sound all the warning bells.

"Some of the gravest matters that Israel has faced in its dealings with the United States" was how Netanyahu defined the contents of the peace initiative presented by US President Ronald Reagan. The words "peace initiative" and "historical opportunity" were placed in scornful quotation marks. But as Netanyahu saw it, the real threat was not Reagan's peace, but rather the likely Israeli response.

In 1982, the young diplomat, still in his early 30s, offered a surprising piece of advice to the Israeli leadership: Don't be quick to reject the dangerous American peace offer, so as to avoid a situation in which "we will be portrayed here as 'opposers of peace.'" It was clear to Bibi that the White House initiative was not to be allowed to succeed, but he preferred that the other side be responsible for scuttling it.

The urgent telegram reflects the understanding that the most important things in the diplomatic realm are public opinion, image, and impression. Not substance. The initiative that Reagan presented in his speech was problematic, but the speech itself, delivered by a wizard of charisma, was simply too good to repudiate.

"In the manner of his presentation the President left his listeners with the profound impression that he was a true friend of Israel, and that he was making the most of an historical opportunity to advance Israel's security and peace in the region ..." Netanyahu opined that the truly problematic sections of the speech "were presented in a most sophisticated manner that blurs their true nature ... Public opinion will no doubt receive it with enthusiasm." This being the case, Bibi recommended that Begin allow the Arab side to be the first to refuse.

"We propose finding a formula that will sweeten the bitter pill of rejection," the young diplomat concluded his telegram to the Prime Minister's Office, "to avoid a head-on confrontation with the President over his peace initiative." Evade it. Cause the process to fail, from behind the scenes, but let the Arabs be the bad guys.

Morning came in Jerusalem, Begin received the confidential telegram from the embassy in Washington, and decided to adopt Netanyahu's recommendation.

Netanyahu has adopted the same strategy that he had recommended in the '80s to Begin with regard to President Reagan in his own dealings as Prime Minister with successive American Presidents, from Clinton to Obama to Trump.

Focused on possible threats, Netanyahu has also missed a number of opportunities. In his first term no less than twelve ministers and MKs resigned or were dismissed by him, along with many of his bureau staff. During his subsequent terms, senior Likud figures such as Reuven (Ruby) Rivlin, Gideon Sa'ar and others were treated as political threats that needed to be neutralized. A sensitive amygdala aids survival, but it perceives every shadow as a mountain.

Netanyahu has at times regarded even political opportunities as threats. On the last day of his term as Israel's ambassador in Washington, Moshe Arens took Netanyahu, his protégé, along with him to an unscheduled meeting in the Oval Room with President Reagan. Netanyahu was officially there to take notes. The future Prime Minister sat on the presidential couch and transcribed the meeting. Afterwards, he sent the protocol to the office of Prime Minister Shamir. The "extremely confidential" telegram which has never been published and which I was able to obtain, reflects the apathy – not to say downright hostility – with which Netanyahu and the Right-wing government reacted to King Hussein of Jordan's desire to embark on peace negotiations with Israel.

In the meeting, Reagan explicitly pushed to pursue the offer. Arens gave a response clearly meant for the protocol, with a clichéd expression of readiness in principle: "Who more than us, having gone through so many wars, wants peace …" but immediately followed by a speech about security and the fact that it could not be secured with a withdrawal to the '67 lines. By the end of the meeting, the American President had not received a response to the message from the King of Jordan. Arens had evaded and skirted the offer as though it were a threat. His concern, as expressed by Netanyahu in other confidential telegrams dispatched to Jerusalem, was that a peace process vis-à-vis

Jordan would entail territorial concessions in Judea and Samaria.

With hindsight, Netanyahu – like the Likud in general, and like Golda Meir before them – missed an historical opportunity that presented itself. Only when the Labor party under Rabin came to power was the government in Israel ready to listen to the Jordanian king, to take up his offer, and to sign a peace agreement with Israel's eastern neighbor.

Fighting for our Home

The screen in the secret intelligence base somewhere in the center of the country showed a number of moving Xs, but only one of them was of interest to the officers watching the Middle East flight map. According to foreign reports, this X was tracing the path of a large Iranian cargo plane making its way towards Damascus. The aircraft, as an anonymous source would later explain to the foreign press, was carrying precision weapons that would allow Hezbollah to strike runways at strategic sites in Israel. The delivery was defined as "game-changing weaponry" and Netanyahu had ordered that any such consignment be attacked.

Secret telegrams from his period as a diplomat indicate that Netanyahu has always acted to prevent advanced missiles from reaching Israel's neighbors to the north. As Prime Minister he would continue this policy in a way that also helped him politically.

On the night following Christmas Day – December 25th, 2018 – Netanyahu didn't sleep. Not only because of the bombing of dozens of targets around Damascus, but also because the next day the Knesset was due to vote on its dispersion and a date for new elections. The command center monitoring the operation to the north received a report from the Hezbollah-affiliated Al Mayadeen TV network, reporting low-altitude IAF sorties over Tyre and Sidon. The Air Force headquarters, manned by senior IAF personnel, conveys the updates it receives to the Prime Minister.

The threat of the Iranian plane was turned into an opportunity. The aim of bringing it down was augmented by a much broader operation, including the bombing of Iranian and Hezbollah ammunition storehouses close to the border. Over the course of several minutes, dozens of missiles hit their targets. The explosions echoed far and wide, and the Syrian army tried to launch missiles at the attacking planes. The Iron Dome system was activated.

A different report broadcast in Israel the same evening mentioned that three heads of regional councils in Judea and Samaria had announced that they would be boycotting the meeting planned for the next morning with the Prime Minister owing to the wave of terror attacks in their areas. There was no apparent connection between these two arenas.

At eleven the next day, the heads of the major regional councils in Judea and Samaria arrived in Jerusalem. They, too, had heard the foreign media-based reports on the radio on their way to the capital, announcing that Hezbollah fighters had been killed in attacks attributed to Israel. But the subject of the meeting with Netanyahu was the murderous terror attacks taking place on the West Bank and the government's failure to transfer budgets to the Jewish communities in this region. Samaria settlers were holding demonstrations outside the Prime Minister's Residence, and some government ministers had taken the unusual step of joining them.

With all of this awaiting him, Netanyahu managed to put a different spin on the whole situation. This was largely thanks to the fact that no telephones are allowed in meetings with him (more out of concern for secret recordings than out of fear of enemy wire-tapping). Thus, the only one in the room with a telephone was the person who has been the Prime Minister's closest confidante over the past decade:

Jonathan Urich.

One of the participants in the meeting introduced his words concerning the security situation with a polite gesture of appreciation: "Thank you for being on top of Israel's security last night, too, according to foreign reports."

Netanyahu brushed it off modestly, "That wasn't my doing." He proceeded to listen to the harsh criticism of the settler leaders in the wake of the intensifying terror attacks. The meeting was tense. At some point Urich showed Netanyahu something on his telephone, and Netanyahu nodded. Notes with updates by the military secretary were brought into him every few minutes, and given due frowning attention.

After an hour and a half of arguing over the de facto settlement construction freeze and the horrific toll of the terror attacks, as the company was passing through the entrance hall on their way out, Netanyahu asked them to wait for a moment. "Chaim," the Prime Minister addressed the Government Press Office photographer who was on hand, "take a picture." Chaim Tzah captured a shot of the council heads alongside Netanyahu in his blue suit and carefully groomed.

As the guests left the Aquarium and turned on their telephones, they were surprised to discover that all the media outlets had reported on the meeting the moment it began. The headline was supplied by the only person in the room who had had a telephone. A tacked-on aside had become the headline that was carried all over Israel and beyond: "Judea and Samaria Council Heads thank Netanyahu for taking care of Israel's security in last night's attack in Syria."

It was important to Netanyahu that the public credit him with the operation in Syria, but since he couldn't say so directly, owing to military censorship, his spokesman fished out a comment that someone had made and blasted it all over the media. Still standing in the entrance hall, before they had even had a chance to react, the council heads received another update on their phones from all the various media channels: "Netanyahu: This is a fight for our home." The news items, full of quotes from Netanyahu, all attached a flattering photograph showing the heads of the Regional Councils in Judea and Samaria standing behind the Prime Minister. The item itself cited Netanyahu regarding the fate of the country:

> "In the upcoming elections we have to win. It's a fight for our home. The fate of the country and of the settlements is not to be taken for granted … Under a Left-wing government everything will turn around in an instant."

All of this media maneuvering was intended to convey messages, and Netanyahu had managed three at once: he took credit for the military operation, delivered a political message against the Left, and presented himself as having widespread support among the settlers.

Both the Iranian threat and the political threat posed by the settlers' protest had effectively been neutralized.

Events are presented and framed this way as a matter of routine. The aim is to control the agenda, to constantly focus on threats and the security issue, and to portray Netanyahu as the answer. The security and political battles alike are framed as a "fight for our home."

▪▪▪

Netanyahu gives the threat a tangible presence and presents himself as the solution, "Mr. Security," who is capable of protecting the Jewish People. In order for Netanyahu to be able to parade himself as "Mr. Security," he needs a threat to be hovering in the air. He will make sure to inflate it so it becomes "unprecedented," and then take up his stance as guardian of Israel. He therefore works constantly to stoke the sense of existential threat facing the Jewish People, along with the constant refrain at election time about the "existential threat" facing the Right-wing government. Netanyahu followed the same thinking to repudiate the demands of the social justice protests in 2011, arguing that "life itself" takes precedence over quality of life:

> "When we speak about the price of housing, the cost of living, I never for a moment forget about life itself. The greatest challenge to our lives right now is Iran's nuclear armament."

Following immediately after safety in Maslow's hierarchy, the next item that appears as a fundamental human need is love and a sense of belonging – to a community, a family, a society, and a nation. Netanyahu works to satisfy this need, too. The belonging that he proposes is very clear: We are the Jews. We are the Likud. We are the Right. Nationalism is a central concept in these messages, and "Netanyahu is good for the Jews." The Left, in contrast, is portrayed as having forgotten its affiliation and what it means to be Jewish.

The sense of belonging proposed by the Left is more complex because it is universalist. Netanyahu remains within the boundaries of the tribe.

While Netanyahu appeals to his political, biological and psychological base, activating primal evolutionary mechanisms, his rivals appeal to the higher, more advanced layers of Maslow's hierarchy: self-actualization and meaning, along with hope for peace and for social justice.

"More and more terror victims; that's what the Left brings," intones a Likud election broadcast, and Netanyahu declares: "They will bring catastrophe upon us." The word is quickly absorbed by the listener's brain and leads to intensified activity in the amygdala. "Exploding buses" – the magnetometer beeps; "the Arabs will annihilate all of us" - cortisol is released. "Gantz is Left, and Left is dangerous" – in the background a military cemetery with rows of soldiers' graves. Life or death. If you want to live, vote Likud.

***

Secret #4: Fear is the Decisive Factor; In War the Stronger Side Wins In the political reality that Netanyahu spearheads in Israel, elections are perceived as a matter of life and death; victory therefore belongs to the side that is strong. Netanyahu, who has managed to brand himself as "Mr. Security," protecting the country's citizens, projects the message that the prospect of him losing an election is an existential threat. In this way he activates a primal survival mechanism. His messages, repeated over and over, concern more immediate concerns and are absorbed more quickly than the messages of his rivals. They also cause stronger emotional reactions, which translate into voting decisions.

5.
COLLECTIVE MEMORY
SYMBOLS

Two people are walking together when suddenly they come upon a grizzly bear standing in their path and growling. They both freeze in their tracks. Then one of them starts to run. "What's the point?" shouts the other. "The bear runs faster, and it will catch you!"

"I don't need to run faster than the bear," his companion shouts back, "only faster than you!"

Terrorists are animals. These three words encapsulate Netanyahu's view of terror. He offered the above metaphor during an interview he gave to the American media during his first term in office, pointing to the need to join forces against the bear of terrorism. It is not by chance that animals feature prominently in his speeches. Human culture has turned animals into symbols that arouses automatic reactions from our evolutionary past.

Bibi's Leopard

Like a ruler in ancient times, Netanyahu keeps a fearsome leopard at his side. It is meant for public diplomacy purposes.

Regarding Hamas he said: "This leopard will not change its spots

- 6 -

For us to make political concessions after four years of Palestinian coddling of terrorism is to reward terrorism.

Only last week Arafat hugged and kissed the leaders of the very group which claimed responsibility for the Ben Yehuda bombing.

To reward him now [terrorism] is to mock the peace process. It can only mean that terrorism pays. As my friend Mort Zuckerman says, you don't turn a tiger into a vegetarian by feeding him meat.

… It doesn't matter how much make-up you smear on its face, it will remain the same Hamas."

The Iranian leopard is a recurring image in his speeches, including this one from 2015:

> "Iran is arming its proxies, its cats' paws – its leopards' paws – with special weapons that right now are aimed mostly at us, but not only at us …"

Two years later, the leopard made another appearance in Netanyahu's speech at the UN: "I warned that when the sanctions on Iran would be removed, Iran would behave like a hungry tiger unleashed, not joining the community of nations, but devouring nations, one after the other. And that's precisely what Iran is doing today."

The leopard is not alone. Wild animals feature prominently in the images that Netanyahu creates when discussing terror. In a speech at the UN in 2011, Netanyahu depicted Islamic extremism as a ferocious crocodile with open jaws:

> "And these critics continue to press Israel to make far-reaching concessions without first assuring Israel's security. They praise those who unwittingly feed the insatiable crocodile of militant Islamas bold statesmen. They cast as enemies of peace those of us who insist that we must first erect a sturdy barrier to keep the crocodile out, or, at the very least, jam an iron bar between its gaping jaws."

The image is planted; it becomes interwoven in our way of thinking. Crocodile, leopard, teeth, blood, shreds of skin – our imagination keeps working. Within a fraction of a second we know that there is no tangible, immediate danger, it is just a metaphor. But the sense of being "devoured" has already been experienced. Feeling is more powerful than thinking. The image forces itself on our mind.

It doesn't stop with a bear, a leopard, or a crocodile. Over the years Netanyahu has enlisted an entire zoo to convey his messages: "If only I could believe Rouhani, but I don't. He is a wolf in sheep's clothing," he said of Iran's new president in his speech at the UN in 2013. Prior to that he had compared the previous president, Ahmadinejad, to a "wolf in leopard's clothing."

Clash of Cultures

For years he has described the conflict with militant Islam as a struggle with no rational basis; a struggle between human and bestial players:

> "It is difficult for cultured men and women to acknowledge that animals of prey are going about in our cities, our flight paths, and sometimes our sea routes, looking to attack the innocent victims they happen upon. When the forces of civilization understand the severity of the problem, they have no choice but to come together in a clear way and to defeat these beasts. These animals have a name: they are radical Islam. This is what is carrying out killings, murders, rapes, burnings and beheadings. We have to stand together and fight together against extremist Islam."

Netanyahu has referred to the perpetrators of many different terror attacks as "human beasts." He once quoted Ehud Barak's metaphor of a "villa in the jungle" as a description of Israel in the Middle East: "We want to protect the villa. In the environment in which we live we have to protect ourselves from wild beasts …"

Netanyahu defines the cause of terrorism as a "deep-rooted tendency towards unbridled violence." He views terrorism as imbedded in barbarous culture: "Terrorism is driven by a culture of death. Its aim is not to liberate a country but rather to destroy a country. Someone who cares about human rights doesn't trample them; he doesn't stab, run over and blow up innocent people. Terrorism is the result of a totalitarian ideology that has stops at nothing to achieve its aims, in our case – the desire to annihilate the Jews and their State."

■■■

Images have a profound impact on the way in which we perceive reality. An experiment carried out in the US divided participants into two groups, showed them reports with crime statistics, and asked for their ideas of how to deal with the problem. The researchers found that the use of different metaphors for the phenomenon of crime in the textual portion of the report led to completely different proposed solutions. The statistics were identical, but the group whose report described crime as a wild animal, proposed strict enforcement and punishment, while the group whose report used a metaphor of a virus that threatened society, proposed social solutions along with reforms relating to education, welfare and community. The metaphor determined the policy.

The web of animalistic images of the enemy causes the public to perceive reality in primal terms and using primal tools, so that voting for Netanyahu is almost an imperative. There is no chance of dialogue or compromise with an animalistic enemy.

Reality feeds this perception to no less an extent than Netanyahu himself does. Savage terror attacks on Israeli citizens in the form of suicide bombers on buses and in restaurants, knife attacks on pedestrians, families shot in their homes, children slaughtered in their beds, drive-by shootings, car rammings targeting crowds at bus stops, rockets launched towards civilian centers, and more, testify to a savage hatred. The cruelty of Islamic terror is indeed inhuman. The perception of reality as an epic struggle between man and beast means that it is not limited to the Middle East, but rather extends globally. The struggle, to Netanyahu's view, is not only up to the Jews, but also all civilized people:

> "Syria is breaking apart, and is spewing from its innards some of the deadliest weaponry in the world. Terror organizations are snatching it up like wild animals pouncing on a carcass."

In his book *Terrorism: How the West Can Win*, Netanyahu described a clash of civilizations as "between culture and barbarism." This was not the East-West conflict proposed by Samuel P. Huntington, but rather the clash between the Judeo-Christian-humanist culture and the militant-Islamist-bestial one. Accordingly, he addresses the entire world when he warns about the animal kingdom that has risen up against humankind:

> "Inhuman barbarians who seek to subjugate the entire world to Islam by the power of the sword are the danger today: when the sword in the hand of those Muslims is a nuclear sword, the world will be a different place. Humanity as a whole will be at a different point in history. We will find ourselves facing new barbarians."

The politico-diplomatic significance of this web of images is that Netanyahu creates political alliances, gets voters onto their feet, and changes reality, all in the name of the battle of human vs. beast.

■■■

An urgent message was conveyed to the Western Wall Heritage Foundation following the Prime Minister's visit to the historical site: "Are you crazy? Cut it out of the video. Not approved." The Foundation staff understood immediately which footage should not be aired, and they managed to block its broadcast.

I was able to obtain the hushed-up video. It shows Netanyahu leading the President of Brazil, Jair Bolsonaro, through the Western Wall Tunnels, deep under the ground of the Temple Mount, where the Al-Aqsa Mosque stands. Netanyahu had chalked up an important diplomatic achievement by bringing the president-elect of the fifth largest power in the world to Israel for his first official international visit.

The tour was closed to the media. The two leaders stood talking alongside the second-largest stone in the world, and listened to a tour guide discuss the location of the Holy of Holies in the ancient Jewish Temple. They then moved to a room at the center of which was a huge, impressive model of the Temple Mount and the city of Jerusalem as it changed over the course of the centuries. The two leaders sat side by side on a white bench facing the reconstruction model, with the Rabbi of the Western Wall next to them. The director of the Foundation started recounting the Temple Mount history. Netanyahu soon cut him off.

"Please pass that to me," he asked, and was handed the green laser pointer that the director had just used. "You see that street?" Netanyahu asked Bolsonaro, pointing the green dot towards a short alley leading to the Temple. "That's the money-changers' road; that's where Jesus walked." The Brazilian president's eyes shone. "Here he overturned the tables," Netanyahu continued. "And from here, Jesus walked to this church," he pointed to the model, and the green laser dot floated over the length of the Via Dolorosa. Netanyahu continued to point out the locations of the churches and other stations on the route to the crucifixion. The President appeared hypnotized. "And then he reached there, where that man is standing," and Netanyahu pointed to the Government Press Office photographer who had been permitted to join the tour and was standing next to the model. The Brazilian president nodded sorrowfully as he watched this presentation of the route walked by Jesus, betrayed by Judah Iscariot, as recounted by the Prime Minister of Israel.

∎∎∎

Netanyahu gave the same presentation to the US Secretary of State, Mike Pompeo, who also asked to visit the Tunnels. Here, too, Netanyahu ignored the rabbis accompanying them and adapted his exposition to the New Testament. Like Bolsonaro, Pompeo was an international leader whom Netanyahu had singled out to stand with him and with Israel via religious messages concealed from the Israeli public.

Pompeo and Bolsonaro are devout Evangelists who revere Jesus and, for this reason, also revere Israel and its leader. They live in anticipation of the Apocalypse and expect the Prime Minister of Israel to play a key role in its unfolding. Netanyahu is familiar with the role of this end-of-the-world war in the bloody process of redemption and uses it to enlist support.

Netanyahu uses a method of influence known as "dog whistle politics," entailing the use of language in a way that passes under the radar of most people but conveys specific messages to an intended audience. His use of animals as a rhetorical device is a way of enlisting support amongst the Evangelist Christian world, speaking to the symbols that lie in the deepest recesses of its consciousness. He speaks in codes. The Christian public knows what he means; the Israeli public does not.

The Children of Light and the Children of Darkness

The distinction between "children of light" and "children of darkness" - the good guys and the bad guys, people and beasts – is what causes hundreds of millions of Evangelist Christians around the world to admire Netanyahu. They believe that he, both personally and in terms of policy, advances their vision of the apocalyptic war that is destined to be fought between good and evil forces; between the human and the bestial.

Anticipation of this religious war is the reason why Evangelists, who comprise more than a quarter of the population of the US, support the Israeli Right, provide funding for the settlement enterprise, and maintain a powerful, secret and influential lobby in Israel. Netanyahu, for his part, fosters ties with them, appearing at Christian events without posting photographs or publicity in the Israeli media.

"You are Israel's best friends," he declares at every Christian conference that he attends. In 2019, speaking before thousands of Zionist Christians, he added:

> "We are witnessing a dramatic change in the relations between Christians and Jews, focusing on our shared values and our shared future.

> "Our vision is to renew our national existence and to renew our heritage here. This heritage is bound up with the Christian heritage: after all, Christianity grew out of Judaism. Here, in this land. What is the Galilee? What is Nazareth? What is Bethlehem? What is Jerusalem? Christianity developed from here."

- 4 -

Bethlehem, where you will be on Tuesday, is the birthplace of Jesus, a Jew whose life of trial and tribulations forged the great religion of Christianity.

And Bethlehem is also where our Matriarch Rachel was buried, and where King David was born --

The same King David who established the capital of the Jewish people in the city of Jerusalem - a city which has never been the capital of any other nation.

Netanyahu has reaped many important political fruits from this religiopolitical alliance. It was the Evangelical lobby, the political base of the Republican Party, which pressured President Trump to fulfill his pre-election promise to move the US Embassy to Jerusalem. There were some Christian leaders who fancied the possibility that such a move would generate a religious earthquake in the Middle East that would advance Armageddon. But the Islamic beast did not rise up from its slumber, and thanks to the alliance with the religious Right that Netanyahu had forged, the Embassy moved despite the protests of Arab leaders.

When the new Embassy building was inaugurated in the Talpiot neighborhood, Vice President Pence – a prominent Evangelist himself – asked megachurch televangelist Pastor John Hagee to deliver the benediction at the ceremony. Hagee believes that the End of Days is approaching, and that Russia and Iran will very shortly launch a great war against the US and Israel, leading to the final Redemption. In his benediction he set forth this vision, concluding with the Messiah who would soon appear. Immediately afterwards, Netanyahu ascended the podium to speak.

Some Evangelists regard Netanyahu, the leader of the Jews, as a forerunner of the Messiah. The role of this herald is to nurture ties with the hundreds of millions of Christians who represent a formidable force on the American continent. Some very wealthy Evangelists have also lent Netanyahu their support over the years.

The ties he fostered with Trump and with Bolsonaro ("Trump of the Tropics") are examples of the Judeo-Christian alliance that he has promoted throughout the world. As part of this effort, a photo shoot of Netanyahu standing beneath the huge statue of Jesus in Rio de Janeiro was planned in 2019. In the end, the commotion caused by the security arrangements interfered and the opportunity was lost.

The Evangelist public is Netanyahu's hidden audience, and the power and influence of the Christian lobby is unknown to most of the Israeli public. Bibi prefers it this way: at the end of the day, the weight of the Church's attitude towards and treatment of Jews throughout history still influences Jewish voters. Hence the dog whistle tactics.

Netanyahu takes care that his addresses at Evangelist congresses are not made known to and do not make waves among the Jewish religious Right, but this son of the historian of the Inquisition heralds the dawn of a new era in Jewish-Christian relations. In the war of religions, Netanyahu has chosen his side. He counters Arafat's famous promise of millions of Palestinian shahids marching to Jerusalem with a vision of millions of Christians standing at Israel's side:

> "I speak to you from the land where Abraham, Isaac and Jacob walked. I speak to you from the land that was once ruled by King David and King Solomon; I speak to you from the land where the Maccabees achieved their wondrous victory. It is the same land in which, two thousand years ago, Jesus preached his gospel of tolerance and love that has echoed throughout the generations. With its return to Israel, the Jewish people has returned home.
>
> "For hundreds of years, the relationship between Christians and Jews was defined by conflict, not by partnership and friendship. But all of this is changing. It is changing in this new chapter in our relations that is being written in our times. Today, millions of Christians stand at Israel's side, because they side with the truth …"

While there is disagreement as to the religious identity of the Messiah who is on his way, there are Jews and Christians alike who view Netanyahu as his precursor. By all appearances, Netanyahu sees himself in this role, too. More than half the responses on Netanyahu's Facebook page are written in English, their formulation leaving no doubt that they come from Evangelist admirers. They praise his kingdom and shower him with verses from the New Testament about the Messiah. Throughout the world, from America to Asia, there are tens of millions of Christians who are waiting for Netanyahu to rebuild the Temple on the Temple Mount, in order to bring on Armageddon, with a view to the establishment of the Kingdom of the Church.

■■■

The top shelf of the bookshelf in Netanyahu's office holds a silver statuette, with two photographs at its side. Three figures were selected by Netanyahu with great care, a snapshot of his world.

The statuette shows Moses holding the Tablets of the Covenant. Netanyahu explains, "He brought us out of slavery to freedom." One of the photographs shows Theodor Herzl, the father of modern political Zionism: "He, too, brought us out of slavery to freedom." The third figure is Winston Churchill, the British Prime Minister who played a key role in the Allied victory over the Nazis: "So I'll always remember to look at the risks." Moses, Herzl, and Churchill. He views himself as their successor.

There is also a photograph of his father; a family photograph dating to his first term, showing his wife Sara and their sons Yair and Avner in the snow at their official Jerusalem residence; and another from his fourth term, again in the snow, this time Netanyahu himself with his sons who are now taller than him. Then, along the length of the wall, there is a map of the Middle East which he uses to show every foreign visitor the tiny size of Israel in comparison with the twenty-two Arab countries. Sometimes his finger slides all the way down to Uganda, where his brother died commanding Operating Thunderbolt.

Netanyahu sees the thread of Jewish history spread over thousands of years, starting with the Exodus from Egypt, and continuing to himself. He even has a small piece of tangible history proving it:

> "In my office in Jerusalem there is an ancient signet ring. It is the signet ring of a Jewish official from the time of the Bible. The ring was found right next to the Western Wall, and it is 2,700 years old, going back to the period of King Hezekiah. The name of that official is engraved in Hebrew on the seal: his name was Netanyahu, and that is also my last name. My first name, Benjamin, dates back to 1,000 years before the ring. Benjamin was the son of Jacob, who was also called Israel. Jacob and his twelve sons roamed around those same hills of Judea and Samaria some 4,000 years ago, and since then there has been a Jewish presence in the land of Israel. And among the Jews, who were exiled from our land, the dream of returning has never ceased."

A Family Mission

Despite his pride in his biblical family name, when he left the country in the 1970s and went to study in the US, he changed his name to Ben Nitay, making it easier for Americans to pronounce.

He chose this name because his father published some of his articles under the name Nitay. The father, Benzion, in turn had chosen 'Nitay' to memorialize his own father, Nathan, as well as a member of the ancient Sanhedrin(assembly of Jewish elders) known as Nitay of Arbel. The grandfather's name, Nathan, was also the inspiration behind the choice of the name Netanyahu, replacing the original family name – Mileikowsky. The names are closely connected: Benzion, Ben Nitay, Benjamin Netanyahu. Fathers and sons. A chain of generations of a family, symbolizing the chain of generations of Jews, in which Netanyahu views himself as a central link.

■■■

On the eve of the elections in 2013, Benzion Netanyahu and his son gave a joint interview. There, at his official residence on HaPortzim Street, Netanyahu promised that in his next term in office there would be no evacuations of Jewish settlements, thereby quieting somewhat the fears of those who were worried about the negotiations with Abbas that had been entrusted to Tzipi Livni. In the interview his father, who was 99 at the time, said: "People are mistaken in thinking that the Holocaust is over. The Holocaust isn't over. It continues. It could still happen. They could annihilate us."

The spirit of the home in which Netanyahu was raised held that "the Holocaust isn't over." Benzion raised his children to save the Jewish People. He believed that his eldest son, Jonathan (Yoni), would be Prime Minister "without question." The death of his son, commander of the General Staff Reconnaissance Unit at the time of his death, for whom he had had such high hopes, only intensified the father's sense of mission.

The Prime Minister recounts:

> "I was a student in the United States when my, Iddo called to tell me of the death of our older brother, Yoni. It was the worst moment of my life, besides one other moment, seven hours later, after a tortuous nightlong journey, when I walked up the path leading to parent's – he was teaching at Cornell University in New York at the time and it was my lot to be the one to break the news. Through the wide window in the front of the house, I could see my father pacing back and forth, lost in thought, his hands joined

behind his back as was his wont. He suddenly looked up and when he saw me, without his saying a word, his expression changed all at once. A bitter cry burst from his throat. I went into the house. As long as I breathe, I will never forget his cry and that of my dear mother. Passing the news of my brother's death to them was as if Yoni had died once again."

Netanyahu's brother Yoni fell in battle against terrorists; his father researched the evils of the Inquisition against Jews and the Expulsion from Spain and believed that the Holocaust had not ended; his grandfather Nathan had been brutally attacked by an anti-Semitic mob and had escaped from the Holocaust. The narrative is real on the personal, family, and national level. Netanyahu believes it with all his heart, and views it as his life's mission to save the Jews: "My main task as Prime Minister is that there will not be another Yad Vashem."[20]

"Our very existence here – that is my mission, which I inherited from my father and my grandfather, may their memories be blessed. This is my mission and it burns within me. This is not spin. It is not a matter of public relations, nor of political advantage. It burns within me. Securing the Jewish People in its land; securing our future, security the future of our children."

---

20 The World Holocaust Remembrance Center in Jerusalem, Israel's official memorial to the victims of the Holocaust.

Judaism's Childhood Traumas

Dominick LaCapra is an historian and theoretician, and one of the world's leading Holocaust researchers. He lectured in the Department of History at Cornell University at the same time that Benzion Netanyahu was teaching there, and the young Bibi met him. In his book *Writing History, Writing Trauma*, LaCapra expands the Freudian concept of trauma from the individual human psyche to the collective, national psyche.

In applying the concept of trauma to social and political contexts, he explains that in the life of a nation there are traumas that keep coming back, never letting up; this leads to a blurring of the distinction between what existed "then and there" and what exists "here and now." The entire nation re-experiences the trauma as though it was happening in the present, and this influences the nation's behavior. LaCapra points to the Holocaust as an example. Netanyahu applies the principle to events even further back in history:

> "Sometimes entire nations undergo traumatic experiences, and these continue to affect their behavior and their world view long after the horrifying events have passed. The Jewish People has experienced extremely bitter events over its history. We have not forgotten the destruction of Jerusalem, nor the Holocaust in our own century."

Jerusalem and the Holocaust. Two strings on the ancient Jewish violin that Netanyahu plays. These are not just events or open wounds, nor even just past traumas that influence the present; they are also central symbols in the tapestry of images that Netanyahu weaves, creating endless connections between the present and the trauma of the Holocaust, whose impact on the Jewish and Israeli psyche continues to be vast and profound. Netanyahu lives and gives life to the Holocaust in the context of current events, causing terror attacks on Jews and international demonization of Israel to echo with overtones of historical persecution and suffering.

Nazis on the Barricades

An official document signed by the Prime Minister's military secretary shows the data on casualties from Israel's wars; in the margin are handwritten instructions to the speechwriter: "Please prepare four nice sentences that the Prime Minister can incorporate, although the Prime Minister has no problem in this area (also a bereaved family)."

The speech itself is devoted to the War of Independence, in which "after half of the nation was annihilated in the Holocaust, there was a danger that the other half would be annihilated too," with an emphasis that the danger still exists.

The request for "nice sentences" to include would seem to arise from the fact that this is an extremely busy time in Netanyahu's bureau, owing to the large number of ceremonies stretching over the week from Holocaust Remembrance Day to Memorial Day and Independence Day. Netanyahu attaches huge importance to his speeches he delivers at these events, owing to their high viewership ratings and official status, and he has developed a fixed format.

Every year, at the opening of the Memorial Day events, Netanyahu takes care to highlight the connection between the Nazis and those who seek "to finish what Hitler began." The Iranian regime is trying to carry out a "second Holocaust." The world powers are also at fault: "The Agreement with Iran proves that the world has not internalized the lesson of the Holocaust." Netanyahu believes that "hatred of the Jews is now directed against the Jewish State," and as at the time of the Holocaust, the rest of the world will stand by: "As to the world's indifference – has anything changed in this regard? The answer is no." The speech concludes with the answer to that potential Holocaust – the power of the IDF.

The juxtaposition of the days of commemoration of the Holocaust and of the casualties in Israel's wars mirrors the close proximity of Yad Vashem and Mount Herzl Military Cemetery. Over the years these two sites have gravitated towards each other, with the distinction between IDF casualties and Holocaust victims becoming blurred in the process. With Netanyahu's encouragement, the winds of the Holocaust blow anew over the Jewish People all the time, invoked in relation to every sort of danger, creating the effect of a merging of present challenges with past fears.

"We shall not allow Holocaust deniers to carry out another Holocaust against the Jewish People," Netanyahu declared at a ceremony at Yad Vashem. A different year he warned, "New adversaries rise up to annihilate us," and went on to name Iran and its metastatic outgrowths.

Iran is not the only Nazi enemy that Netanyahu refers to. In his speech to the World Zionist Congress in 2015, he said that Hitler had not originally wanted to eradicate the Jews but rather to expel them, but the Grand Mufti of Jerusalem told him, "If you expel them, they will all come to Palestine." When Hitler then asked what he should do with the Jews, the Mufti answered, "Burn them." The suggestion that Hitler had not intended to annihilate the Jews, and embarked on his plan only at the Mufti's urging, aroused furious responses throughout the world, with many understanding it as an exoneration of the Nazis and a distortion of history. Netanyahu recanted, but in his clarification he took care to emphasize that the Mufti is a venerated Palestinian figure and that in Ramallah there is support for the Holocaust. In a different speech, three years earlier, he had characterized the Mufti as "one of the leading architects of the Final Solution," and declared:

"The Palestinian state will not allow a Jewish presence. It will be 'Judenrein'. This is ethnic cleansing. There are laws today in Ramallah according to which someone who sells land to Jews can be sentenced to death. This is racism. And you know which laws they recall."

Qalqilya and Treblinka

Netanyahu chose to hold the first Likud election rally in 2006 at the Park Hotel in Netanya, where dozens of Israelis had been murdered on the Seder night, the first night of Passover, four years earlier. He attacked the Kadima party, under Olmert's leadership, comparing Hamas's rise to power in Gaza to the rise of the Nazi party in Germany: "A new adversary has arisen," he warned Israel's citizens. "When Hitler rose to power, they said then too that he didn't mean it, and that being in power would moderate him."

He also compared the European conciliatory attitude towards terror to Chamberlain's appeasement of the Reich, and in a speech at the UN he drew a connection between ISIS, Iran, Abbas, and Hitler:

"[M]ilitant Islam's ambition to dominate the world seems mad. But so too did the global ambitions of another fanatic ideology that swept into power eight decades ago. The Nazis believed in a master race. The militant Islamists believe in a masterfaith. They just disagree who among themwill be the master ... of the master faith. That's what they truly disagree about ... In what moral universe does genocide [the charge leveled at Israel] include warning the enemy's civilian population to get out of harm's way? Or ensuring that they receive tons, tons of humanitarian aid each day, even as thousands of rockets are being fired at us? Or setting up a field hospital to aid for their wounded? Well, I suppose it's the same moral universe where a man who wrote a dissertation of lies about the Holocaust, and who insists on a Palestine free of Jews – Judenrein - can stand at this podium and shamelessly accuse Israel of genocide and ethnic cleansing."

One year, at a Memorial Day ceremony, President Rivlin responded in his speech to this recurring theme, making no effort to hide his criticism: "It is important to clarify: we are not in the 1930s; we are not standing on the brink of a second Holocaust, or anything like it." The Left, too, has accused Netanyahu of scare tactics and exploiting the Holocaust.

Both Ben-Gurion and Begin likewise drew comparisons between the Nazis and contemporary troubles. "We do not want the Arab Nazis to come and slaughter us," was how Ben-Gurion justified the need to approve the reparations agreement with Germany. "The Russian tanks wreaking havoc in Hungary show what these Communist Nazis are capable of doing," he wrote, in a different context. Begin justified the attack on the nuclear reactor in Iraq by referring to the need to protect the nation that had "a million and a half of its children annihilated by the Nazis in gas chambers." In a government meeting he explained the necessity of invading Lebanon: "The alternative is Treblinka."

As in the title of Professor Moshe Zukerman's book, *Shoah [Holocaust] in the Sealed Room*, on the subject of the Gulf War, every war in Israel – like every election campaign – has had the ghost of the Holocaust hovering over it. Iraqis, Lebanese, Egyptians, Palestinians, Iranians - in Israel, Nazis don't die, they simply replace each other.

"To describe: the loss of twelve million." In a hotel suite, a few moments before going down to address community leaders, Netanyahu scribbles next to this instruction some data that will help him to do the math, showing how twelve million Jews have been lost since the Holocaust, through assimilation. Once he used to call this the "silent Holocaust," and was criticized for it. Now, with a blue pen, he calculates in the margins that it works out to 29,500 Jews marrying out of the faith every month, multiplied by the years that have passed since the Holocaust.

A knock at the door and the shuffling of the bodyguards in the corridor indicate that the time for corrections and playing with figures is over. The Prime Minister straightens the stack of papers and hands them over to his spokesman, who will have them ready in place for him (so that when he is filmed ascending the podium to speak, he will not be holding a sheaf of papers). On the same page that shows his computations, there is a reminder in an especially large font, so there is no chance of confusion or forgetting: "Do not compare to Holocaust."

King Xerxes I

Netanyahu visited a synagogue on the festival of Purim. Children in fancy dress costumes gathered around him. "Who knows what we are celebrating?" he asked them and then answered himself, "That's right – they tried to wipe us out. And where did that happen?" "In Shushan, the capital," shouted one of the children. "Quite correct," Netanyahu praised him, adding, "in Persia. The Persians are trying now, too, to eradicate us, and this time, too, they won't succeed."

Throughout his years as Prime Minister, Netanyahu has made mention of the Esther story dozens of times in different speeches, drawing a parallel between Iran and its efforts to obtain nuclear weapons and the attempts by the wicked Haman to annihilate the

Jews. "We read the Book of Esther, which describes the attempt to destroy the Jewish People. They failed then. They will fail today. We will never allow Iran to develop nuclear weapons," he said in 2018. He had expressed the same idea in his speech at the UN, in 2012, when President Obama had warned against an attack on Iran. "We are not living in the days of Esther. We are responsible for our own fate," he declared.

One year, his comparison between Persia, Iran, and the Nazis drew a response from Teheran. Iranian Foreign Minister Zarif tweeted in 2017 that Netanyahu was inventing lies about the Iranian people, which had saved the Jews three times in history. He referred the Israelis to the relevant texts: "The Book of Esther tells of how Xerxes I [King Ahasuerus] saved the Jews from a plot hatched by Haman the Agagite." The second time: "During the time of Cyrus the Great, an Iranian king saved the Jews — this time from captivity in Babylon." And again: "During the Second World War, when Jews were being slaughtered in Europe, Iran gladly took them in."

Netanyahu not only keeps goes back to the Holocaust, but connects contemporary threats to the ancient, biblical past, too. Iran is the "new Amalek," in his words, trying to establish "a thousand-year Islamic Reich."

"In every generation all kinds of adversaries rise up against us. But the great change that has happened in our generation is the rediscovery of the Jewish People's ability to defend itself," echoes Netanyahu's narrative.

The Symbol of Symbols

> "From my experience I know that there is nothing that causes enthusiasm and solidarity among Jews everywhere in the world like the mention of the name Jerusalem. The city and the nation are one and the same."

It is a short time before the speech that Netanyahu will be delivering at the official Jerusalem Day ceremony on Ammunition Hill. After some thought he erases the sentence that would reveal one of his methods, as a speaker, to arouse enthusiasm.

Netanyahu has written points on the pages in his handwriting: "The revival of the nation, Rachel's Tomb, wiping a tear … the quest for peace will continue, but this peace will include a united Jerusalem. We shall not go back to a division of the city; it is ours. It shall remain ours forever, for thousands of years we prayed …"

Jerusalem is not just a place; it is a symbol. So is Rachel's Tomb, and Ammunition Hill, and, of course, the Holocaust. Ernst Cassirer, who developed a philosophy of symbolic forms, demonstrates how symbols in the hands of the state and its leader create consciousness and culture: "Man … lives in a world of symbols. Language, mythos, art, and religion are the parts of this world. They are the different threads that are interwoven to form the network of symbols, the events and the workings of human experience."

The mention of the name "Jerusalem," as Netanyahu wrote in his notes (and then erased), arouses immediate enthusiasm and solidarity among Jews everywhere in the world. There are words whose mere mention causes an outpouring of emotion.

These legendary symbols create a picture that is based on an ancient mythos; a picture so powerful and direct that everything else pales into insignificance beside it. A picture not only is worth a thousand words, but also silences a thousand words. And when a person is deluged with symbols and images, he becomes almost incapable of perceiving the actual reality – that which the symbol is supposed to symbolize, that which lies behind the image.

The symbols have pushed reality aside. Netanyahu, who himself has become a powerful symbol, makes use of mythical thinking, based on national and religious legends, and this imbues his words with a sort of magical power. The symbols are like political consciousness dynamite that Netanyahu places in his speeches, devastating the slower processes of logical thinking. And the symbol of symbols is Jerusalem.

■■■

For Bibi, Jerusalem is a code word. "When a Jew says 'Jerusalem' – that one word encapsulates all our history, our dreams, and our values," he declared one year at a ceremony marking the anniversary of the city's liberation. This explains the frequent inclusion of Jerusalem in his campaigns ("Peres will divide Jerusalem," and more).

Jerusalem has been there for him throughout the serial succession of his opponents – Peres, Barak, Olmert, Yachimovich, Herzog, Gantz. The rival, whoever he or she may be, endangers Jerusalem. The approach that fuses the Holocaust, Jerusalem, militant Islam, and political rivals served him in the 2006 campaign against Ehud Olmert:

> "He decided to give them money, and instead of keeping Hamas at bay, he is bringing them closer to Jerusalem, and Jerusalem is threatened. He takes the fence and brings them closer. Four hundred meters from the road to Jerusalem is where Hamas will be sitting. I acted to stop their spread towards Jerusalem. These instances are evidence of

a lack of logic and a lack of understanding, and they are evidence of weakness. We [the Likud] are not weak. We do not bend. We know how to stand up to international pressure. We know how to put up an iron wall against anyone who comes to annihilate us."

Olmert is bringing Hamas to Jerusalem; the Left is aiming ISIS at Jerusalem; Gantz and Lapid will give up Jerusalem; Peres will divide Jerusalem; Barak has relinquished Jerusalem. Netanyahu formulates his messages to correspond precisely to the national traumas that still influence Israeli worldviews. Even his most up-to-date campaigns are based on ancient history.

The destruction of Jerusalem is an event much further back in history than the Holocaust, but Netanyahu knows that among his traditionally-oriented voters, the ancient destruction is still relevant. In every prayer, blessing, wedding ceremony and funeral, it is present. Jerusalem, like God, is a presence in the lives of Israelis – even those who have been out of touch for some time.

∎∎∎

"Jews in Spain, on the eve of the Expulsion; Jews in Ukraine fleeing from pogroms; Jews fighting in the Warsaw Ghetto when the Nazis were closing in on them – they never ceased praying, never ceased longing. They continued to whisper, 'Next year in Jerusalem.'"

The idea of historical continuity extends from the rivers of Babylon, to the palaces of Persia, the dungeons of the Inquisition, the Kishinev pogroms, the extermination camps, and exploding buses, all the way to the bureau of the Prime Minister in Jerusalem, where Netanyahu sits beneath the likenesses of Moses, Herzl and Churchill, acting to save his nation from another Holocaust, which is approaching and threatening the Third Commonwealth.

> "Faced with threats of annihilation, Israel will not stretch its neck for slaughter. Unlike what happened in the time of the Holocaust, we are capable of and determined to defend ourselves, by ourselves."

The Chosen People is persecuted. It might be a Holocaust, or a pogrom in Kiev; it might be Esau who threatens Jacob, the wicked Haman plotting against Mordecai, or Hamas against Jerusalem – it is always seen through the same spectacles. Any narrative, seeking to organize disparate events within the same overall scheme, must be sufficiently simple and inclusive to be able to accommodate many different elements.

Throughout the years, Netanyahu's narrative has been a simple frame story. It includes archetypes, symbols, and images, good guys and bad guys, human beings and beasts. In every election campaign, Netanyahu revives the storyline of the Jewish People from the dawn of history.

Underlying elections in Israel is the Judeo-Christian mythos, and the central symbols of Jerusalem, beasts, and the Holocaust. The persecuted Chosen People. The leader chosen by the people must be Netanyahu, who himself is persecuted. Netanyahu will redeem his people.

■■■

Secret #5: Jerusalem and the Beast Using a web of images and symbols, Netanyahu creates a primal, ancient discourse that presents the conflict as a collision of civilizations – beasts vs. human beings. He bases himself on principles that are common to Judaism and Christianity, and maneuvers between local and distant messianic movements. The traditional Right adopts the narrative offered by this son of an historian, who revives Judaism's traumas, highlights his connection to the Bible, and warns that the Holocaust and the destruction of Jerusalem will repeat themselves if he is not there to save the nation from those threatening to obliterate it.

6.
THE LEFTIST LABEL
PROPAGANDA

The team of actors recruited for the job was comprised of five men. The chosen location was a sandy area on the outskirts of one of Israel's coastal towns. The license plates of the white pickup truck that had been rented the previous evening had been replaced. The rear of the truck had been splattered with mud, to look more authentic. This was to be the terrorists' vehicle.

Displaying the ISIS flag is prohibited by law in Israel, but Netanyahu's campaign production team had two black flags printed with the white circular seal of the prophet Mohammad in its center, along with the inscription in Arabic, "There is no God but Allah." The flags of the Islamic caliphate were handed to two actors, who were stationed in the back of the open truck. One of the terrorists, designated as the driver, wore a black balaclava over his face, and a camouflage uniform. The other terrorist had his face exposed, with the addition of an artificial beard.

The truck drove up and down the sand dunes not far from the coastal road. The ISIS fighters stood in the back of the truck, each holding a side rail with one hand and waving the flag with the other. The vehicle was filmed over and over from different angles.

The truck drove to the main road and pulled up next to a car waiting at a traffic light. The actor playing the driver was a bespectacled

Ashkenazi man who appeared rather apathetic towards his surroundings. "Which way to Jerusalem, bro?" the terrorist asked him in an exaggerated Arab accent. "Take a left," answered the bespectacled driver.

A black slide appears on the screen. Three pistol shots are fired, each blasting a small hole in the slide. After the first, in red letters: "The Left" … Another shot, another small hole, and more red lettering: "will capitulate" … Another shot, "to terror." The sound: joyful celebration in Arabic. The terrorist at the back of the truck fires some more. "The Left will capitulate to terror." A slide in blue and white: "It's us or them." The Likud, led by Netanyahu.

■■■

Perhaps Netanyahu's greatest political achievement is his manipulation of the word "Left" to create negative connotations amongst the Israeli public. With the help of the Right as a whole, and within a reality saturated with terror, he succeeded in creating an associative continuum in which "Left" is first and foremost a four-letter word.

The public presumably knows that the word "Left" is not a slur or insult, but as we already know, there is a difference between what the public knows and what it feels. Netanyahu, who directs his message to the associative limbic system, has turned the word "Left" into a curse in the mind of the voter. He brandishes this label in pursuit of his political opponents, seeking to stain them with it. Leftist leaders are aware that their political affiliation is their weakness, and over many years, opposition politicians have become careful not to identify themselves or their views with the word "Left." Barak, Olmert, Livni, Yachimovich, Herzog – everyone who has run against Netanyahu - have each claimed not to be a leftist. In its 2019 campaign Blue and White made every effort to distance itself from this label. The party recruited well-known Right-wing figures – some defectors from Netanyahu's own bureau – who went so far as to claim, "We are the real Likud." One of the party's main slogans was, "There's no Left or Right; Israel comes before everything," in an attempt to avoid Netanyahu's "Left" stamp.

"They camouflage themselves. They're Left - even extreme Left, and we have to expose them … Be like parrots," Netanyahu instructed, reverting to images. "Our job right now is to keep drumming in that they're Left." And the Likud indeed drummed this incessantly. Every clip that Bibi disseminated concluded with the inscription, "Weak Left."

How does he do it? How did he take a simple, innocent, legitimate, ideological word and imbue it with such negative connotations? How did "leftist" come to mean "traitor"?

The Diffusion Method

The pilot opens the throttle and the helicopter flies lower, towards the long semitrailer cruising along the Jordan Valley. It hovers just a few meters above, so anyone standing on the roof of the truck can see the pilot's face, covered with his helmet: a smiling Yair Lapid. The helicopter lowers itself even closer to the truck, which is loaded with crates of beer. The future candidate for the office of Prime Minister, dressed in a flight suit, grabs the side of the truck, jumps over to the rear section of the helicopter (seemingly leaving the control wheel and flight controls unattended) and reaches out a muscular arm to sweep up a crate off the truck, dumping it into the helicopter's interior. The driver of the semitrailer gives a friendly wave, and Lapid gives a charming smile in return. A voice reads out the inscription that appears on the screen: "Goldstar [beer] – a man's word."

As a presenter, Lapid was worth a fortune. It didn't matter whether he was lying in mechanics' overalls under a car, advertising Bank Hapoalim; talking to a fish about renovating its house; or selling a new brand of wine. Lapid's method of selling products was exactly the same method that Netanyahu would come to use against him and the Israeli Left: the diffusion method.

Lapid, who hosted a talk show on TV and wrote a weekly newspaper column, was considered the epitome of Israeliness; surveys and focus groups found that most of the Israeli public knew his name and attributed positive qualities to him. He also featured on a "sexiest men" list. "The ideal husband for your daughter," was the PR company's recommendation to Bank Hapoalim. And sure enough, Lapid became the face on the bank's commercials.

The idea was that the same positive qualities that the public associated with Lapid would now also be associated with the bank. A process of diffusion, as it were, with feelings passing between the two entities appearing in juxtaposition. Lapid as a symbol of appealing masculinity – beer as appealing masculinity. Lapid as a symbol of Israeliness and empathic humanity – the bank as the same.

Scientists were long puzzled by the mystery of how two pendulum clocks hung on a wall, or suspended from a beam, will gradually achieve synchrony. The synchronization was eventually found to be attributable to the tiny vibrations that traveled through the air, or the wall, from one clock to the other. In a similar manner, images that are juxtaposed come to achieve synchrony. Lapid-bank; militant Islamists-beasts; Left-terror. Peres-fear. Herzog and Livni-ISIS. The one image seeps into the other.

The Weapons of Propaganda

The "hypodermic needle model" was first proposed by Harold Lasswell, a pioneer of communications theory and political science. It suggests that the government and media "inject" propaganda directly into the "vein" of their audience, causing them to draw specific conclusions and make specific decisions. What ingredients are contained in this injection? What turns a claim or assertion into propaganda? Lasswell found that the two essential components of propaganda are manipulation and symbols. In Netanyahu's case, the manipulation is carried out on and by means of symbols. Jerusalem, Hitler, beasts, the flag – these are some of the symbols that Netanyahu uses against the Left. Through repetitive mention of certain terms, "Left" ceases to be a word and becomes symbolic of a whole system of values that are wrapped up with it. "Left" is transformed from a concept into an image.

This is how propaganda is created. Terminology from one world is superimposed on concepts from a different world. The message is then repeated enough times that eventually an illusion of truth is created, and the two concepts seem somehow interlinked. Metaphor is the weapon of propaganda.

Metaphor was also our weapon of choice when I served as commander of the Military School for Communications during the Second Lebanon War. At Sokolov House in Tel Aviv, home to the IDF Spokesman's Unit, we designed posters depicting Nasrallah as a snake. These posters were dropped by IAF planes over Beirut.

The same weapon was used by early Christianity, when it created a connection between Woman, the serpent, and primordial sin. Martin Luther defined the Jews as poisoners of wells, as vipers, and as children of Satan; Iranian leaders call Israel the "little Satan," and extremist Islam refers to infidels as pigs. The metaphor establishes a link between concepts drawn from disparate realms, which then influences consciousness, voting, and action.

■■■

At a press conference that he held jointly with Netanyahu, French President Macron was asked about a strained phone conversation he had had with President Trump. Macron evaded the question by invoking a saying attributed to Bismarck: "Laws are like sausages: it's best not to watch how they're made." Bibi laughed out loud. He knows only too well how ugly politics can get.

Bibi is a great believer in smear campaigns. He will never forget the moment when, in the midst of an election campaign, he was forced to race over to the TV studio to reveal to the public that his political rivals were trying to blackmail him by means of a video tape showing him cheating on his wife Sara. He doesn't hesitate to use the same methods against his competitors, and instructs his staff to gather negative information about rival candidates. His indictment on bribery charges details how he intervened personally on dozens of occasions to have negative reports about other candidates promoted on a news website, in return for regulatory benefits worth hundreds of millions of shekels.

His interference has at time extended beyond the Israeli media. "Please collect information for me linking the PLO/Arab countries/extremist Islam to drugs," he instructs the head of the research department in the Foreign Ministry, with a view to using the information to sway public opinion abroad. As Deputy Foreign Minister he sent a telegram complimenting the French embassy for having managed to place a photograph of Arafat with Sadam Hussein in *Le Figaro*. "Nice work. Well done."

A secret telegram, whose existence is being revealed here for the first time and which was addressed to Bibi during his service as a diplomat, reveals how the Israeli consulate tried to obstruct the appointment of a US ambassador to the UN because the candidate, Vernon Walters, was regarded as not sufficiently pro-Israel: "AIPAC has prepared a dossier including various details and points of vulnerability in the man's career. The dossier has a strong negative emphasis and could provide preliminary material for those senators interested in raising difficulties during the confirmation proceedings." The Israeli diplomat writing to Ambassador Netanyahu added that the AIPAC smear campaign had come to the knowledge of the candidate, "who reacted angrily. At this stage AIPAC decided to approach Walters with a view to mitigating the tension that had been created. Attached is Steve Rosen's report following the conversation."

Bibi read the report in its entirety and decided to intervene. A week later he was already able to dispatch a secret telegram of his own to Jerusalem, reporting on his intensive lobbying at the highest levels of the US administration: "I accompanied Schultz to the airport and spoke with him in private, in his car, for about half an hour. The meeting took place at my initiative." According to his own testimony, Netanyahu managed to obtain a commitment from the US Secretary of State that good relations between the US and Israel would be maintained even though the new ambassador to the UN was "tough minded."

■■■

The amygdala in the brain is constantly monitoring reality and applying its binary categorization: threat or opportunity. Black or white. Left or Right. Intuitive, instantaneous thinking uses shortcuts in the form of generalizations or stereotypes. According to a simplistic worldview, there are good guys and bad guys; it's us or them, life or death.

Netanyahu couldn't do it without the help of the media. The limbic system merges effortlessly with the media system. Mass visual communication, which allows only brief speech, pictures, and images, invites a division of the world into "them and us." Scandal or celebration. Bad or good. Left or Right. Netanyahu's campaigns frame the elections as a war, in which there are two sides. It's either one or the other. One has to stand either here or there. It's us or them; man or beast. We are the Jews, eternally persecuted and threatened with annihilation. The Left? They're on the side of the beasts. The Nazis.

How do we get from Left to Nazis? Via a progression of images, symbols, and connotations that Netanyahu has built up through propaganda. The steps are as follows:

STAGE 1 – THE LEFTISTS ARE NOT JEWS

As on every festival, on the holiday of Jewish democracy – the Election Day public holiday – the Jews have to defeat their enemies, the Israelis, the leftists, who had arisen to destroy them.

In order for this story to work, for each election Netanyahu recreates the Jewish sense of persecution, stretching from the siege of Jerusalem to the siege of the Warsaw Ghetto, reiterating that we – we, the Right – are Jews. The fact that the Left is losing its Jewish identity is an important element in the molding of public opinion and in Netanyahu's story.

It was on the basis of this approach – "We are the Jews" – that Chabad activists ran a national campaign in 1996 under the slogan, "Netanyahu is good for the Jews," which changed the voting map, leading to Netanyahu's victory and Peres's defeat. Afterwards Peres angrily charged, "The Jews beat the Israelis." Even after five terms in office, Netanyahu is still floating the question of "Who is a Jew?" His answer: Whoever is not a leftist.

> "The Israeli Left has to undergo some soul-searching. It has to ask itself why a fundamental concept of Zionism – "the Jewish nation-state of the Jewish People in its land" – has become a vulgar concept, a dirty word, an idea to be ashamed of. We aren't ashamed of Zionism. We are proud of our state, of its being a national home for the Jewish People."

As studies by Lasswell and others have shown, a precondition for effective propaganda is that it must contain a kernel of truth to serve as the basis for manipulation. What truth is there in the lie that the Israeli Left is not Jewish? Why does this accusation "stick"? The Israeli Left emphasizes the idea of "a nation like all nations" as a positive value. It promotes integration into the family of nations, normality, humanism. Every human being is a human being, regardless of religion or race. These are the universal values of the liberal worldview.

But political warfare doesn't allow for complex messages; there is only a binary division: you're either Jewish or not. The discourse is "us or them". The Jews against the world. Universal values are therefore portrayed as anti-Jewish. Secular humanist ideals are invoked as support for the claim that the Left has lost its Jewish values. For example, a humanist approach towards illegal migrant workers is viewed as anti-Jewish. Western culture is viewed as assimilation.

> "There are also those [on the Left] who fight for the illegal infiltrators to come here and to stay here. You have to understand the absurdity of this: We built the [security] fence. We've built the obstacle, and are working intensively to send back the remaining infiltrators – and they want to keep them here. That being the case, is it any wonder that Ahmad Tibi supports Bougie [Herzog]? Is it any surprise that Bougie says he would be glad to see the Arab parties joining his list?"

"The Left is in favor of infiltrators" was Netanyahu's accusation against the heads of Blue and White who, he claimed, opposed building a fence. They aren't Jews, he repeats the message. During the time he served as head of the opposition, he heaped withering criticism on the Rabin government for its abandonment of Judaism:

> "Mr. Peres – Mr. Rabin, especially - I listened to your speech. I heard you mention Jewish values. Don't tell us stories. Don't pretend that what motivates your policy in this regard is Jewish values. Your government is the most distant and disconnected from Jewish values that we have ever had."

Netanyahu portrays the Left as having lost its Jewish identity with the support of the Arabs, and points to the religious education system as a model and ideal:

> "Arab propaganda has succeeded in causing us to question the justice of our cause. There is no doubt that the Oslo process and the explanations that were given for it in the past, blurred and dimmed our understanding. But the source of the problem is the nihilistic influences on our children, and our feeble response to them. The education that our children are receiving does not build resilience in the face of unceasing attacks on Zionism and on our aims. Many of our youth aren't imbued with faith and ideals. They don't have the necessary knowledge. They've lost their awareness of the uniqueness and destiny of our people, and they seek their identity in foreign pastures.

> "In this area, the religious education system serves as a model. That doesn't mean we all have to take this path, but

we have to conclude something from the fact that the percentage of skullcap-wearing soldiers in the IDF is so impressive, that crime and moral corruption are almost unheard of among them, and that their devotion and readiness to sacrifice is a source of inspiration and pride to all of us."

■■■

The leftists, to Netanyahu's view, have lost not only their Jewish identity, but also their patriotism:

"We have the People of Israel and we have the Israeli flag, which we carry with honor and pride. We will continue to carry it for many more years. The media, and the Left that serves it, has a hard time accepting that, so they create endless scandals, endless items, endless headlines, so that perhaps something will stick …".

In other words, those who proudly display the flag, those who are patriotic and Jewish, are the Right; those who try to bring down Netanyahu are those who have forgotten the flag. The Left, which was ready to relinquish the great symbol of Judaism – Jerusalem – is also ready to relinquish the symbol of Israeliness – the flag. Netanyahu's answer to the investigations by the leftist police is the flag.

The Left, pushed into a corner, responds with defensive apologetics. Yair Lapid emphasizes his Jewish identity and tries to woo the ultra-Orthodox sector. Gantz's advisors make sure to photograph him at the Western Wall and donning Tefillin (phylacteries), in light of surveys showing that most of his voters are traditional Jews. At meetings of the Left campaign leaders, a central topic of discussion is how not to appear leftist. In a closed meeting in 2014, Herzog rebranded the Labor party as the Zionist Union, to combat the perception that the Left is no longer Zionist. Ehud Barak had taken the same measure in 1999, renaming the party One Israel. Avi Gabbay, who succeeded him as party chairman, restored the name "Labor" but explained the party's weak state with an acknowledgment that indeed, as Netanyahu had asserted two decades earlier, the Left had "forgotten what it means to be a Jew."

Netanyahu tosses all this aside. "They camouflage themselves," he claimed against his adversary, Barak, in 1999. In 2019 he charged that Gantz and company were "leftists in disguise." He repeats the message over and over, allowing it to spread slowly but surely. In every election campaign, he systematically links his political rivals with the adversaries of the State of Israel and those who are not part of the Jewish People:

> "When you listen to what they say in Hebrew, they don't sound like great Zionists. Listen to Bougie, who said that the expression 'Jewish state' is completely misunderstood. Other members of his list say that the Palestinian identity is stronger than their Israeli identity. That women don't need to send their children to serve in the army. That Zionism is something that doesn't speak to them."

Netanyahu's conclusion: "They aren't the Zionist Union; they're the anti-Zionist Union."

STAGE 2 – THE LEFT IS ARAB

Having declared the Left un-Jewish and un-Zionist, the next step is to link the Left and Arab terror:

> "The leftists have forgotten what it is to be Jewish. They think they'll put our security in the hands of the Arabs.

The Arabs will take care of it: give them part of the country, and they'll take care of us."

More than a decade later, Netanyahu is still trying to link Gantz and the Arabs, with the repeated claim that Gantz will set up a government with the support of the Arab parties. Quotes from different candidates on the Blue and White list were collected to prove this; they were repeated by Likud spokesmen in interviews, and became video clips for the Likud campaign warning against a "Left-Arab government". The hyphen connecting "Left" and "Arab" is more important to Netanyahu than the hyphen connecting "Jewish" and "democratic."

"A leftist government could arise, with the support of the Arabs," Netanyahu warned. Blue and White, panicked by the image, did all they could to disassociate themselves from the Arabs in the public consciousness. Along with security-related statements about toppling Hamas, Yair Lapid and Benny Gantz instructed their list to deny vehemently any possibility of joining an "Arab bloc" to prevent Netanyahu from forming a government. The fact that the Arabs did ultimately recommend Gantz to form the government was proof for Bibi that his assessment had been correct all along.

On the day of the first round of elections in 2019, Netanyahu again made sure that the public understood that it had to choose between the Arab enemy and the persecuted Jew, and sought a way to recreate the effect of the "Arabs streaming to the polls" warning from the previous elections. This time his weapon was a secret recording of a conversation between two Members of Knesset, Amir Peretz of Labor and Ofer Shelah of Blue and White. The barely audible recording has the two men discussing what Likud later referred to as "the deal with the Arab parties to bring down Netanyahu." The clip was disseminated via instant phone messaging in the middle of Election Day, to hundreds of thousands of voters.

It has become a sort of routine that Netanyahu convinces the public that the Left will go with the Arabs. Netanyahu himself is the hyphen between the Left and the Arabs:

> "There are Islamic parties there, anti-Zionist parties, and that's its essence; that's the Left. Therefore, in these elections it's either Tibi or Bibi."

Put "Left" together with "Arabs" often enough and the diffusion effect sets in. Gantz. Left. Weak. Arab support. A political defeat to the Left means terror. The obvious cognitive shortcut becomes, "The Left will bring terror." After watching the clip showing the driver on the coastal road directing the ISIS terrorists to Jerusalem, Arab Supreme Court Justice Salim Joubran, in his capacity as chairman of the elections committee, defined it as "using motifs that ostensibly connect the political Left with a terror organization."

STAGE 3 – THE LEFT IS IN TANDEM WITH TERRORISTS

Bibi doesn't need to say that Benny Gantz is a terrorist. It's enough that he mentions over and over that Gantz attended a memorial for Palestinian terrorists. There is no need to say that Blue and White collaborate with the Arabs; he need only repeat "Tibi or Bibi." The Left will capitulate to terror; Gantz is easy for the Iranians to access, they have information about him; Hamas and the Israeli Left have overlapping interests. After a barrage of rockets from Gaza targeting an event that Netanyahu attended, he was quick to attack his rivals:

> "Hamas, too, prefer Gantz and Lapid, because they are weak. The only thing that competes with the great celebration that went on in Gaza over their shooting at us – and perhaps even surpassed it – was the glee of Gantz and Lapid, while citizens of Israel and the Prime Minister were under fire."

In other cases, the indictment of the Left includes the charge of "aiding the enemy." The Left tries to help the Arab Joint List to get elected to the Knesset, with the aim of "introducing inciters and spies against Israel." Again, there is no need to use the word "traitors" explicitly:

> "Visits in the past by Left-wing MKs to convicted terrorists who murdered Jews show how distorted and dangerous the leftist path is."

■■■

Election Day (again), September 2019. Fifty minutes to the close of voting booths. Netanyahu's voice is already hoarse from his Facebook broadcast. He is still peddling the leftist label and attacking the exultant "leftist media":

> "We're going to lose everything! They're already celebrating! They've prepared the candies – in Ramallah, too, and in Teheran, in Gaza, and Hezbollah, too, and in Damascus."

A clip entitled "Lapid-Gantz and Iran – a love story" amassed some two million views. On a different occasion, he had declared: "Khamenei, the leader of Iran, said that he prefers Gantz."

Perhaps the hoarseness had developed a few hours earlier, when the Prime Minister dragged his bodyguards to the Machane Yehuda market to dramatize his fear of a low turnout amongst his base. He stood there with a megaphone and yelled, "The Palestinian Authority is calling to bring me down!"

"Gantz supported the Iran nuclear agreement, which allowed Iran to obtain nuclear weapons," read an election poster. The wording was somewhat clumsy, but the clumsiness did the trick: it created a mental shortcut. "Gantz is in favor of the Iranians and is helping them to obtain nuclear weapons." Gantz is with the Iranians. The Iranians are enemies. Gantz is an enemy.

...

> "It is infuriating that while the American administration recognizes the legality of the settlements in Judea and Samaria, Benny Gantz is putting together a government with supporters of terror who don't recognize any of our rights in our land."

Netanyahu's hopes of creating a government had run out. The mandate was handed to Gantz. Netanyahu appeared with a large banner behind him that read, "Emergency Conference." The sub-heading was highlighted in red: "Preventing a dangerous minority government dependent on supporters of terrorism."

Netanyahu's spokesmen weren't content with the visual composition on the screen. To bolster the standing of the leader of the country who was facing criminal charges and had twice failed to put together a government, all the senior Likud figures were enlisted to sit behind him and applaud while the Likud chairman spoke out against what he called "an historical national terror attack." Behind the scenes the ministers griped, but at broadcast time they all sat in front of the cameras as per instructions from the Prime Minister's Office. When Netanyahu entered, the audience welcomed him, singing, "Bibi, King of Israel."

"When you're on live TV, the whole country can see whether you're really applauding or just faking it," one of the ministers shared his distress with me after the event, when we met at a workshop on appearing on camera. "Don't laugh," he chided me as a smile crept over my face, "it's really hard!" The minister and his colleagues had served unwillingly as walk-ons, applauding along with the audience while Netanyahu accused his rivals of committing a terror attack. From the podium Netanyahu charged former Chiefs of Staff Gantz and Ashkenazi with collaborating with the enemy in wartime:

> "What got into your heads? Benny, you – and Gabi [Ashkenazi], too – received briefings and updates just last week about the security situation; you got everything. You knew exactly what was at stake, and despite it all, while we were in the midst of a military operation, being attacked with missiles, with our citizens sitting in shelters – at the very same time you were conducting negotiations with the same MKs who support the terror organizations and want to destroy the state … Elections are bad for Israel; we don't want elections. But there's something much worse – a dangerous minority government with the backing of Ayman Odeh and Ahmad Tibi. Such a government is an existential threat to the State of Israel … Such a government is an abandonment of the security of the state."

STAGE 4 – THE LEFT IS NOT HUMAN

Faced with criminal investigations and a decision to indict him, Netanyahu activates the image that he has taken pains to implant in the Israeli consciousness: the image of man vs. beast. This time, he plays the role of the hunted animal:

"I am being subjected to unprecedented hounding"; "A blood libel"; "An obsessive witch hunt aimed at toppling the Right-wing government"; "A hounding of me and of my wife"; "When the truth emerges, it will turn out that it was an organized witch hunt"; "The public understood long ago already that there is a transparent media witch hunt against me."

Who are the hunters? Whoever they may be. They are evil, malicious people who are after Netanyahu's blood.

"This is a lynch," Netanyahu told Likud MKs with reference to investigations into suspicions of a massive graft scheme involved in the multi-billion-shekel state purchase of naval vessels and submarines. He demanded that they defend him in the media, using the word "lynch," with all its gruesome associations in the public mind. In an interview to Channel 12 TV he claimed, "My blood and the blood of my family is being spilled." "They're putting me in front of a firing squad." Referring to the investigations against him, he stated, "This is a blood libel."

Netanyahu's discourse concerning the criminal investigations against him echoes the situation of the Jew persecuted by savage beasts throughout history. It's a lynch, a blood libel. Netanyahu views himself as a modern Dreyfus, and his legal troubles are just another incarnation of antisemitism on the part of ruthless beasts. This is the covert meaning of the image of the witch hunt and all the accompanying discourse. "I'm also a human being," he has repeated over and over in his responses to police questioning.

"They are committing a terror attack against democracy. A terror attack against democracy," he repeats in a live broadcast via Facebook. The topic is the media leaks from his interrogations; the discourse is existential. "A terror attack against the Israeli democracy," he accuses the media and the leftists, repeating the term for the third time. After the elections he referred to the police searches conducted on his aides' telephones, too, as a "terror attack on democracy."

It is not for nothing that Bibi's images with regard to his legal affairs are characterized by the recurring theme of human beasts and terrorists. Here, too, he manages to bind together elements that are unrelated to each other: the police with the Left, with the media, with the beasts, with terror.

"This well-orchestrated campaign includes media personalities who are functioning here not only as journalists. They are also the investigators, the judge, and the executioner. At play here are considerations not of editing [in Hebrew, *arikha*], but of beheading [*arifa*]."

The word "beheading" conjures up a visual image. The Prime Minister's silver, coiffed head, bent over; a leftist journalist standing over him holding a knife, a guillotine, or an executioner's rope. This is how pictures are conjured out of words. The image is not a random one. The statement comes at a time when the entire world watches aghast as ISIS executioners behead their captives in front of cameras. The shocking picture from ISIS clips slides into place in the mind, aligning with the picture of journalists trying to behead the Prime Minister. The leftist journalists take on the role of executioners, Netanyahu's head is hacked off. This is the scene that Netanyahu plants in the unconscious of the Israeli citizenry, hidden within the political drama that they are following closely.

Already in the very first political clip that Netanyahu produced for the first election campaign in 2019, he associated the Left with louts lacking humanity:

"The Left-wing demonstrators and the media are exerting thuggish and inhumane pressure on the Attorney General to indict me at any cost."

The appending of the term "inhumane" to the Left is an attempt to convey the idea that the Left has not only forgotten what it is to be Jewish, but has also forgotten what it is to be a human being. We are people; they have forgotten what it is to be humane.

This comparison was made more boldly and forcefully by one of the Likud ministers, Tzachi Hanegbi, who defined the Left as a gang of bloodthirsty scavengers. A recording of his words to a convention of Likud activists includes the following: "We are not scavengers! We don't lie in wait, like vultures circling over a carcass that they plan to devour. We are human beings."

STAGE 5 – THE LEFT IN TANDEM WITH THE NAZIS

Like a skilled and experienced chef, Netanyahu gives his creations time to simmer and attain their full flavor. The next stage in the chain of association is to allow the manipulative stew of symbols to brew until it produces the link between the Left and the Nazis.

Following the publication of an unfavorable item about him in *Haaretz*, Netanyahu responded:

> "For years, *Haaretz* has been a newspaper that slanders the IDF and Israel throughout the world, and represents not even a fraction of the range of positions held by the broader Israeli public. It is no wonder that the public at large has lost confidence in you. We can only hope that the fact that the German media concern DuMont Schauberg, which disseminated Nazi propaganda during World War II, has purchased a 20% stake in *Haaretz*, is not connected to this trend."

This identification of a Nazi trend wafting through *Haaretz* in 2019 was not the first time that Netanyahu had bound up the Left with the Holocaust. In 1993, as chairman of the opposition, he claimed that Yitzhak Rabin was insane and was emulating the appeasement policy towards Nazi Germany:

> "Mr. Prime Minister, there are instances in this century of prime ministers losing their sanity. There were instances

in this century of entire governments that lost their sanity; my colleagues always cite the example of the British Prime Minister, Chamberlain … You are much worse than Chamberlain … You are endangering the security and freedom of your own people."

Three weeks before the repeat elections in 2019, during a visit to Ukraine, he responded to a clip released by Blue and White against the ultra-Orthodox:

> "The incitement by Prime Ministerial candidate Yair Lapid carries an anti-Semitic tone … I am standing here today on European soil, in a place where vicious things were said about Jews. It pains me greatly to hear these expressions, these images, this trampling of people's dignity."

Netanyahu sees around him not only anti-Semitic Jews consumed with self-hatred, ("They hate the nation," he said on one occasion in reference to the Left,) but also their collaboration with the radical Left in Europe:

> "Antisemitism and its lies did not die with Hitler in a bunker in Berlin … This incitement has its source in extremist Islam and in the Arab world, but in recent years there has also been incitement just as venomous from the western world. British Members of Parliament, senior officials in Sweden, public opinion shapers in France.

> "I have to say that antisemitism in our times creates strange alliances. Members of elites that supposedly represent human progress join up with the most primitive barbarian zealots on earth who behead people, oppress

women, persecute homosexuals, and obliterate cultural treasures. They have made a pact to spread the virus of antisemitism against a single target – us."

...

In comparing the Left to Nazis, Netanyahu follows in the footsteps of Begin. "They [the Labor] haven't learned yet what the red flag symbolizes in our time," Begin asserted in 1981. "It is the flag of Communism and of Nazism. It is the flag of hatred of Jews and supplying arms to Israel's enemies all around. The flag of persecution of Jews and persecution of Hebrew. The flag of concentration camps and human oppression. Subjugation." Many years previously, in a speech against the Reparations Agreement with Germany, Begin had accused the Left of leading the country to a second Holocaust, and described the rightists detained at demonstrations against the agreement as being led to Mapai (Labor) concentration camps.

The comparison between Left-wing actions and Nazi actions has become a common theme in Israel. Examples include the infamous picture of Rabin dressed in an SS uniform; residents of Gush Katif[21] affixing a yellow star to their clothing and writing numbers on their arms; members of the Disengagement Authority referred to as "Judenrat" and IDF soldiers sent to evacuate residents as "Gestapo." During the period of the Oslo Accords, Moshe Feiglin declared, "Rabin is the Judenrat loading us onto the trains."

Actually, this charge didn't start with the Right. Ironically – and Netanyahu never misses an opportunity to mention this – it was Ben-Gurion who first referred to Begin as a "distinctly Hitlerist type."

---

21   The bloc of Jewish communities in the Gaza Strip that were forcibly evacuated by the IDF and then razed to the ground, as part of the Israel's unilateral disengagementfrom the Gaza Strip in 2005.

Zeev (Vladimir) Jabotinsky, the Betar leader so admired by Netanyahu, was referred to by the Mapai chairman as "Vladimir Hitler," and Herut, Betar and Revisionist adherents were labelled "our Hitlerites." Yeshayahu Leibowitz, an outspoken Orthodox intellectual and polymath whose political views placed him on the extreme Left, coined the phrase "Judeo-Nazis." Yair Golan, a former IDF Deputy Chief of Staff, delivered a controversial Holocaust Memorial Day address in which he warned of trends in Israel recalling "horrific processes that developed … in Germany". Bibi himself has been compared to Hitler on several occasions.

The Right compares the Left to Nazism citing its harm to security, the country, and the Jewish People, while the Left compares the Right to Nazism citing its harm to democracy, the Palestinians, and minorities. At the root of this exchange of allegations are vastly different perceptions of the collective memory of the Holocaust – and, accordingly, of its lessons for the present. Holocaust remembrance in Israel is political, partisan remembrance.

The Left and Right stand on opposite sides of the ghetto wall, and the only question that remains to be resolved is, "Who is the Nazi here?" Netanyahu wields this question just as the Left does. Among the symbols that cram every election campaign in Israel, there is one central, key player. Hitler.

STAGE 6 – LEFT EQUALS DEATH

Election Day approaches. The Holocaust is repeating itself. The threat of slaughter is imminent. The question of who to vote for is critical. Netanyahu, along with his good friend cortisol, lets the amygdala know that the elections are a matter of life and death.

In order to translate this narrative into votes for the Likud, Netanyahu makes it clear that a vote for the Left means death in Israel's cities and annihilation of Jews. Exploding buses, pictures of soldiers' graves, Arabs in droves. Gantz sitting with terrorists. "Without Netanyahu, people will be slaughtered here," says his wife Sara. In short, Left equals death.

In 1995, a few months before Rabin's assassination, Netanyahu – then-chairman of the opposition – spoke from the Knesset podium, describing the Left as being possessed by a death wish. He employed a visual image:

> "Mr. Chairman, a group of fools is standing on the roof; they want to jump, drawing an entire nation along after them to smash themselves to smithereens, and they ask us, 'What is your alternative?'
>
> "Well, our alternative is not to jump; not to commit suicide. To live and not to die. Our alternative, Mr. Prime Minister, is to do the complete opposite of what you are doing. Faced with raging terrorism, we would do the exact opposite. We would fight the terrorists ..."

The choice between life and death is the choice between Right and Left. The biblical dictum[22] is clear: "You shall choose life."

Anyone Opposing Me is a Leftist

After emptying the word "Left" of all its values, Netanyahu undertook a fierce rebranding of the Israeli Left and imbued the "leftist" image with new, malevolent meaning. Through sophisticated forms of propaganda and using symbols, manipulation, and reiteration, he

---

22 Deut. 30:19

succeeded in turning the political war between Right and Left into a negative image of the wars between Israel and the Arabs.

The struggle between man and beast is duplicated as a political struggle. The war against the Jewish race is reflected in the war of political parties. And vice versa.

Anyone who opposes me is a leftist; anything negative is leftist. So goes Netanyahu's thinking. It doesn't matter whether it's the leftist Chief of Police, the court, Benny Gantz, the New Israel Fund, Yair Lapid, President Ruby Rivlin, the social protests, the Deputy State Attorney handling Netanyahu's prosecution, the Attorney General, employees at the Prime Minister's Residence who have sued him, or Naftali Bennett. These are just some of the many figures who have earned Netanyahu's designation as "Left."

During Obama's term in office, Netanyahu would repeatedly remind his interlocutors that the full name of this adversarial American president was Barak "Hussein" Obama. Ilana Dayan, an investigative reporter who publicized an in-depth and damning report on the workings of Netanyahu's bureau, was labelled "an extreme leftist." After failing in his attempts to form a coalition after the 2019 elections, Netanyahu lashed out at his former Minister of Defense (who had resigned in the wake of a ceasefire in Gazawhich he characterized as a surrender to terror): "As of now, Avigdor Lieberman is part of the Left."

■■■

Angry lettering spatters all over the page, a far cry from the customary order of his speech notes. Angry and accusatory, he scribbles notes for himself ahead of his evening appearance in which he will respond for the first time to the investigations against him. The Prime Minister has just emerged from several difficult hours answering the questions of police investigators at his official residence, followed by a frustrating discussion with his lawyers. The reporting on TV is only adding to the level of agitation in the house, and Netanyahu decides: "It's time to move to the offensive. It's time to meet the press."

The rest of the speech was apparently shredded; only this page somehow found its way to Netanyahu's personal files, and there I found it. The handwriting, after some deciphering, reveals ten points on the basis of which Netanyahu intended to fight for his innocence. Ten items that would reinforce his weakening hold on the Prime Minister's seat. The ninth point reads as follows:

> "There is a clear attempt here to topple a Prime Minister in a non-democratic way.
>
> Political rivals
>
> Opposed to our policy
>
> Opposed to our policy in Jerusalem
>
> Opposed to our firm policy against a Palestinian state."

Following the three-fold "opposed to our policy," suggesting it was leftists – the same leftists who are ready to give Jerusalem to the Palestinians - who filed the criminal charges against him, Netanyahu writes the opening sentence and numbers it as the last of his Ten Commandments for dealing with his interrogations. He draws a square box around the heading, as always, to remind himself to stand tall and look straight into the camera: "What they failed to achieve in the voting booth, they're trying to force onto the public in an unlawful way." He is pressing so hard with the pen that it makes a small tear in the page: "The truth will win out."

At the top edge of the page he scribbles, "Police investigation, interrogation, indictment." The agitated handwriting becomes increasingly difficult to understand. A point relating to public servants who are elected directly and can be unseated only by the nation or the court makes it suddenly clear that this page actually belongs to the investigations against Netanyahu during his first term in office, concerning the Bar-On Hebron Affair.[23] It is an easy mistake to make because twenty years later, exactly the same messages mount the podium together with Netanyahu to respond to the charges against him: "This tainted process ... is intended to bring down a Prime Minister of the Right; it is intended to bring me down ... They are pursuing me, not the truth ... I shall continue to lead the country with responsibility, with devotion, with concern for the security and the future of all of us. For the country's sake, we have to investigate the investigators."

Nothing has changed. Netanyahu was and remains well prepared, and continues to operate in a systematic and consistent manner. He keeps repeating his message: the future of all of us. The Left, the Arabs, security.

■■■

It's a battle for the home front. An existential threat. The beasts are growling. Out of the windows of the villa in the jungle we see him standing there, facing the world, saving our lives with his polished English, and when he returns, the enemy from within is waiting for him. Those who have forgotten, who haven't learned the lesson, who will divide Jerusalem up for the Arabs, who don't believe in God and in the land; those who want to open the door of the villa to beasts of prey.

Netanyahu manages to divide the world into contrasting pairs in the Israeli consciousness: animals vs. beasts, Jews vs. Nazis, the West

---

23 A 1997 scandal surrounding the personal and political considerations behind Netanyahu's appointment of a new Attorney General, who resigned the next day in view of the backlash.

vs. terror, Jews vs. Arabs, Right vs. Left, Netanyahu vs. the media; the Right vs. the media, Netanyahu vs. the legal system, the nation vs. the elites, the Jews vs. the Israelis; Netanyahu vs. the police investigators; people of culture vs. barbarians; Netanyahu vs. Obama, traditionalists vs. secularists; life vs. death; us vs. Arafat; Netanyahu vs. terror; the Right vs. the Attorney General's Office; the Likud vs. the Left; Netanyahu vs. the Attorney General; Jerusalem vs. Peres; the people vs. sour pickles; life vs. death; us vs. death. And on and on.

It's not logical, but who has time to think logically when cortisol is flowing and the screen in front of us is showing an eternally invalid circular equation that reads: Nazis=beasts=Arabs=Left= investigations=media=terror=death.

■■■

Secret #6: The Enemy in Our Midst Through repetition of images, symbols and claims, Netanyahu has turned "Left" into a slur and created the subconscious idea that the struggle between Right and Left is another stage in the Jewish struggle to survive.

7.
WE ARE ALL RIFFRAFF

COVENANT

The first round of elections in 2019; 41 minutes left for voting. Netanyahu has the results of the Channel 2 TV exit polls, which were leaked to one of his advisors. The core team gathers around, and everyone listens tensely.

The numbers are worrying; things don't look good for Netanyahu. Gantz-Lapid's Blue and White has received more votes. The chances of Bibi forming a coalition seem small. For a moment it looks like defeat is approaching. He reveals no emotion, just says quietly, "It could happen." And then, "It certainly could happen." The expression on his face gives it away: it might be that this is the end.

"He looked like someone who grew old all at once," commented one of the aides who was present. Someone else tried to inject some hope, repeating the familiar claim that the Right always does less well in opinion polls, and that voters don't always report honestly how they voted.

A few minutes later, the leak from Kan 11 came in, and a moment after that, Channel 13. Their results were more encouraging. It wasn't clear yet whether the New Right had passed the election threshold. Netanyahu spoke with his wife. Then he said, "I'll watch the results alone," and walked slowly to his office, a heavy weight on his shoulders.

Netanyahu remained secluded in his room. Outside, his advisors started adding numbers on their phone calculators and spun different political scenarios. At ten, the exit poll was made public. More data came in. The door of the Prime Minister's room opened. Only those closest to him went in and out. Slowly the smiles returned to their faces. It looked like a victory for the Right and for Bibi. It was at this moment that the campaign staff decided that he needed to project victory to the public and to the media, establishing it as fact. At precisely the same moment, Gantz's team likewise decided to announce victory, on the basis of the sole exit poll that predicted that Blue and White was the party that would emerge with the largest number of mandates.

As Gantz and the rest of the Blue and White leadership quartet stood ready to deliver a victory speech, Netanyahu's team glanced at the screen, grimaced, and continued writing. They knew that Bibi had won, by a good margin. An historical, strategic, tremendous victory as Netanyahu would later describe it. A few weeks later, he would suffer a crushing and historic defeat in forming a government.

"It could happen, it could definitely happen," Netanyahu tells his aides during the dark moments when he thought that he had lost – and indeed, he knows that his majority is fragile. He claims that the people are with him, but knows that in actuality it's only half the people: the nation is split between tribes – Left, Right, ultra-Orthodox, Arabs – and only constant, intensive maintenance of his "base" gives him the political power, brittle and splintery as it is, to bring together a coalition. With his constant fear of abandonment, Netanyahu acts to maintain a sense of coalescence around him, which is essential to keep the voting numbers up.

He creates a sense of siege that unites the Right and serves to close its ranks. Then he counters it with a defensive wall, which he builds using the same bricks that served Menachem Begin in his time.

Jewish and Ethnic

The 1981 elections redrew the division of political and social forces in Israel.

On one side was the Ashkenazi[24]-secular-veteran-socialist Labor hegemony. On the other side were the dark-skinned Mizrahim[25], the Right-wing, the religious, residents of the periphery, the traditionalists – in short, the "second Israel."

In political terms, the elections were a choice between the Alignment (Labor), headed by Peres, which according to the polls was expected to return to power, and the Likud, led by Begin, who had just completed his first term as Prime Minister. In actuality, the elections were a battle of kibbutzim vs. development towns, white skins vs. dark skins, Ashkenazi vs. Mizrahi, East vs. West, establishment vs. periphery. The level of antagonism reached the point of arson against party branches and physical violence in town squares (at a time when both the town square and the encounters between conflicting viewpoints were physical and tangible, before the age of the Internet and social media).

That momentous election embodied the underdog experience, the sense of persecution and "everyone against us" among the voters of the Right. That feeling persists to this day, and Netanyahu stokes it because it helps him to get elected.

The sense of victimhood and being a persecuted minority that Netanyahu nurtures stands on two pillars – the Jewish and the ethnic.

---

24   Ashkenazi Jews are those whose ancestors settled in Central and Eastern Europe during the Middle Ages.

25   Mizrahi Jews are descendants of the local Jewish communities that existed in the Middle East and North Africa from biblical times into the modern era.

The Jew has been persecuted since the dawn of history by non-Jews; the Mizrahi is oppressed by the Ashkenazi hegemony. There is an external threat and an internal one. There is one single answer to both enemies: "us." We the people. We the public. We the Jews. We will win.

The Orator in the Town Square

There are instructors at theatrical schools in Israel who teach their students acting techniques by showing them old footage of the great orator of public squares, Menachem Begin, delivering his famous "riffraff speech" in Tel Aviv.[26] For Netanyahu, too, the speech is a source of inspiration and a guide to public appearances and conveying messages. Netanyahu has analyzed the speech in depth, and he delivers it anew, with slight changes, for each election campaign.

Begin's rhetoric is music: it is not so much a speech as a kind of concert, structured like a musical composition, following a crescendo and leading to a symphonic climax, with Begin's voice as the sole instrument and the audience filling in with a choir of applause and whistles.

At a certain stage in the speech Begin tells the crowd, "Now – silence. Not a peep. Absolute silence." A moment later, he rouses them with a rhetorical question. His pauses give him the strength, at the

---

[26] June 28th, 1981. The previous night, entertainer Dudu Topaz had spoken from the same stage at a rally for the Alignment (Labor). Tens of thousands of people turned out for the rally and Topaz greeted them, "It's nice to see this crowd tonight. Theriffraff over there in Metzudat Zeev [Likud headquarters] - they barely even do sentry duty. The combat fighters and the commanders are here tonight. Here is the beautiful Israel."

moment of climax, his fist waving in the air, to roar the words that send the crowd into a frenzy: "Jews! Brothers! Fighters!"

The versatility and variety of Begin's voice is equally apparent when he tells a personal story that includes dialogues. He changes intonation depending on the speaker. When he quotes Dudu Topaz too, he performs a disdainful imitation, intentionally mispronouncing the entertainer's last name, and exaggerates the theatrics when he mentions the slur that had been used against Likud voters. All this adds to the contemptuous humor:

> "I must confess – until this morning, I had never heard the word "*tchach'tchachim*" [riffraff, punks], and I didn't know what it meant. In the underground, during the days of the revolt [against the British], Galili[27] once said to me, 'How did you solve the problem of the Middle Eastern immigrants in the Irgun?'[28] I looked at him in amazement, and said, 'I don't understand your question. What problem?' He said, 'Come on, don't you know? Haven't you heard? The problem with the Middle Eastern immigrants.'"

> "So I said to him, 'What problem? We don't have any problem! We're all brothers, we're all Jews, we're all equal, all of us! The great commander of the regions was a Yemenite. Uzi was Sephardi. Gidi, who carried out the historical operation at the King David Hotel, was Sephardi. The person

---

27 Chief of Staff of the Haganah, the main paramilitary organization of the Jewish population in Mandatory Palestine prior to the establishment of the state.

28 An offshoot of the Haganah, representing the policy of Revisionist Zionism. Begin was the last commander of the Irgun before its fighters were incorporated into the newly formed IDF in 1948

in charge of all the prisoners in Latrun was Yemenite, and all our boys stood at attention in front of him! What problem? We don't have one! We're all Jews! We're all brothers! We're all fighters!'

"But listen: when that – what's his name? Dudu Too-paz – said that nonsense, that utter rubbish, the whole audience that was standing here applauded. Now I'll tell Dudu Topaz who he was talking about.

"Our Middle Eastern brothers were heroic fighters, already in the underground. Some of them were executed by the British, and until their last moment they sang Hatikva,[29] and amazed everyone with their outstanding bravery. They went to prison, to concentration camps. They fought and did not bend. They shouted before British judges, 'We don't recognize your authority. You should get out of the Land of Israel!' Feinstein was of European origin; what do you call it – Ashkenazi. Moshe Barazani was Sephardi, from Iraq. At night, after they had been sentenced to death, and were due to be led in the morning to be hanged, the rabbi insisted that he should be the one to come and lead them. They didn't want to harm the rabbi. They placed a hand grenade between their hearts … and detonated it. Ashkenazi? Iraqi? Jews! Brothers! Fighters!

"No one has ever insulted an entire sector of Jews as the Labor did yesterday, right here.

---

[29] Composed at the end of the 19th century, this poem served as the anthem of the Zionist Movement and, after the establishment of the state, became Israel's national anthem.

"What I ask of you is that tomorrow, from morning to evening, there should be a marathon of phone calls. What is needed, what is important, is to call everyone you know in Jerusalem and in Haifa and in Rishon LeTzion and in Nes Tziona, in Rehovot and in Beersheba. Just tell them what Dudu Topaz said here. Everyone in Israel has to know that. One sentence, that's all: 'The riffraff are at Metzudat Zeev [Likud headquarters].' We are truly fortunate that they are at Metzudat Zeev ..."

In his article entitled "We are the People (You're Not!)," Professor Dani Filc analyzes the speech and defines Begin's aim as "dismantling the Labor party's mythos of the warrior pioneer who came from Europe to a desolate land, replacing it with the mythos of the Jewish fighter who gives up his life for the entire nation. It's the same sacrifice for Ashkenazim and Sephardim, who are both essentially Jews. [Begin] does this with great success, enlisting the masses (the 'simple people,' the 'riffraff from Metzudat Zeev') to fight against the veteran Mapai elites."

Netanyahu continues Begin's path, connecting the persecuted Jew with the snubbed Mizrahi and writing a new historical mythos for the State of Israel.

Politics Writing History

Netanyahu believes that there is an entire public that has been excluded from the Israeli story. In the face of the Labor's self-image as the party that "built the state," Netanyahu champions the right of other sectors to be included in this definition. He fights not only for his own place in history, but also for the place of his voters, and this is the foundation of the covenant that Netanyahu has forged with his supporters.

With each passing year, his words at the official government ceremony commemorating the Altalena Affair[30] have placed increasing emphasis on the place of the Right in Israeli history:

> "For decades, there was no real battle for the historical truth ... For decades there was something else – an entire camp that was simply pushed aside. Others sought to mold the public consciousness, in their image and in their likeness, and history was written (and sometimes rewritten) by those who saw themselves as the victors who had vanquished the losers. It is only by virtue of our insistence, your actions – the dear public that is here, and the work of our government – in education, in culture, in commemoration – that the fighting family[31] is receiving the place it deserves in Israeli history."

The above is an excerpt from Netanyahu's speech in 2019. Obviously, he is not talking only about the honor due to the Irgun. Paralleling the stories of the pioneers of the Jezreel Valley, he touts the "pioneers of the development towns"; paralleling the heroic ghetto fighters

---

[30] The *Altalena* was a cargo ship which had been loaded with weapons and fighters in Europe by the Irgun. It arrived in Tel Aviv in the midst of the War of Independence, after an agreement had been signed for the absorption of the Irgun into the IDF, but while the Irgun's Jerusalem Battalion was still fighting independently. A violent confrontation ended in the death of 16 Irgun fighters and 3 IDF soldiers.

[31] The Irgun has traditionally been called the "fighting family" by its members and veterans.

memorialized by the Labor hegemony,[32] he recalls the Revisionist underground fighters in the Warsaw Ghetto. He upholds Jabotinsky's role in the establishment of the IDF as no less important than that of the Haganah; he equates settlers in Judea and Samaria with the early pioneers, and – especially – insists that the value of the contribution made by religious and traditional immigrants in the early years of the state is no less than that of the secular pioneers.

"I am a descendant of the 'Vilna Gaon,'"[33] Netanyahu declares proudly, and describes how this 18th century sage urged his disciples to move to the Holy Land several generations prior to the appearance of the secular Zionist movement. In Netanyahu's history book, many previously unknown or underrated heroes are revived. History is written by the victors – and Netanyahu uses his political victory to rewrite the past:

> "[The Likud's rise to power] gave the Irgun's legacy a new lease on life, with the suppression of its role in achieving Israeli independence giving way to overt pride. Even today I meet youngsters who are eager to hear the stories of the legacy of the underground movements."

The elections are about not just the country's future, but also the nation's past. Should the mournful tunes commemorating the Holocaust reflect the shame of sheep led to the slaughter, or pride in the steadfastness of Jewish faith in the face of such evil, and acts of

---

32 For instance, in the names of the kibbutzim Lochamei HaGetaot ("Ghetto Fighters", in northern Israel) and Yad Mordechai (named after Mordechai Anielewicz, leader of the Jewish Fighting Organizationwhich led theWarsaw Ghetto Uprising.

33 Rabbi Elijah ben Solomon Zalman (Poland, 1720- 1797), the foremost scholar and leader of non-tle of the chapter and the chppe in Hassidic-Jewryof the last two centuries.

religious heroism? Did the preservation of Jewish tradition have a role in bringing about the establishment of the state, or was it all due to the rebellion against tradition on the part of the early pioneers? Should we be reviving the works of forgotten Revisionist poet Uri Zvi Greenberg or promoting the works of Mahmoud Darwish?[34] Is the literary world of the Talmud and Jewish Law a relic of the Middle Ages, or the nation's greatest cultural treasure? Netanyahu's path for the country's future includes the right to retell its past.

■■■

In almost every election campaign some Left-wing figure or another supplies Netanyahu with new ammunition in the form of arrogant expressions recalling Topaz's rant in 1981. Each time, he reverts to the historical conflict with Mapai, the original incarnation of Labor. The party holds no political weight today, but its presence is important as a nemesis that the Likud can continue to confront.

It has usually been Ashkenazi, Left-wing "cultural" figures that have uttered the unfortunate and offensive comments that Netanyahu pounces on, knowing how to milk these incidents for their full worth, and – like Begin in his time – to ensure optimal diffusion of the sense of persecution and humiliation at the hands of the Ashkenazi elite.

> "They silence and slander the Right; they called us riff-raff, punks, baboons, kissers of amulets, and now they call us bots," he summed up the insults by the Left over five election campaigns, speaking in the first-person plural, in response to an investigative report in the media claiming that Likud wasoperatinga network of bots to promote the party on social networks. Although Netanyahu

---

34 Regarded as the Palestinian national poet.

has occupied the premiership continuously for the past decade, he added: "For four years they held the power; next week, on Election Day, the power moves over to you. On Election Day we'll show them."

As the second round of elections in 2019 rolled around, and some figures voiced the opinion that Netanyahu's voters were ignoramuses, he was quick to respond on Twitter: "And now we're 'ignoramuses'. There is no limit to the arrogance of the Left towards Likud voters. Our answer will come in the polls."

Prof. Daphna Canetti, head of the School of Political Sciences at Haifa University, and political psychologist Dr. Eran Halperin, conducted a study that showed that the main impetus driving voters is hate. They found that hate is "the factor that makes it possible to make stronger predictions concerning political approaches than other psychological phenomena such as fear and anger." The conclusion that hate is deliberately stoked from on high because "hate can easily lead people to change their original political positions." Professor Canetti told *Globes* financial newspaper: "The party that we support represents not only who we like, but also who we hate. When you characterize the parties, you notice that they are differentiated from one another mainly in negative formulation."

Netanyahu unites the public in their sense of hostility towards their nemesis. The enemy, whether real or imagined, is "the other," the "them" who are not us. The Leftists, the media, the elites, the Army Radio station, the Supreme Court.

Hatred as Impetus

The Prime Minister, on a pre-election tour of the market in Tel Aviv, didn't notice one of the cameras that caught him talking about the elites and the Left, and telling Likud activists, "They hate the nation, the Sephardim, the Russians, the Ethiopians …"

This slip of the tongue – The Left hate the people – whether deliberate or not, is the essence of Netanyahu's approach. It is the same idea expressed in other statements: "The Left have forgotten …", "they are afraid," "us or them," and a host of other overt and covert messages that Netanyahu conveys with the intention of maintaining and reinforcing his voters' sense of being besieged by the Left, which has supposedly disengaged from the nation, the land, and Judaism. "The people are us," Bibi declares, implying the exclusion of the Left from the term "people."

Scholars both in Israel and abroad, who are part of the elites under attack, define this as "Right-wing populism" and note a similar trend of separatism, extremism and nationalism gaining traction in Europe over the last two decades. The "populist Right" is a somewhat vague term referring to a large-scale convergence around a leader in confrontation with a different group within the population, perceived as an enemy, using simplistic and sweeping messages against the elites, the Left, liberalism, and – especially – foreigners and immigrants.

Returning to the comment at the market, Bibi's team decided not to deny it but rather to up the ante and to attack the Left. More than Netanyahu is hostile towards the Left (which he has invited to join his government more than once), what is important to him is that his public feels that the Left is hostile towards *them*. The circle of hostility feeds itself.

■■■

He sits at the center of the government table in the Knesset plenum, gazing with disappointment – perhaps anger – at the many empty seats around him. This is where Neeman sat; over there was Meridor's place; this seat was Benny Begin's. All spirited away by the winds of contention that have blown through his first term in office, leading to about half of his ministers resigning or being fired. Netanyahu will shortly be firing his Minister of Defense, Yitzhak Mordechai, on live TV. He gathers up his papers, scribbled all over with handwritten comments, and strides towards the podium.

He already knows that this will be his last speech in this 14th Knesset, and he decides to muster the entire rhetorical arsenal at his disposal.

There is endless heckling, and this suits his purposes. He lashes his audience with a mixture of the destruction of Jerusalem, them and us, who are the real Jews, images, the persecuted Mizrahi, quotes, scorn, rhetorical questions, a direct appeal to his listeners, and more:

> "On this sad day, the eve of the 9th day of the month of Av – the day that recalls the terrible price that we paid in our history for baseless hatred - I wish to address myself especially to the Mizrahim, and specifically to the Jews from Morocco, and I want to tell you on behalf of the Israeli government and on behalf of the Jewish People: 'We' are you; 'you' are us. No one is going to take us 50 years backwards …
>
> "After the previous elections, a certain person [Shimon Peres] was asked who had lost, and his answer was, 'We, the Israelis, lost.'
>
> "The Israelis are you! Minister of Defense Yitzhak Mordechai [born in Iraqi Kurdistan] – isn't he an Israeli?

[Persian] Chief of Staff Shaul Mofaz – isn't he Israeli? Avigdor Kahalani, an Israeli hero [born to Yemenite parents] – not Israeli? What is he then, Chinese? Thai? What are you? Who is protecting us in Lebanon? Who enlists in the elite IDF units? Israelis from all over – from Poland, from Morocco, and those born in Israel. Who makes a big deal out of this?

"One of our traditional prayers reads: Bless us, our Father, all of us together as one, in the illumination of Your countenance; Blessed are You, Who blesses His people, Israel, with peace." All of us together – that's peace, but you evidently don't want that togetherness. Today you are proposing to disperse the Knesset … This poison has to be stopped right now. Disperse the Knesset if you have the guts.

"Who are you going to enlist for your election campaign? The religious sector? You've already made them persona non grata. The ultra-Orthodox? You've declared them all but untouchable. The Sephardim? But they're not Israelis. The Moroccans? They can't tell good from bad. So who are you left with? What are you left with? Northern Tel Aviv?"

■■■

Donald Trump became president because he was the issue. He started out as a political oddity, but the fact that he was the candidate who received the greatest coverage, the candidate that everyone was talking about, is what led him to the Oval Office. The commentators who had insisted "Anyone but Trump" served to bolster and boost his campaign. Trump won because of the attacks on him. The media devoted vast amounts of broadcast time to him, with a view to belittling, deriding, and attacking him, but all the exposure he received was a boon for his campaign. In its attempts to cut him down and write him off, the media ended up crowning him. True to its inability to think rationally, the American media fumed and fussed over every gimmick, oddity and provocation by this reality star. The coverage was negative, but Trump was the central item on the agenda.

As time went on, the attacks on Trump not only awarded him exposure and publicity, but also caused his supporters to close ranks in support of him. Amongst many conservative groups throughout the US who were sick of political correctness, there was a sense that Trump was saying openly and bluntly what "we think," and any attempt to silence him was "silencing us."

The American public, which felt undervalued and put down by the New York liberal elites, perceived the disdain for Trump as disdain for itself, and its response was to vote for the provocative candidate who said what they were thinking. Much of this scenario applies to Netanyahu and has been consciously imitated.

"Like Trump," he would direct his advisors, adopting many of the former American president's methods. A review of Netanyahu's media activity shows that after Trump entered the White House, the number of interviews with Netanyahu started to increase, as did the frequency of his tweets, and he started to express himself in tougher and more confrontational language. He sees "Trumpicity" as a model for a protest vote, in which many Americans voted for Trump not because of any hopes that he offered, but mainly as a venting of anger against the Democratic elites. Although directed against him, the "Anyone but Bibi" campaign serves Netanyahu because it places him at the center of public discourse and allows him to show how he is attacked from all sides. The point is for the entire Right to identify with him.

The Persecution Prism

Netanyahu knowingly blurs and merges three dimensions - the personal, the popular, and the national. On the national level, there is the Jewish People, persecuted since the dawn of history by a succession of malevolent enemies: Amalekites, Egyptians, the Church, Cossacks, Nazis, Iran, Arabs, and many more. On the popular level, there are the Mizrahi Jews and all those who feel relegated to the category of the "second class Israel," rejected and downtrodden. On the personal level, Netanyahu himself is persecuted by the Left, the media, the Attorney General's Office, police investigations, and political opponents. He works to have the public view all this as part of the same story.

When he calls on the public to boycott a TV channel (popular level), as he did in 2019, claiming that it is broadcasting a series that is anti-Semitic (national level) and is publicizing leaks from the investigations against him (personal level), which he defines as a "terror attack on democracy" (national level), he is deliberately mixing all these elements together.

Netanyahu takes care to formulate his statements according to a covert code that equates the national with the personal, suggesting that "the country is me":

> "Keshet and Channel 12 have crossed a red line. They are devoting an entire series to slandering Israel. It is horrific propaganda. Intolerable. I'm not surprised – Keshet maligns me on a daily basis, as it maligns Israel."

When Netanyahu finds himself in legal hot water, he asks the public to view the situation through the persecution prism: "They don't just want to bring me down; they want to bring us all down – the Likud, the nationalist camp," he quotes one of his supporters, in a response to the police recommendation to indict him.

"We are witnessing an attempted coup," he announces in response to the Attorney General's decision to press charges. It's not against me, it's against the Right. It's against us." I am us. The people are us.

Here, too, Netanyahu recycles the very same formulas that he used in relation to the criminal investigation against him during his first term, twenty-five years previously. Then, too, he had defined the drive behind the investigation as "an attempt to topple the government and to negate the will of the people." The main difference between his protests then and now is that then there were fewer TV channels for him to criticize:

> "Driven by political motives, some people from the media, and especially people at TV Channel 1, are still unwilling to reconcile themselves with the nation's decision in the recent elections … They refuse to reconcile themselves to the fact that we are keeping the Golan Heights. In short: they refuse to accept your decision in the last elections."

■■■

Netanyahu likes it when he is under attack. The attacks on him are translated in the minds of his supporters into attacks on the people. They are regarded as a symptom of the same old hatred of the white elites against the repressed, Right-wing, traditional, Mizrahi "us." The message that Netanyahu has repeated for years – "You are us, and we are you" – has succeeded in arousing a sense of persecution amongst the Right whenever Netanyahu is under attack. In 2015, Livni and Herzog ran for election under the slogan, "It's him or us." Netanyahu's bureau was delighted with this free gift. In return, his slogan read: "It's us or them."

Thus, mainly in view of a common adversary, Netanyahu manages to create points of contact between the personal and the popular. "I am just like you," he tells his audience. "My family and I are being humiliated by the same elite and the same media that ignore and dismiss you."

Netanyahu (TV interview): Let me finish what I was saying, like you allowed Gantz to finish.

Presenter: I just want to tell you that you've already spoken for four minutes longer than Benny Gantz spoke for.

Netanyahu: But if you count how much time Lapid gets, and how much Gantz gets, and how much Ashkenazi gets …

As Prime Minister, (also known to be a serial refuser of interviews,) Netanyahu could appear, if he so desired, at any hour, in any studio, for any amount of time. But what matters to him is not to get more screen time; what matters is that the public should see that in relation to his rivals, he is given less time.

■■■

Another related technique is that Netanyahu echoes the hatred of him to highlight the sense of persecution. Of course, he doesn't need to make much of an effort: the hatred aimed at him is patently real. Nevertheless, he chooses to highlight it intensively:

> "I heard the sanctimonious and feigned innocence on the part of Tzipi Livni and Shelly Yachimovich today. They said that there's no incitement from the Left; no calls for murder, not even allusions to murder. So I'm reminding them of the art exhibition at Bezalel Academy, with the hangman's noose around my neck, the guillotine in the public square at Left-wing demonstrations against me, and the response to the post published by Rabin's

granddaughter, who spoke today. She wrote – I quote: 'Maybe [the day of] Netanyahu's assassination will be a holiday.' Incitement should be denounced no matter which direction it comes from. Likewise hypocrisy."

Sociologist Charles Cooley offers a definition that fits Netanyahu: "The function of the great and famous man is to be a symbol, and the real question in other minds is not so much, 'What are you?' as, 'What can I believe that you are?'"

Netanyahu is no longer an individual, a human being. He is a concept, a symbol. For the Left, he symbolizes all that is bad. For a broad section of the public, he symbolizes affliction, persecution, harassment.

His status rests on people who view him as a great man. The public needs an object of identification. Netanyahu's power lies, among other things, in his ability to cause people to believe that he is the right object, or symbol, for them. He has become the man upon whom an entire public projects the resentment it has carried for so many years, and he carries the mental images and expectations of the citizens of Israel. He is the proud answer to all internal and external enemies.

He grew up in the wealthy Jerusalem suburb of Rehavia, was educated in the United States, is Ashkenazi and secular, and, by all sociological logic, he should belong to the secular Left. Instead, he forged an underdog alliance with major sectors of the population that feel left out and discriminated against.

■■■

The Mizrahim, the "Arabic Jews," found themselves in a bind. The "white Jews" – the Ashkenazim – having forged an alliance with the Christian West and its "progressive" values, had placed them on the opposite side, as part of the "archaic" Arabic civilization.

The more the Ashkenazi establishment regarded the Mizrahim as Arabs, the more resentment the Mizrahim felt towards both Ashkenazim and Arabs, for in the absence of either of these two factors, the traditional Mizrahi Jewish culture would still be flourishing.

This is one explanation of the secret of the connection between the Right and the Mizrahim, which has been the subject of countless sociological studies, and which led to Netanyahu becoming Prime Minister. The elites are still "white." Netanyahu appropriates the Mizrahim in his struggle against them:

> "The country no longer belongs to a small elite in northern Tel Aviv … The Left … want to take us backwards. They want to discriminate and separate, to cause splits and rivalries. They refer to most of the nation as "extremists." They hide their leftist identity behind a mask … Without the ultra-Orthodox, without the settlers, without the Russian immigrants, with the Ethiopians, and without the development towns. That's the same old path of the Left."

Prior to visits and speeches in cities and regions all over the country, Netanyahu's staff make sure to conduct a preliminary survey of the area so that Netanyahu can be the one who comes bringing good news and a budget for whatever is needed. For example, for a speech that he delivered in the northern town of Shlomi, an asterisk is attached to a reminder written in parentheses on the page: *(Comment: they want an amphitheater. The damage: NIS 700,000.)

The Silenced Right

The sense of persecution felt by the Right and residents of the country's periphery is also related to the security situation, and it intensified greatly in the wake of the Disengagement, when the entire Right felt that it had become a silenced minority trampled by aggressive elites. The missiles from Gaza that rained down after this withdrawal were followed by the Second Lebanon War, which was similarly perceived as a response to the IDF withdrawal from southern Lebanon. All of this made 2006 a turning point.

Following his analysis of all the media reports around that time, Dr. Eitan Orkibi points to the change that occurred that year in the political discourse in Israel: "The security crises were framed in the Right-wing discourse as a moment of awakening, when the public freed itself of the illusions of the Left and returned to the Right's embrace. While the Right is framed as a minority capable of seeing reality and voicing consistent positions, the Left is framed as a belligerent camp that silences rivals' opinions and constantly acts to create de-legitimization of the Right and its spokesmen. Thus the political rift in Israel was presented as an unequal struggle, in which the Right was viewed as an 'excluded minority' – a symbolic, public-consciousness victory over the Left, which was presented as an 'aggressive elite'. The Right-wing rhetoric formulates the events of the summer of 2006 as another chapter in the historical narrative of the Right as the underdog of Israeli politics."

Netanyahu remained Minister of Finance in Sharon's government long enough to make sure that the Disengagement would be carried out, resigning only as the plan reached the stage of execution. He is a millionaire who lives in affluent Caesarea – the only town in Israel managed by a private company. As Minister of Finance and as Prime Minister he has adopted many measures (including privatization and cutting government allowances) that have hurt the weaker socio-economic groups. He has not gone out of his way to actually implement Right-wing policy in terms of building new settlements or applying Israeli sovereignty to Judea and Samaria. In addition, he is not religiously observant, and has formed governments with the Left. Despite all of this, in the eyes of the religious-Mizrahi-Right, he is one of their own.

The "us" that Netanyahu addresses himself to is not the entire nation. His voters make up only a third of the voting public. He has no desire or intention to appeal to the Left and bring them around to his way of thinking. All he needs is to bring together a sufficient number of rightists, traditionalists, and residents of development towns to become the largest party in the Knesset. In Israeli politics, 30 Knesset seats (out of the 120 total) can be the key to forming the coalition.

The target audience can change from time to time, as necessary. At election time, the "base" is sacred. Immediately after the conclusion of the campaign, the target audience changes, as reflected in a change of style and the commitment to be the "Prime Minister of everyone." Before the elections, the aim is to unite the Right against the Left. After elections, the aim is to appeal to the vast majority of the public, possibly even with an apology about some of the tactics employed in achieving victory, or calling for a unity government with the leftists, who had been depicted during the campaign as traitors.

Netanyahu doesn't need to go far to meet his most hard-core supporters. A municipal boundary and a few hundred meters are all that separates his mansion in Caesarea from the neighboring development town of Or Akiva. Despite their proximity, the differences between these two locations are marked, as are their voting patterns. The proportion of Caesarea residents with tertiary education is 2.5 times the proportion in Or Akiva. The average income is three times the level of the immigrant town, which in the past was a transit camp for new immigrants. Or Akiva is home to twice as many Asian- and African-born residents as its neighbor.

Only 15% of the residents of Or Akiva voted for the Center-Left in the first round of elections in 2019. More than 50% voted for Netanyahu. If the election results throughout the country had mirrored the voting patterns in Or Akiva, the Right would have made up a coalition of more than 100 MKs.

If, on the other hand, the results had reflected the voting in Caesarea, the Left would have ended up with 85 mandates, and it would have been Blue and White – who received more than half the votes – that would have formed the government. Notably, the distribution of votes in the successive elections in 2019, in Or Akiva and in Caesarea, are almost identical to their distribution in these localities in 1981.

■■■

Netanyahu's consuming sense that the media elite and the Left don't recognize him and his talents comes from his father. Benzion Netanyahu was an historian who was rejected by the academic establishment. After failing to receive the status he felt he deserved and the appointment he had hoped for at the Hebrew University (to his mind, solely because of his Right-wing views,) he was forced to uproot his family, including three young sons, and move from Jerusalem to the US to teach at universities there.

In the eyes of Benjamin Netanyahu, the elitist Left that discriminated against his father, is the same Left that attacks him, and now this chain continues with attacks on his elder son Yair, and of course on his wife Sara. As he sees it, his brother Iddo has also been a victim of discrimination by the country's elites. Iddo Netanyahu is a playwright who enjoys international success, but was rejected by the cultural establishment in Israel. The family believes that the reason is that no theater in Tel Aviv is willing to give the stage to a brother of Bibi.

■■■

In an interview he granted on the eve of the first elections in 2019, Netanyahu distanced himself from a Likud Facebook webcast making fun of the appearance of prominent reporter and political commentator Amnon Abramovich. (Abramovich, who covered the criminal investigations of the Prime Minister, has a severely scarred face, from burns incurred while fighting in the Yom Kippur War.) Immediately after denouncing the clip, however, he returned to his usual narrative of victimhood. His pain, anger, and humiliation were plain to see in his agitated responses, which bound up the bullets of enemy terrorists with those of the leftist-media enemy:

> "Night after night, it's someone else's turn to be ridiculed by you. I don't think I'm considered wounded, but I did take a bullet here; five times I nearly lost my life, I was in dozens of very courageous operations, I fought in battles. I am mocked, my wife is mocked, my son is mocked, they're portrayed with pigs' faces. Pigs! Pigs. Did you have anything to say about that?
>
> "What you do here night after night is satire; you malign and malign and malign. I'm also a human being, also flesh and blood; when you offend me, when you when you offend my wife, who I love, when you offend my sons, who I love … they are attacked in a manner that has never yet been seen. They are simply placed in front of a firing squad; they undergo terrible character assassination."

The Polling Booth at Army Radio

The draft we see shows no erasing and no hesitation. The opinion polls aren't good. A moment before leaving for another Likud rally, to deliver a speech timed to coincide with the evening news, Netanyahu writes in large letters:

> "The media is cut off from the people. It doesn't read the people's feelings. It has mobilized itself, with clear intent, against us. The people want *us* in power. Not the Left.
>
> "The people will prevail. We will prevail. Together with the people. Not just a narrow sector; the entire people is with us. Despite the media. In spite of the media."

Netanyahu take care to use the word "we" as representative of the people who are with him. On the other side are "them," and he takes care to underline these terms, so that the contrast will come through in his voice, too. The whole nation is with us. It's us or them. *We* are the people; *they* are not.

> "Evening after evening you see the biased, distorted media … Once in four years you have a chance to give them a crushing answer – the commentators, correspondents, and propagandists of the Left. You can tell them very simply: it won't work. You won't be the ones to decide. We will decide. The people will decide. Because the people are sovereign, not the media."

Netanyahu should rightfully have sent large bouquets of flowers to certain political commentators after election campaigns that he won thanks to their opposition to him. Indeed, the Israeli media is the main factor underlying his consecutive electoral victories, because its hatred towards him helps him to get reelected. In the struggle of the media against Netanyahu, the people are with Bibi.

Netanyahu cracks his whip at the media, but he doesn't really intend to subjugate it. Rather, he wants to maintain a constant threat in the form of the regulator. This inhibits the press from going too far in its criticism of him, while at the same time serving Netanyahu vis-à-vis his voters, reinforcing the persecution prism. What is important to him is not so much to speak rather than to show that there are those who try to prevent him from doing so.

Steve Linde, a former editor-in-chief of the *Jerusalem Post*, describes that during one brief encounter with Netanyahu, the Prime Minister told him, "You know, Steve, we have two main enemies." Linde thought he was about to hear about Iran or Hamas, but no: "*The New York Times* and *Haaretz*."

The media is Netanyahu's sworn enemy, and they have been at odds since the 90s, at varying levels of intensity: on low flame during each term in office, and at full power with the approach of elections. In 1996, it was "the media is against us," in 1999, it was "They are afraid"; in 2015, "Noni Mozes [owner and publisher of *Yedioth Ahronoth* daily] is Voldemort"; and in 2019, "The media are Bolsheviks."

The media isn't leftist in the narrow party sense of the word. The point of using the expression "leftist media" is that it creates the sense that there are those who aren't represented in and by the media. The word "leftist" in the media context encapsulates all the bitterness of the minorities who don't belong to the tribe that is shown on the screen. Throughout its programming and staffing, the media is white, hegemonic, Ashkenazi, elitist, and liberal. Studies have shown that the same categorization applies to guests and interviewees. The media is centered around Tel Aviv, it sanctifies discourse about the rights of the individual rather than the national collective, and is perceived by a majority of the population as biased and disconnected. People love to watch it and love to hate it.

■■■

Media advisor Shai Bazak carefully cut out the small item that appeared in the *HaTzofe* daily newspaper, and, at Netanyahu's request, pasted it at the center of a large sheet of grey cardboard. It was to be presented before the cameras in an upcoming speech, somewhere during Netanyahu's first term in office. The headline announced that most of the population believed that the media had a leftist bias. Over the years, this datum has remained unchanged. Although in the interim Bibi left the Prime Minister's Office and then returned, a survey presented at the annual Eilat Journalists' Conference that was held during his fourth term indicated that 72% of the public believed that "the media is leftist."

The media hates Netanyahu. Shelly Yachimovich, speaking as a media figure, acknowledged this openly: "Let's make no pretenses. The media will mobilize en masse to bring down Benjamin Netanyahu as Prime Minister … The media has a very clear political preference, and it will be working against Bibi." Amnon Dankner, editor of the *Maariv* daily, boasted, "Never in Israel's history has there been a press assault on the Prime Minister like the one on Benjamin Netanyahu." He added, "It's true that the media is leftist. Leftist isn't a dirty word. The media has killed Netanyahu."

Journalist Raviv Drucker, whom I replaced as political correspondent for Army Radio, has many high-profile investigative reports to his name, but one of his most courageous revelations was when he wrote, "If you place a polling both at Army Radio, 80% would vote for Center-Left parties. You would obtain the same results from polls at Channel 10, Channel 2, *Maariv*, *Yedioth*, and *Haaretz* – well, there maybe it would be 95%."

"Our Planes" or "The Air Force Planes"

I was nervous. Sitting around the table were the top-level Channel 2 personnel, who had gathered to discuss a special report that I had been asked to prepare about the channel's functioning during the Second Lebanon War.

The data was grim. Surveys indicated that most of the public thought that the media had harmed public morale, had not fulfilled its role properly, and should not have aired Nasrallah's speeches. According to the viewers, the media had devoted little attention to strikes on the enemy, while highlighting strikes on the home front. This was the first war to be broadcast live, via TV and the internet, and officers and soldiers were quoted as saying, "Hezbollah is shooting at us from inside and the media from behind."

"I'm not the NCO responsible for public morale," argued Ilana Dayan when I cited the fact that more than 90% of the Jewish public believed that the role of the media was to strengthen public morale during wartime. The Channel 2 bigwigs didn't like hearing their viewers' opinions. "It's specifically in times of crisis that criticism is necessary, in order to expose failures," one of them insisted. Some of them tried to suggest that the findings were simply a matter of "shooting the messenger" – in other words, that the criticism aimed at the media was the result of the media having done its job and informed the public about mistakes and faults.

Yair Lapid eventually had his turn to speak and addressed scathing criticism at his colleagues: "Why didn't you call me? Why didn't you invite me to present programs with the soldiers, instead of just negative news all day?" (A few days later, Lapid published a very candid op-ed: "We failed. All of us. Me, too. The Israeli media failed during this war. We failed the responsibility test and the restraint test, the humility test and the solidarity test, the fairness test and the consistency test, the chatter test and the reliability test.")

On the way out after the discussion, one of the attendees whispered to me, "Don't take Yair too seriously. The whole way through the war we begged him to come and broadcast, but he wouldn't. Now he's preparing to enter politics. We all know he just wants to appear patriotic."

■■■

Media discourse during crises also fuels the public aversion. Since the Yom Kippur War, news reports are no longer formulated in the first person – "our planes returned safely to their bases," or "our forces were active" – but rather in the more neutral third person: "the air force planes returned to their bases," "IDF soldiers were active last night …"

Media studies have shown that today, when soldiers are killed in military operations, they are no longer presented in a heroic, patriotic light, (the "Silver Platter", in the famous poem by Natan Alterman, upon which the state is given,) as in the past, but rather as victims of a war that was badly managed. Senseless victims. The coverage no longer refers to "our soldiers" having given their lives for the country, for an important purpose, but rather to "our children" who have become victims.

Widely viewed as a white, discriminatory elite, the media is likewise accused of being "soft," devoid of patriotism, and unrepresentative of the people, both at election time and in wartime. Beneath the surface, Netanyahu's battle against the media is a mirror image of Israel's wars against its enemies. Us or them. The people are us. Our planes. Our soldiers. Our forces.

Beginnings of Movies

The sound of a teaspoon tapping against a whiskey glass was the cue for conversation in the Caesarea mansion's expansive sitting room to die down. The 30-odd guests, including Bibi and Sara, were led by their host, film producer Yoram Globus, down to the enormous basement. They all settled into the comfortable armchairs for a private viewing. No one had any doubt that within a short time, some gentle snoring would be heard, as always, from Bibi's direction.

Bibi enjoys the beginnings of movies. Even in the private viewing room of his close friends, producers Moshe and Leon Edri, on the marina in Herzliya, he would fall asleep while Sara would keep up a social presence and sometimes wake him if it became uncomfortable. This has made him the butt of many friendly jokes, but he still likes to watch the beginning of a movie in a home theater from time to time. Perhaps this is his way of reliving the experience of watching Westerns as a boy in the US, along with "Gone with the Wind," "The Good, the Bad and the Ugly," and "Casablanca," all of which he still quotes.

He deemed anti-Semitic a miniseries that aired in 2019 ("Our Boys"), admitting afterwards, rather sheepishly, that he had only seen the beginning, and then had fallen asleep. His eyes also closed after the beginning of a movie about himself entitled "King Bibi" – which likewise earned his censure. He watches few movies and even less theater, and rarely listens to music. His TV viewing is limited to copious, daily doses of news. Reading biographies and historical books remains his almost-sole cultural activity.

When he comments on cultural issues, he usually does so in the context of current events. When he sneaked away to watch *Hamilton* on Broadway, he used the opportunity to chat with the director and to suggest that Jewish aspects of Hamilton's character receive greater emphasis. When, before election time, he was asked on a satire show whether he had watched the series *House of Cards*, he replied:

> "I live it. What do I need to watch it for? Sometimes reality is even worse. But there's one difference between *House of Cards* in America and *House of Cards* in Israel. It's simple – in America, the politicians use the media; here, the media - especially someone starting with the letter 'N' - uses the politicians. That's the real *House of Cards* in Israel. I'll tell you his full name – Noni Mozes. That our country's *House of Cards*."

While a personal friend of producers and leading cultural figures in Israel, Netanyahu's general attitude, like that of Right-wing Ministers of Culture (Limor Livnat, Miri Regev), maintains that the world of Israeli culture is "leftist."

Over the years, government funding has been awarded to films that achieved international success by engaging in self-castigation over the "occupation." "Leftist cinema." Netanyahu has also chosen to speak out against Israeli films that have been perceived as damaging the country's image. Most of the Ministry of Culture budget goes towards institutions identified with bastions of the Left in the center of the country. In contrast, state support for many popular annual events that have a traditional, religious character is as scanty as the media coverage of them.

The political struggle in the cultural realm extends to music, and the question of the proper proportion of Mizrahi music to be included on radio playlists. Literature, too, is a political issue, with the major Israeli publishers identified and affiliated with the Left. There is a widely held perception that Right-wing writers – Uri Zvi Greenberg being Netanyahu's favorite example – have not received the exposure and promotion that they deserved. Netanyahu and the Likud argue that the traditional and Right-wing public are under-represented in all areas of culture, from cinema to theater to music. Neither the screen nor the stage shows the real people.

Like the cultural and artistic realms, academia in Israel is also regarded as white, arrogant, and Ashkenazi. It is the same academia that refused to embrace Professor Benzion Netanyahu. The same academia that produces petitions by "leading intellectuals" protesting against the Right-wing government and Right-wing policy in the name of the enlightened values upheld by the Left. In contrast to these petitions, letters signed jointly by a number of leading rabbis are regarded as missives from a primitive and anti-democratic world. Indeed, the animosity that Netanyahu reinforces between "the people" and the intelligentsia has a solid basis.

The legal system, too, has become a symbol of the same elite. The Right, headed by Netanyahu – the product of an elitist background and educational system – attacks the Supreme Court as a stronghold whose power needs to be tempered. The very waging of a political war against the Supreme Court is worth points amongst "us."

The legal system, the cultural establishment, academia, the media, the literary sphere – all are characterized by a leftward slant even after dozens of years of Likud in power. A vast public goes about with the feeling that it has been discriminated against and silenced for decades, and remains unsatisfied. Netanyahu takes care to voice this dissatisfaction endlessly, reiterating his messages that mix everything together: the law and politics, the Supreme Court and Army Radio, the criminal and the national.

There is an all-around sense that there are the people with power and the intelligentsia, and there is us, the people; us, the underdog. The elections are our opportunity to speak out in the voice that was silenced. We are the majority who feel like a minority. We are the weak.

In a reversal of the official slogan, Netanyahu pushes a covert election message: "The Right is weak; the Left is strong."

■■■

Secret #7: I, We, The People Netanyahu merges the persecution of Jews with persecution of Mizrahim and persecution of himself, intensifying hostility towards the leftist elites and the media (which themselves are hostile towards Netanyahu), forming a single Right-religious-traditional-Mizrahi-nationalist entity that feels like a disadvantaged underdog after facing years of discrimination. This creates the desired merging of "the people is me and us," such that the minorities become the majority that votes for him.

8.
CONTROLLING THE MEDIUM
COMMUNICATIONS

I sat down in front of Netanyahu for the meeting that had been scheduled for us in his office in Jerusalem. Offered a drink, I requested tea with lemon; he asked for a can of Sprite. He lifted a small lever on his chair to lean it backwards, put his feet up on the desk, and opened a drawer to take out a box of cigars. "What's news at Army Radio?" he asked. I had come to hear about his political plans after his last-minute resignation as Minister of Finance in Sharon's government.

Ten minutes into our meeting, his bureau chief walked in and announced, "There's been a terror attack in Jerusalem. At a roadblock, apparently. There are casualties." These were years of mass killings by suicide bombers. Netanyahu put out his cigar and we stood together at the window, surveying the city spread out below, looking for smoke. We saw nothing out of the ordinary. The IDF beeper that I carry with me began displaying more details about the attack, but he asked not to talk about politics or security. "Let's talk about the media," he asked, in the wake of an article that I had published, criticizing the conduct of the media during the Disengagement. "How's it going for you? What responses did you receive? How are your relations with Arik [Sharon]?" He peppered me with more questions, including about my family and background.

When it seemed that my answers had satisfied him, he put his feet back up on the desk, made a great fuss of re-igniting his cigar, inhaled, and declared, "What the country needs right now is an Israeli version of Fox News." He enumerated the shortcomings of the leftist media, defined the press as a critical factor in the war against terror, and went into great detail about the economic viability of a channel that would be the voice of the Right-wing, nationalist, and traditionalist public. The notes I took at the meeting include the phrases, "There is a vacuum," "Whoever gets in now will do well," "This is the time," "It's happening all over the world,", "No reason why the Israeli flag can't be displayed on the screen throughout the broadcast, just like Fox has done since 9/11." Netanyahu spoke as though I was the face of the wave of Israeli journalism, and hinted quite heavily that adopting a Right-wing journalistic line was the right thing for me personally.

At the end of the meeting he asked me if I already had all of his books, and mentioned that he hoped to write more in the future. Since he had already given me *A Place in the Sun* on a previous occasion, he pulled out a copy of *Terrorism: How the West Can Win*, and scribbled "To Kave Shafran, in friendship" on the first page. "Keep in touch," he said, and sent me on my way. As usual, he wanted to keep meeting off the record, and continued holding off on my requests for interviews.

■■■

Shortly after that meeting, I was invited to a meeting with businessman Shlomo Ben-Zvi, who had started a new free daily newspaper named *Israeli*. The concept was a "thin" publication that could be read cover to cover in less than fifteen minutes – the average commute on an intra-city bus. At the time, no one knew that Ben-Zvi's behind-the-scenes partner in this initiative was the recentlydeceased billionaire, Sheldon Adelson. I refused Ben-Zvi's offer to become a correspondent. Not for a moment did it occur to me that my meeting with Netanyahu could be connected to the meeting regarding the new freebie newspaper.

In the statements of claim that were later exchanged between Adelson and Ben-Zvi, it emerged that it had been Netanyahu who had named Amos Regev as the right editor for the newspaper. Ultimately, when *Israeli* closed down and Adelson made a public announcement launching *Israel Hayom*, Regev, with Netanyahu's encouragement, was appointed editor. Netanyahu, acting systematically and consistently, managed to change the Israeli media landscape most significantly by means of *Israel Hayom*, along with additional platforms identified as Right-wing, such as Channel 20 and Galei Yisrael radio, where I presented a morning news program for three years.

The day that *Israel Hayom* first appeared, in July 2007, is viewed by many as the day that Netanyahu paved his way back to the Prime Minister's Office. He himself has stated that the day that the *Israel Hayom* Law[35] passed its first reading in the Knesset (it never passed subsequent readings) was the day he decided to break up the government, sack ministers Lapid and Livni, and head for new elections. Netanyahu believes that control of the media equals control of the country.

One method of control is for him to maintain an open war against the media, to ensure that it retains some measure of restraint while simultaneously helping him to gain the support of the public in the face of its attacks against him. Another method is exactly the opposite: undercover cooperation and influence by building and maintaining

---

35   *The Law for the Advancement and Protection of Print Journalism,* proposed by a Labor MK and sponsored by members of five other Knesset parties, sought to make it illegal to distribute free of charge any full-sized newspaper that was published six days a week. While the law's stated intention was to protect Israel's newspapers at a time of economic hardship for the printed press, the law was clearly aimed against Israel Hayom - the only Hebrew daily that met its specific requirement.

ties with publishers, editors and owners. The general public, watching Netanyahu's ongoing combat against the "leftist media," is unaware of the extent of Bibi's connections and cooperation with that same media. The recordings of his secret discussions with Noni Mozes – whom he had attacked endlessly in public – attest to the gap between what happens on the media stage and what happens behind the scenes.

Behind the scenes, Netanyahu pulls innumerable strings of control. Since his election in 2009, with the support of *Israel Hayom* – which has become Israel's most widely-read daily – Netanyahu has been involved and influential in a long list of media platforms via influence over their owners, their economic stability, and their appointments. He controlled the Israel Broadcasting Authority)IBA) by approving office-holders, and he controls its successor – the Israeli Public Broadcasting Corporation – by means of government funding. He tried to influence *Yedioth Ahronoth* through secret discussions with its publisher, Noni Mozes; he shaped the content of *Maariv* via the newspaper's editor-in-chief, Nir Hefetz, who became his spokesman; he determined the future of Channel 10 by means of decisions regarding its debts and its continued existence; he was involved in the appointment of the commander of Army Radio; he influenced the Walla website extensively through his ties with its owner, Shaul Elovich, and Channel 12 News (the News Company) via his personal acquaintance and discussions with shareholders. He also advanced the establishment of new broadcast stations identified with the Right and with himself. The covert influence that he wields as media regulator is one of the ways in which he tries to shape public opinion – and a major theme running through the charges for which he is currently on trial.

There are five important areas of activity via which Netanyahu influences the mass media. Two have already been mentioned: overt ongoing war, and secret cooperation. The others include sloganeering (he is a serial producer of catchy phrases and unforgettable sentences); interviews (he knows better than any other Israeli politician how to appear on screen and convey a message); and spin (his control of the agenda). David Margolick, contributing editor to *Vanity Fair*, wrote in his profile of Netanyahu: "He is less Israel's prime minister than its editor-in-chief."

Each Day with Its Agenda

The name Joey Skaggs strikes fear into the heart of the American media. Skaggssatirizes social issues by means of elaborate hoaxes which are then reported and covered by the unwitting mass media. He was producing fake news years before Trump invented the term.

Skaggs defines himself as media prankster. Time and time again he manages, with a combination of patience and creativity, to mislead newspaper and TV editors, to receive widespread coverage, and to be interviewed as any one of a diverse collection of completely fictitious identities. He has created stories about a dream holiday in which the vacationer's fantasies are fulfilled while he sleeps in a drug-induced coma; computers with artificial intelligence replacing judges; a group of vigilante sidewalk etiquette enforcers to patrol the streets; and a brothel for dogs that supposedly opened in New York.

He views his work as an art form. The media view him as a source of embarrassment and as a threat; there have been several unsuccessful attempts to put him on trial. The astonishing ease with which this con artist succeeds again and again raises some serious questions about the gullibility, irresponsibility, and superficiality of the press, and it is not for nothing that his pranks are studied in communications departments in the US. Of course, any decent journalist who put in the effort to check things out, correlate information, and dig a little deeper into the stories offered to the news editors would uncover the ruse, but the media is lazy and easy to manipulate. Skaggs uses his "art" to convey the message that the "hype, hypocrisy, propaganda, and disinformation fed to the media, is consequently fed by the media to the public" and "how vulnerable the public is to abuses of a media … for whom the bottom line is the first priority."

■■■

"You have to feed the monster," is the typical resigned attitude of spokesmen towards the limitless appetite of the correspondents and reporters for the dozens of internet sites, TV programs, newspapers, and radio stations that have sprung up in Israel in recent years.

Being Israel's "editor-in-chief" is hard work. One has to keep creating the media agenda. On Sundays, at the weekly cabinet meeting, Netanyahu delivers a speech focusing the media spotlight on what he considers to be important. On Mondays, he tries to shape the discourse at Likud faction meetings. On week nights, he and his staff usually coordinate the main headlines with *Israel Hayom*; on Wednesdays, attention is devoted to briefing political commentators in anticipation of the columns they will publish in the weekend papers. Prior to a broadcast of "Friday Studio," Bibi speaks by phone with the journalists who are expected to participate in the panel.

When he raises topics for media consumption, he usually warns his spokesmen who brief the correspondents: "Don't let one story gobble up another." When elections are approaching, control of the discourse is especially important and he tries to float issues and initiatives – sometimes by means of empty promises to annex the Jordan Valley or Gush Etzion, a commitment to changing the system of government, or calling special press conferences on various diplomatic or security issues.

Netanyahu's campaign manager, Ofer Golan, defined control of the discourse as Netanyahu's central objective. He explains the strategy behind the campaign poster showing photographs of journalists with the inscription "They won't decide" as follows: "We invented the wheel. We put up one poster; we had to decide where to put it. It cost us NIS 120,000 for nine days. A poster as tall as a building. We deliberated about four different locations, and eventually we put it in the Pi Glilot area. Within seconds it was on Twitter, and then it spread. A poster that cost NIS 120,000 created a buzz worth millions of shekels. On [satire program] *Eretz Nehederet* they talked about the poster and our campaign. That was the challenge of the campaign: to create an agenda; to control the discourse."

In 2003, Bibi decided to reinvent himself as the "new Netanyahu" who had learned lessons from his first term and was conducting himself responsibly as "Mr. Economy." In 2006, during the Second Lebanon War, he gathered his close circle at the Likud headquarters and defined their task as positioning him as Israel's spokesman to the world. Indeed, he fulfilled this function well, and made sure that the Israeli media gave him coverage: "How would you, in Paris/New York/London, feel if you had fifteen seconds to take cover from an incoming missile?" he asked his listeners, earning him the title, "one-man public diplomacy machine."

At the end of the war he gathered his team of advisors and aides (Naftali Bennet and Ayelet Shaked among them) once again, and told them that henceforth the aim would be to maximize media exposure, support, and funding for the army reservists' protest, so as to heighten the sense of failure in the war and to lead to the government's fall.

Netanyahu raises topics that are aimed to divert the media discourse. The Iranian threat is always relevant and valid. Some other issues that he has raised were trial balloons, not necessarily having any real substance: intensive attention to threats, such as flotillas from Europe in support of the Palestinians that never arrived; nationally-motivated instances of rape; Rivlin's inclination not to award him the chance to form a government; the "hot tape affair"; plots to overthrow him; potential new laws; cameras in polling booths to prevent voting fraud in the Arab sector. Most of this was nothing more than smoke-screening.

"It's less important to Bibi what the media says about a certain subject. What's important is the subject that they're talking about," one of his spokesman explained. To be more precise – most important is what they *aren't* talking about.

■■■

In the control rooms of sports and news broadcasts, there's always someone in charge of switching cameras. His role is to press the button that determines which camera is on air, while the others are not. It is somewhat like the light board operator in charge of stage lighting for large musical productions. Netanyahu is that operator. It is he who angles the spotlight toward one particular corner of the stage, directing the media floodlights in the same direction.

The TV medium doesn't allow for in-depth, complex thought or clarification of the truth. For this reason Pierre Bourdieu, for example, called for intellectuals to boycott the media. He warned that the media focuses on specific types of conflict and selected issues related to current events; hence, media discourse by definition is meant not to reveal but rather to conceal.

Netanyahu is a sophisticated censor who exploits the national obsession with news to prevent discussion of the deeper issues that are important to people's lives, or to prevent discussion of failures or of criminal investigations. He controls the media agenda by raising issues not with the aim of discussing them, but rather as a way of hiding and removing other issues. Hilary Clinton once mocked the media obsession with trivialities: "If I want to knock a story off the front page, I just change my hairstyle."

For Netanyahu, the routine tactic for knocking items off the front page is to aim the spotlights on a statement by some leftist/anti-Semite/journalist/Palestinian/European, and to criticize it in public, usually via Facebook. Since idiotic and annoying statements are in ample supply, there is always someone to attack, a "storm" is quickly formed, and other topics are pushed out of the way. The shelf life of any topic in the media is short. Netanyahu knows how to change internet headlines quickly.

When he is suspected of zig-zagging to the Left, he makes a Right turn. He reaches a ceasefire with Hamas and then immediately launches a scathing attack on a Supreme Court decision allowing Palestinians to attend an alternative Memorial Day ceremony together with bereaved Israeli families. He backtracked on the agreement concerning infiltrators from Africa and tore right into the New Israel Fund. When Netanyahu detects trends that point to any weakness on his part, he deals with them by drawing attention to other issues instead.

Pulling the Strings

Razi Barkai waits in the studio for the green light for his broadcast. I am on the fifth floor, the Army Radio commander's floor, standing tensely next to the fax machine that will at any moment spit out a letter from Netanyahu's lawyers who are attempting to block the release of my investigation. It's not a big story, but it does have the potential to bring a criminal inquiry in its wake. The subject is an important, social, non-profit organization whose fundraising evenings in Israel and abroad have been attended by Netanyahu, as well as other senior members of the Likud, who have written letters of support and recommendations for funding. My investigation has found that resources of this non-profit helped Likud figures indirectly in the primaries.

The fax duly produces a letter of warning from a prominent law firm. The first page rolls out slowly: a long list of names, in two columns – all the partners in the firm. The list continues onto the second page. The third page emerges: there is a denial of any connection to the activities of the non-profit, a demand that the investigation not be aired, and a threat that I will be sued for damages and slander. Along with the fax from the lawyers, two Likud ministers are breathing down the neck of the Army Radio commander, and in addition there is pressure from Ehud Olmert who, as Mayor of Jerusalem, had also encouraged contributions to this non-profit. All these forces have joined to thwart the report. The coercion has the desired effect; the report receives a minor mention on the news. It was meant to be the opening item.

Netanyahu, like the Iron Dome system, is able to shoot down negative news items about him. Early obstruction is part of his method of controlling the agenda. Throughout his years as Prime Minister, quite a few investigative reports have been relegated to dusty files owing to pressure that he exerted and threats of lawsuits. Many other reports were toned down significantly following intervention by his lawyers or spokesmen. He takes care to obstruct the publication of negative items even in gossip columns.

"The questions need to be submitted a week in advance, in writing." This was the demand that arrived in the office of the mayor of Beersheba in advance of Netanyahu's visit to the city and the encounter that awaited him there with hundreds of high school seniors. The students wrote out their questions; the ten most important were selected and conveyed via the office of the mayor to the government precinct in Jerusalem, to the Prime Minister's spokesman, who reviewed the page of questions carefully and was unsatisfied.

Question 2 was a question posed in critical language by a student at Regional High School E, concerning the salaries of teachers in the southern region. Question 6 came from Regional High School H and concerned Rabin's assassination and the incitement that had preceded it. The other questions were easier to deal with. The spokesman wasted no time: he picked up the phone and did his homework so that on the drive down to Beersheba, by the time Netanyahu opened the detailed itinerary that had been planned, he found the page of questions with the spokesman's handwritten note: "Questions 2 and 6 are cancelled!"

A list of suggested responses was also ready and waiting in the itinerary folder, along with quantitative data on government investments and achievements in Beersheba. The visit, of course, was a success.

■■■

"Throw the telephone into the toilet right now and flush." According to *Haaretz*, this was the message conveyed to personnel from the Walla news site in light of rumors that a police inquiry was being opened concerning Netanyahu's involvement in the site's content. The telephones weren't destroyed, and the messages – including detailed correspondence – reached the police and later the public, revealing the extent of Netanyahu's involvement in every word carried in the media.

In their messages, the Walla personnel referred to Netanyahu as "Kim" - an allusion to North Korean dictator Kim Jong-un. Netanyahu, for his part, demanded (, sometimes via his spokesman, sometimes directly,) the replacement of certain photographs with others, or the rewriting of headlines. He also conveyed incriminating information to the company concerning his rivals, and demanded that activities of the wives or family members of his rivals receive coverage. He suggested highlighting negative reports about the President of Israel, while working to have negative reports concerning himself minimized.

Netanyahu formulates messages to the press, conveys demands at all hours of the day and night concerning specific wording, is involved in the video editing of his interviews before elections, and haggles over the positioning of every item on the site. He asks for positive items to remain at the top of the main page for some time, while requesting that negative items be "pushed down."

A Bridge to the Message

Netanyahu not only dictates the media agenda and controls the spotlight, but also knows how to appear on stage. The use of spin is one way to influence what people are talking about; interviews is another.

Three days before the elections, Netanyahu launched a blitz of interviews. Rina Matzliah of Channel 2 addressed the Prime Minister on live TV and chose to start off with a polite, bland and banal question: "Mr. Prime Minister, Mr. Benjamin Netanyahu, good evening. How are you?"

Netanyahu answered, "I am well, but I'm more concerned about the state of my country, and therefore I call from here upon all those who care about Israel's security to go out and vote …" Matzliah cut him off, claiming that he was engaging in election propaganda.

Even if Matzliah had asked Netanyahu, "Excuse me, sir, what is the time?" he would undoubtedly have answered, "Time to shore up Israel's security, and in order to make that happen - vote Likud." A message has to be repeated in relation to every issue and every question. When the Prime Minister was discharged from the hospital in 2013 after undergoing surgery, he approached the cameras next to the Emergency Room, thanked the doctors and "the citizens of Israel who expressed the hope that I would make a speedy recovery. So I'm making a speedy recovery, and will continue to care of the security of our citizens, the security of all of us."

Ayelet Shaked, who previously worked in Netanyahu's office, once described what she learned from him: "In the media you have to refine the message and repeat it again and again so it will sink in. The most important thing that I learned from him is to create a bridge." She quickly goes on to explain: "In other words, it doesn't matter what the question is; the answer has to be the message."

...

The answers are printed and ready in front of him before he hears the questions. The pages I obtained from Netanyahu's files contain many pages with the heading "Points for Interview" – sometimes at the level of detailed scenarios of questions that are to be anticipated and suggested responses. One of the pages features the answer, "Concerning General Claims." A different page is headed, "Concerning Sharon," and a third page lists the messages that should be conveyed concerning "the claims regarding lack of experience." He never goes to a press conference without a page of messages.

In the first debate against Peres in 1996, Netanyahu was asked difficult questions about having moved to the US, about Rabin's assassination, and about contradictory statements that he had made. One of his responses to the interviewer was the following: "I thank you for the question, but before answering, I have to respond to the statement that Mr. Peres made concerning Jerusalem. Mr. Peres, it doesn't matter what you say here this evening, because in actuality you are dividing Jerusalem!"

This answer was taped down on the table in front of him, undetected by the camera, on one of a series of notelets that he had placed as reminders for himself before the debate. He had planned his messages carefully, practicing over the course of a series of simulations in which Dan Meridor played the role of Shimon Peres. When the interviewer addressed a difficult question at him, Netanyahu chose the most appropriate message from the list that he had prepared and written on the notelets. When asked about the "hot tape," he answered, "I made a mistake," and then immediately built a bridge to his message: "But the mistake that Mr. Peres is making …" went on to accuse Peres of sowing fear, inviting terror, and dividing Jerusalem.

Professors Tamar Liebes and Shoshana Blum-Kulka, who analyzed the Bibi-Peres debate, define this television appearance as the reason for Bibi's victory in the elections. What was the secret of his success? The researchers found that the secret lay quite simply in his grueling rehearsals: "Netanyahu was better suited to the medium. TV appearances are an environment in which he thrives. He can be tense and nervous, as he was before the debate, and recover in front of the cameras. He looked young, energetic, and sure of himself. He is an expert in packaging his messages in accordance with the circumstances of each appearance, and he makes sure, by means of grueling practice, that he does it properly. The strategy of pre-planned attack boosted his self-confidence. Peres, in contrast, failed in all three areas. He expressed disdain for the very idea that there was a need to practice for an appearance, believing that his actions and his vision would 'do the trick'. His answers were overloaded, he didn't manage to consolidate them into a slogan, or to organize himself within the time allotted to him."

The recipe for success in the media, as in most areas in life, lies in preparation and practice. Netanyahu is an international public diplomacy machine and a genius in front of the camera, because all his knockout sentences have been prepared beforehand. Catchy rhymes and images aren't brainwaves that strike him out of nowhere. It's all written down in advance. He is able to recite it all quite naturally. He has a good memory for messages, and it's difficult to divert him from them. Like a guided missile that hones in on its target, nothing will stop him from pursuing the messages that he has prepared in the desired direction.

When Netanyahu goes on the air, he sees it as stepping onto the battlefield. "For me, TV is a boxing ring," he declared in 1987, as a young Israeli diplomat in the US, busy presenting Israel's case. "They put you in front of someone who wants to attack all that you stand for, and you have to decide when, what, and how to respond." In a smug interview on the day the Knesset was sworn in after the first round of elections in 2019, he told journalist Amit Segal jokingly, "Your job is to ask questions, and my job is not to answer."

It's All Talk

Netanyahu, who has studied and practiced public speaking, is consistent in producing clear messages and polished interviews, while his rivals made mistakes on air. During the 2019 elections, Gantz was responsible for a string of gaffes, and although they didn't damage his overall effort, each blooper was seized upon by Netanyahu's campaign. The media enjoyed mocking him, too. Here and there he stuttered. In one interview he made a statement that sounded like an agreement to join a unity government with Netanyahu. Then he denied it, claiming that his "M-16 ear" hadn't heard the question properly.

Netanyahu offers the media his best, most-carefully chosen words, along with his rivals' worst blunders. He knows that in the public mind, someone who speaks with confidence on the screen is perceived as a leader. Slips of the tongue on air are perceived as a weakness of leadership.

As elections approach, the name of the game is "Who said to whom." Reams of quotes are collected by politicians as ammunition against their adversaries, and shared with the media. In 2019, the Likud hired investigators whose entire function consisted of gathering statements by Lapid, Gantz, and Barak and their fellow party members. After poring endlessly over the internet and protocols of meetings and producing whatever they could find, they were sent to Labor headquarters in Tel Aviv to scrutinize newspapers from bygone years for statements that could be quoted out of context for the benefit of the campaign.

At the same time, Netanyahu prepared video clips discrediting Lapid, Gantz, Livni, and Herzog, presenting their lesser command of English as an obstacle that would prevent them from speaking to international audiences. As evidence he showed moments of hesitation or stumbling in their interviews. They, in turn, searched the archives for mistakes that he had made in the past.

∎∎∎

A third tactic that Netanyahu uses to control the media – along with spin and interviews – are slogans that linger in the mind.

There is a rhetorical pattern leading all the way from his first term in office ("They give – they'll get; they don't give – they won't get" concerning the Palestinians) to the present ("There won't be anything, because there isn't anything," concerning the police investigations). Despite the twenty years separating these two sentences, it's easy to point out their double-barreled common denominator. This technique is what makes these sentences unforgettable.

The same technique is applied against enemies: "Let it be clear to anyone who tries to harm us – we will harm them"; "Those who tried us, suffered; those who try us, will suffer."

Netanyahu fills the linguistic mold with whatever the relevant content may be, thereby packaging policy in a catchy message ready for the media and the masses. The secret of the technique lies in the parallelism, with repetition of the same word or phrase, the comma in between serving as a sort of mirror. "If the Arabs lay down their weapons, there would be no more war. If Israel lay down its weapons, there would be no more Israel."

This two-part wonder-formula is especially useful for describing two contentious or contrasting sides; the difference between us and them: "Israeli used its missiles to protect its children; Hamas uses its children to protect its missiles." Or, "Israel does everything it can to minimize civilian casualties; Hamas does everything it can to maximize civilian casualties." "Israel isn't what's wrong with the Middle East; Israel is what's right with the Middle East." And of course: "Hamas is ISIS, and ISIS is Hamas."

It's a contrasting or complementary parallelism, using the same words, with a slight change. "It's not an historical agreement; it's an historical mistake," Netanyahu declared with regard to the Iran deal, and warned, "The most dangerous regime in the world cannot have the most dangerous weapons in the world." While drawing the red line on his famous bomb visual at the UN, he used the opportunity to convey a verbal knockout: "A red line doesn't lead to war. A red line prevents war."

Even when he changes his views, he packages his words in the same formula: "Yes to a Jewish state is No to a Palestinian state." Later he agreed to a Palestinian state, using the same formula: "The Palestinians have to be ready for concessions, and we too shall be ready for concessions." Likewise, "Our aim: to achieve maximum self-rule for the Palestinians, and maximum security for Israel." Addressing a different topic, he said, "Israel has to watch over the Golan, because the Golan watches over Israel." A few years later he entered negotiations with the Syrians and agreed, according to reports, to a full withdrawal from the Golan Heights.

For many years Netanyahu tried to persuade the public that he was in favor of peace, and blamed the Left for its "idiotic attempt to divide the nation into two camps: lovers of peace and eschewers of peace."

The first time he used the parallelism appears to have been in 1984, at the UN. The draft of his speech shows that he entitled it, "Jordan is

Palestine," and the key sentence is underlined for emphasis: "Jordan is Palestine, Palestine is Jordan." Years have passed, the policy has changed, but the rhetorical tactic remains the same.

Parallelisms abounded in Netanyahu's savoring of the peace agreements signed with Arab countries: "This peace wasn't attained because Israel weakened itself; it was attained because Israel strengthened itself," he emphasized, and promised: "We invested in peace over many years; now peace will invest in us." Reveling in the negation of the "land for peace" formula touted for many years by the Left, he repeated his own doctrine of "peace for peace" and "economy for economy."

❙❙❙

In Netanyahu's euphemistic terms, territorial withdrawals were referred to as "pulses." These, he stated, were "not an ideal solution, but there is no ideal solution." "The conflict isn't about a Palestinian state, but rather has always been about the existence of a Jewish state," because "they ask us to recognize their state, but they don't recognize our state." When he agreed to a ceasefire with Hamas, contrary to the position of the Minister of Defense and of most of the general public in Israel, he offered an elegant justification: "Leadership isn't doing what's easy; leadership is doing what's right."

The formula works for any subject. Regarding the rising prices of housing: "I said: Buy apartments. Some people heard me and did so; some people heard me and didn't." On Gantz: "While I gave instructions to break into Iran's nuclear archive, Iran broke into Benny Gantz's cellphone." Justifying the call for a viewers' boycott: "The media ignores us – we'll ignore the media."

At a Holocaust Memorial Day ceremony he described the cold that he had experienced himself on a visit to Poland: "Whoever wasn't cremated, froze to death; whoever didn't freeze to death, was cremated."

At a ceremony on Ammunition Hill: "We liberated Jerusalem, and Jerusalem liberated us." Freedom of religion is "not in spite of our control of the city, but rather specifically *because* of our control of the city."

Bibi speaks in slogans, and is proud of his ability to present any message in clear, simple, and memorable form:

> "I come from a home in which I was taught that clarity of expression is an asset. It's a sign not of shallowness or simplistic thinking, but rather of the essence of the processing of an idea."

On the other hand, when participating in a discussion at a research institute in Britain, he exclaimed to the organizers, "God, I can speak here! It's not sound-bites. It's not TV. We can develop an idea!" So perhaps even Netanyahu finds it challenging to formulate every idea with the linguistic speed required of participants in media formats.

Most of Netanyahu's campaign slogans have also remained true to his formula: "A strong Prime Minister – a strong Israel," "A strong hand in security, a strong hand in the economy," "A strong leader for a strong nation," "No peace – no security"; "A strong Likud – a strong Israel."

The formula, the parallelism, and in many cases (in Hebrew) the rhyme, have also been employed by other politicians in Israel: "We shall proceed with negotiations as though there was no terror, and we shall fight terror as though there were no negotiations," declared Rabin and Peres in the midst of an avalanche of terror attacks. This echoed Ben-Gurion's policy during the Second World War: "We must help the British in their war as though there was no White Paper, and we must oppose the White Paper as though there was no war."

A special parallelism was planned in advance for the moment on prime-time TV when Netanyahu rolled up his sleeve to become the first Israeli to be vaccinated against COVID. This moment was carefully staged and publicized with a view to encouraging the public to have the vaccination – and perhaps to vote for him, too. Viewers who were watching carefully a moment before the vaccination was administered saw Bibi's spokesman approach the nurse standing behind the Prime Minister and instructing her in an authoritative whisper to move aside, out of the frame, so as not to detract from the Prime Minister's glory. Bibi's personal physician administered the shot. A second later, the Prime Minister looked directly at the cameras and, recalling a different pioneer who took mankind's first step onto the moon, declared, "One small vaccination for man; one great healthcare leap for all of us."

If it Rhymes, it Must be Right

Indeed, Netanyahu didn't invent the technique. Several memorable statements and mottos attributed to other leaders and famous figures have been formulated in this mold, with the same intention. An example is Kennedy's patriotic call, "Ask not what your country can do for you; ask what you can do for your country." Churchill praised the Royal Air Force's efforts against the German Luftwaffe: "Never in the field of human conflict was so much owed by so many to so few." In fact, Bibi himself was the subject of Shamir's skeptical evaluation: "The sea is the same sea; the Arabs are the same Arabs, and Netanyahu is the same Netanyahu."

The same formula is to be found in non-political settings. Ahad Ha-am[36] noted, "More than the Jewish People have kept the Shabbat

---

36 Pen name of Asher Zvi Hirsch Ginsberg, known as the father of cultural Zionism.

(Sabbath), the Shabbat has kept the Jewish People." Of course, there is the famous opening line of Tolstoy's Anna Karenina: "Happy families are all alike; every unhappy family is unhappy in its own way." From the realm of classical Jewish sources we have, for example, the Mishnaic[37] aphorism: "One who is pleasing to his fellow men, is pleasing to God." The long and diverse list of examples ("To be or not to be? That is the question") illustrates the effectiveness of the technique in impressing many ideas and observations on our historical human memory.

Although the formula has been employed by many great orators, Netanyahu seems to have been the first in Israel to make such systematic, consistent, and ongoing use of it. It's not a matter of a few entertaining phrases that are to be found if one combs through his many speeches over the years. He talks this way all the time. He never delivers a speech that doesn't contain a trademark parallelism. His famous address before Congress in Washington on the eve of the 2015 elections, where he had been invited to speak (to the great chagrin of President Obama) contained dozens of examples:

> "Iran's regime is not merely a Jewish problem, any more than the Nazi regime was merely a Jewish problem."

> "America's founding document promises life, liberty, and the pursuit of happiness. Iran's founding document pledges death, tyranny, and the pursuit of jihad."

> "The deal will not prevent Iran from developing nuclear weapons. It would all but guarantee that Iran gets those weapons, lots of them."

> "[This deal] doesn't block Iran's path to the bomb; it paves Iran's path to the bomb."

---

37   Avot 3:10

> "So this deal won't change Iran for the better; it will only change the Middle East for the worse."
>
> "This deal won't be a farewell to arms. It would be a farewell to arms control."
>
> "If Iran changes its behavior, the restrictions would be lifted. If Iran doesn't change its behavior, the restrictions should not be lifted."
>
> "If Iran wants to be treated like a normal country, let it act like a normal country."

The entire media campaign against the Iran agreement ran under the slogan, "Fix it or nix it." Rhymes such as this one are among the most widely-used techniques in persuasion and marketing. Matthew McGlone and Jessica Tofighbakhsh, two psychologists based at Lafayette College, Pennsylvania, explore the phenomenon in their discussion of the "rhyme-as-reason" effect - a cognitive bias that causes people to award greater accuracy to an aphorism if it rhymes. One of the reasons proposed for the effect is the Keats heuristic, according to which the aesthetic qualities of a statement influence our evaluation of its truth. The persuasive power of the rhyme was clear in the famous "If it doesn't fit, you must acquit" argument offered at O.J. Simpson's trial for murder.

In their study, McGlone and Tofighbakhsh asked participants to rate the ostensible accuracy of rhyming aphorisms and of semantically equivalent non-rhyming statements, and found that the rhyme played a significant role. For instance, "What sobriety conceals, alcohol reveals" rated higher on the accuracy scale than "What sobriety conceals, alcohol unmasks." A majority of participants viewed the rhyming aphorisms as richer and more profound than the corresponding non-rhyming statements.

Stories and especially songs meant for young children are full of rhymes, for the same reason. Long before it was proven by academic research, people knew instinctively that the human mind absorbs and remembers messages better when they rhyme.

Studies have shown that companies with catchy names are more successful in their public offerings on the stock exchange than similar companies with complicated names. It is no coincidence that Yair Lapid chose to call his party Yesh Atid (, literally, "There is a future,") to rhyme with his name. A musical note is a reason to vote.

■■■

As a political correspondent during the period of the Disengagement from Gaza, I was sternly reprimanded by the office of the Prime Minister, Ariel Sharon, for using such terms as "expulsion," "withdrawal," and "evacuation" with regard to the uprooting of Jews from their homes in the Gaza Strip. The preferred official term was "Disengagement" – a sterile euphemism, whose terms offered "pitzui temurat pinui" (compensation for evacuation). Discussions in the Army Spokesman's Unit in anticipation of the Disengagement produced the slogan that was meant to mold the mindset of those who would be called upon to carry out the operation: "be-regishut u-ve-nechishut" ("with sensitivity and with determination").

The mind absorbs a rhyming message quickly and easily, and that is precisely the danger: the ease with which the phrase passes through the cognitive process creates an illusion of truth, which lowers our level of alertness and critical thinking. The mind creates a shortcut to the conclusion: "I understood the statement quickly and easily, so it must be logical and correct."

Look at Me, Look at Yourselves

Netanyahu is the most media-savvy and publicity-aware Prime Minister Israel has ever had, but is that the only explanation for his repeated re-election? Are his arguments persuasive, or is it just his rhymes that win the public over? Is anything real or is it all illusion?

This question – which, obviously, ignores Netanyahu's ideological underpinnings – misses the broader picture: a new era in which form dominates substance in all areas. Netanyahu's habit of formulating his messages in rhymes and parallelisms reflects a reality in which the supermarket of opinions (just like every other store) offers shiny, impressive-looking wrappings that are essentially opaque and don't allow one to view the product itself. In our times, greater weight is awarded to how the message is presented, and less to the substance.

Journalists often accuse Netanyahu of engaging in "shallow discourse." They are watching Netanyahu but actually seeing and hearing themselves: single-dimensional, brief, superficial, full of slogans and word-plays. The differences between the respective styles associated with headlines, advertisements, and leadership have long been erased. The same style now characterizes all three genres.

News has become a form of verbal and visual entertainment, selling advertisements to the extent that it is captivating. This trend has come to be known as "infotainment," a term that hints to the trend away from formal, serious, or in-depth treatment of a subject towards the gossipy, personal, soft angle. In his book *Amusing Ourselves to Death*, educator Neil Postman analyzes how the transition from the print era to the TV era sounded the death knell for the written word and created a shallow discourse centered around visual images, impacting the partners in the discourse and teaching children that entertainment is the central value in life. The main aim is to boost pleasurable consumption while preventing discourse and thinking.

A review of the public relations and advertisement campaigns in all the election cycles shows that the political campaign staff are at the same time commercial campaign staff, and their openly-stated approach is that the leader is a product that has to sell itself via entertaining branding techniques. The Prime Minister is "sold" to the public in exactly the same way as toothpaste is. The news itself sells superficial political entertainment so that the audience will remain glued to the screen for the toothpaste advertisement. Sometimes it's the same advertising agency selling both products.

In communication studies this is referred to as mediatization: the process by which the whole of society comes to be shaped by and dependent on the media.

Netanyahu cannot be faulted for using easy-to-remember phrases because the media encourages it, leaving no possibility for politicians to act or speak in any other style. Those who obey the rules of media format are rewarded with broad coverage. Thus, Netanyahu and the media, in fact, form their own parallelism. It is Netanyahu's media show-trial. This mirror reflection of Netanyahu's relations with the media may also be one of the reasons for the loathing that many journalists feel towards the Prime Minister.

Thinking in Brief

The media's demand of politicians to speak in brief, memorable slogans becomes more insistent with each passing year. The length of the fragments picked out of speeches and interviews for broadcasting is growing constantly shorter. In the US, where the sound bites from the presidential debates are carefully measured, it was found that for the 2016 US presidential elections, the sound-bites were less than seven seconds long. (In 1968, by way of comparison, they lasted 43 seconds.) The significance of this finding is clear. Politicians who want to feature in the news have to speak in sentences that contain ten words at most.

"Answer questions, but as briefly as possible," Netanyahu urged the Likud ministers in a sort of workshop for public appearances that he held for them a month before the first round of elections in 2019. The session was intended to give clear definition to messages and to instruct the participants in the art of media interviews.

"There's no such thing as not answering questions," he told them. "But don't waste time on the answers. Respond as briefly as possible, and then move to your message." "And what's the message?" asked one participant. The Prime Minister replied, "The most important thing about the message is that it should be summarized in one word. Two words max. No more."

Immediately after this session with Netanyahu, the Likud ministers ascended the stairs leading from the Aquarium up to the cabinet meeting room. The press was waiting for them. Miri Regev was the first to be interviewed that morning: "The public has to make a very clear choice today between Bibi and Tibi." Next came Ofir Akunis, who repeated: "It's as clear as daylight that these elections are 'Bibi or Tibi.'" Gila Gamliel followed: "Gantz and Lapid prefer Tibi to Bibi." Next was David Bitan, who dutifully recited, "It's Bibi or Tibi." A short, catchy, rhyming slogan. Exactly the same slogan that Bibi had used 23 years previously, in his first run for the premiership. Netanyahu knows that the media has no time for full-length, well-considered arguments, and he keeps his statements shorter than anyone else.

It's all a matter of getting the message across in a couple of words. Bibi-Tibi. Weak Left. Witch hunt. They're afraid. A secure peace. There won't be anything. House of cards. If they give, they'll get. The Left is with the Arabs. We are the people.

Politicians still tend to talk at length, so how does the media choose the sound-bites for broadcasting? There are rules for how discourse is created, and Netanyahu knows how to use them. Analysis of media discourse reveals that the focus isn't on positions and opinions, but rather on bashing the rival candidate. Almost 40% of the sound-bites broadcast leading up to the US presidential elections consisted of criticism of the other candidate. The format demands slogans and invites conflict.

Another 30% of the sound bites that were broadcast in the US concerned the progress of the campaign and who was in the lead. In communication studies this trend is known as "horse race journalism," dedicated to comparative polling data rather than candidate policy. The question that occupies the media is which horse will win (i.e., which is stronger and faster than the other,) rather than who is right.

Within the vicious cycle that has been created, the media covers only conflicts and provocations, while cynically scorning politicians for creating provocations and pointing to this as the main reason for the public's lack of faith in politicians.

The media that made Netanyahu the way he is, and that hates him, is the same media that created Trump, and hated him. Trump spoke in sentences that averaged seven words. According to one study, even first-graders could understand him.

Politicians the world over have learned the trick. They keep their messages simple, short, sharp, and critical. They talk in tweets and images. They all know: if there's no picture, there's no story. News broadcasts feature much fewer words uttered by the candidate himself, and many more visuals of the politician while the journalist speaks.

The visuals have a greater impact on viewers than the verbal content. The media doesn't want lengthy answers; brief slogans are enough, preferably with pictures. Netanyahu hatches conflict, presents images, and formulates policy in rhyming phrases and brief aphorisms as a mirror image of the media's preferences.

In his book *Nineteen Eighty-Four*, George Orwell describes the principles of "Newspeak," a controlled and simplified language introduced by the regime with a view to limiting the range of citizens' thought to those areas and concepts deemed "acceptable." The state of the media in Israel is in some ways reminiscent of this scenario. Formulation of policy in accordance with a uniform rhetorical structure serves to constrict conceptual horizons and leads to simplistic, rigid ways of thinking among the citizenry and leadership alike. The ability to conduct a different type of discourse and discussion has all but disappeared: issues seem to be caged within the simplistic framework of Left-Right, yes-Bibi or no-Bibi, guilty or innocent, Israeli or Jewish, and who is stronger. Other, more complex subjects that entail greater complexity and encompass a broader and more human range of responses – such as children's education, the future of the elderly, hopes and dreams, loneliness, alienation, and identity – are almost impossible to discuss. They are certainly not to be dwelled or elaborated upon. Time is short, dialogue is diminished, thought is constricted, perspectives are narrowed. Israeli society is increasingly hardnosed, unyielding, and morose. Language molds society.

This was all aptly described by Netanyahu's father, Professor Benzion Netanyahu:

> "The problem is that there is no serious representation of any outlook or worldview. There is no in-depth, systematic analysis of any kind. There is no logical debate over the fundamental issues. Imagine that someone maintains the view that all the territory of Judea and Samaria should be relinquished. Well, fine: let him write an article that provides a basis for his arguments in international law, in historical fact, the diplomatic and security situation,

and considerations of possible developments in the near future. But no such article has been written. You can look everywhere; you won't find it. Because what we have here is a terrible emptiness. A tendency to turn away from rational analysis, replacing it with shallow slogans and baseless generalizations."

■■■

In 1985, the *New York Times* published a report about the quality of the speeches at the UN, deeming them long and boring. The report made favorable mention of the Israeli ambassador to the UN, one Benjamin Netanyahu, noting in particular his sarcasm and inner drive. With the years, and his accumulated experience, Netanyahu became well known in the US and a sought-after guest with the most popular interviewers, including Larry King. Israelis were not cognizant of the fact that their future Prime Minister was grooming himself for the job, and that the media was part of his strategy.

> "By means of newspapers, pamphlets, faxes, and broadcasts; with the help of lobbying groups and personal diplomacy with lawmakers; and through the use of email, which I have recommended in the past, I succeeded in introducing our concerns and arguments into the world's consciousness."

It is no wonder that Netanyahu is proud of having touted the use of email. During the Second Lebanon War, he dispatched an email to a Jewish community in the US presenting Israel's position, and they forwarded it on. The word "viral" hadn't yet entered the digital vocabulary, but Netanyahu was fascinated and energized by the possibility of creating a message that could be disseminated widely, and encouraged his staff and colleagues to write emails to their friends.

Netanyahu has progressed in parallel with the historical development of communications. He knows how to adapt himself to each new age, moving from written communication to electronic forms; from one single channel to the multi-channel revolution; from television to internet, and from internet to the world of social media. This man in his 70s, who doesn't use a cellphone, posts updates on social media platforms where most users are under the age of 18.

Neo-Netanyahu

The advisors were surprised by the data coming in. "Halt the production," Topaz Luk ordered, and went to show the report to Netanyahu. His son Yair and spokesman Jonathan Urich were at his side. Surprisingly, the numbers showed that internet users showed the highest levels of involvement in the cheapest and least-polished video clips that had been uploaded over the last week.

It was a few weeks before the elections, and Luk and his colleagues realized that they were wasting a lot of money on expensive TV productions while a video of the Prime Minister talking from the back seat of his bullet-proof car, or standing under the pergola at his official residence, caused many more people to stop and pay attention to the messages, and to respond. "So what are you saying?" the Prime Minister asked. "That less is more?" From that moment, preference was given to video clips of non-professional standard, filmed on a cellphone, in Netanyahu's natural environment.

The campaigns since 2015 have relied on the feedback figures from social networks. The budget for promoting different posts, running into tens of millions of shekels, has likewise been channeled by campaign director Ofer Golan on the basis of the respective number of responses anticipated. Randomness disappeared, analytics took over.

After later findings showed that the word "emergency" in the title of a clip was effective, Netanyahu's advisors used it in more than twenty different videos, warning of defeat in the elections and the rise of a leftist government. The entire day of broadcasting of the second elections in 2019 was designated an "Emergency Broadcast."

The Likud invested tens of millions of shekels on social network advertising for the elections in 2019. More than any other party. Everywhere that Gantz appeared, there was an accompanying negative ad about him. The Likud simply bought up all the media advertising space adjacent to Gantz's ads.

The times of Netanyahu's live broadcasts on the social networks were also carefully calculated. In order to catch viewers watching the TV news broadcasts via various apps on their phones, the Likud bought the ten-second advertisement slot that shows before the news begins. Viewers found themselves watching a live broadcast by the Prime Minister, and were forced to choose whether to continue with Netanyahu or to switch to the news studio. The data showed this to be a successful strategy. Only a few days later did the news company realize why the ratings for news via the phone had plummeted. Netanyahu was standing at the gate and snatching away the viewers.

■■■

Netanyahu has explained his wide-ranging activity on the internet as facilitating direct contact with the public and a way of by-passing the media with its biased editors and journalists. He deliberately ignores the fact that the internet has an editor, too – a particularly cruel one.

The editor of Facebook is an algorithm. Its editorial considerations have nothing to do with Left or Right; all that matters is popularity. The formula that determines the intensity with which posts are promoted on social media is based on the number of views and responses. Whatever doesn't arouse interest is pushed down to the bottom of the pile, even if it's important. In the absence of oversight by a human editor, who is capable of appreciating the value of the content, the sole determining factor is the numerical bottom line – a factor that invites the most bizarre and extreme content. The more provocative a message is, the more viewers it will have, and thus the algorithm knows that the video should be given higher priority on the feed. And each additional click on such content only serves to reinforce its priority status.

The escalation and intensification of political messages, as practiced by Netanyahu and his rivals, is the result of political discourse controlled by media consultants, who possess figures and data showing that extreme messages and heavy attacks on competitors make ideal click bait. And leaders have learned to appease the algorithm. Guided by the ruthless editor of the internet and encouraged by the audience's responses, politics becomes more callous and relentless. At the same time, it also becomes a lot funnier.

Facebook has turned Netanyahu into a sort of stand-up artist. Short, amusing clips in which Netanyahu plays the leading role, have become a major tool for conveying messages to the public, his advisors having successfully convinced him that "this is what works today."

Professor Rafi Mann researched the history of humor in elections since the founding of the state, and found that in Ben-Gurion's time, humor had no place. Today, politicians prefer appearing on satire shows to appearances in news broadcasts. Along with the technology, there has been fundamental change in the discourse. Mann's definition of the current stage is "the politician as comic."

When Netanyahu made a real-life appearance on the *Eretz Nehederet* (A Wonderful Country) satirical comedy show, he prepared himself with the help of a string of top-rate stand-up artists, and conditioned his arrival in advance on a flattering final question.

"Ben-Gurion is remembered as the founder of the state; Begin is remembered for the peace agreement with Egypt. What do you think you will be remembered for?" the host asked, as had been agreed.

Netanyahu paused, thought a bit, pursed his lips and pretended to be weighing up his words carefully. Then he sat up, looked straight ahead, paused another second for effect, and slowly and deliberately enunciated the answer he had prepared a week in advance: "Guardian of Israel's security."

■■■

Secret #8: **Appear and Impact** Netanyahu influences the various news systems and controls them by means of spin, trial balloons, personal contacts, and economic leverage. He grants interviews in order to convey his messages. The question that he is asked is of little importance; his message is the answer. He speaks in parallelisms and rhyming slogans that are quoted as headlines. He devotes time, effort and resources to digital and new media and is proficient in their use, establishing his image via social networks. The world keeps moving forward, and Netanyahu keeps up with it. That's how he survives.

9.
WITHOUT WORDS
BODY LANGUAGE

Although the bullet-proof vehicle is quite spacious, it's difficult to get dressed sitting in the back seat. "Can't we just let this go?" Netanyahu grumbles as he removed his jacket. "It's so hot here." "It's essential," the head of the security unit insists. "It's an open area, too," he adds, as Netanyahu tries to adjust the bullet-proof vest so it will fit more comfortably.

"Give me the speech again," he asks, as he finishes organizing his attire and takes the red pen out of its compartment in the car door. The convoy keeps driving; in ten more minutes they will be in the Negev. There is just enough time for final corrections.

The Prime Minister, sitting in the car, also writes himself instructions concerning non-verbal messages; these comments are noted in the margins.

> "Had the 1,200 residents of the Negev not held back the invaders, the way to Tel Aviv would have been open to them and who knows what would have happened."

Netanyahu ponders how to present this fragment. Then he writes to himself, "Lift hand!" These are his stage instructions. He will raise his hand, pointing northward towards Tel Aviv, to demonstrate.

He is as deliberate and careful with his body language as he is with his words. Elsewhere in the margins of the speech he marks, by means of two diagonal lines, where to pause to take a breath. Every move is planned in advance; every breath, every inflection of the voice.

Each page of his notes contains only two paragraphs. During his first term in office, he used font size 42. Now, in his fifth term, he uses size 48. All along, the sentences have been short. Where a Hebrew word may be read in more than one way, he carefully adds the vowels that determine the appropriate pronunciation. Here and there he adds a comma. Hearing an announcement that the event is about to begin, he folds the pages and steps out of the car, the door held upon for him by a bodyguard armed with a sub-machine gun. The master of ceremonies invites the Prime Minister to speak.

"We have come here to celebrate a great holiday …" he starts. He is feeling very hot, and perspiring. Uncharacteristically, and to his bodyguard's dismay, he removes his jacket, placing it behind him on a small chair. He continues speaking in his starched white shirt, striped tie, and constricting bullet-proof vest.

When he reaches the point in the speech mentioning Tel Aviv, the Prime Minister sees the stage instructions written in red pen; he raises his hand towards the north and lifts his voice: "Had the 1,200 residents … the road to Tel Aviv would have been open …" To the audience, the gesture appears altogether spontaneous.

From Word to Picture

September 1960. In the studio, John F. Kennedy and Richard Nixon stood facing three large cameras and one moderator. This was the first debate ever aired on television between two candidates for the presidency of the US. It would change politics forever, its results leading to a series of studies that molded the way in which leaders act in the public arena, at the recommendation of their media advisors, to this day.

Vice President Nixon arrived at the debate feeling slightly unwell, after some long flights and no rest. He refused makeup, and wore a heavy grey suit. The combination of no makeup, heavy fabric, and bright camera lights made Nixon's perspiration clearly visible. The color of his suit was unflattering, especially against the studio backdrop. The two candidates stood throughout the debate, and the Vice President, whose left leg was afflicted with phlebitis, shifted his weight constantly throughout. Kennedy, in contrast, appeared young and vibrant. On the other hand, Nixon had far more experience: his answers were more organized, his policy was clear. He was proficient in the details and answered all questions capably.

"Who won the debate?" the researchers asked in their survey, and were surprised to discover that the answer depended on whether respondents had watched the debate or just listened to it. Those who had heard it over the radio maintained that Nixon had won, because his arguments were far more convincing than those of his rival. Respondents who had watched the debate on television, however, had seen the glowing Kennedy and the sweaty, swaying Nixon, and chose Kennedy solely on the basis of his non-verbal messages and image. The packaging decided the election.

The transition from radio to television therefore also marked a new era in politics and global culture: the era of visibility. The first music video to launch on MTV was *Video Killed the Radio Star*. Television had defeated radio; the image had vanquished the word. Tragically, form had prevailed over substance.

Television in its time wrought a complete transformation of politics, just as the digital revolution has changed our world today. It wasn't merely a technical change in the medium, but rather a fundamental change in how decisions were made and matters conducted.

To a certain extent it was a change in people's way of thinking. The advent of television sealed the incontestable supremacy of the sense of sight. The overuse of this one sense, in the screen era, causes attenuation of the others as a protection against sensory overload. Thus, visual technology suppresses other senses that might be more critical.

In 1960, with television debuting in the lives of Americans, the elections were the closest of any in the 20th century. Kennedy won by a margin of less than ⅔ of a percent. In the race between Netanyahu and Peres in 1996, Netanyahu won by a margin of around 30,000 votes. Just because of visibility. Voters watched on television as the young Netanyahu, following a series of simulations and practices, and with slogans taped to the edge of his table, faced off against the older Peres, who had refused to invest any serious effort in preparation and displayed unconcealed rage towards his opponent. In the decades that followed, too, Netanyahu would adapt himself to the new medium and made optimal use of most-watched TV broadcasts as a springboard to victory.

Televised debates for the US elections have been called time and time again on the basis of body language. In 1992, incumbent President George Bush, Sr. lost to Bill Clinton after he was caught on camera glancing at his watch impatiently at the precise moment that a woman in the audience was asking the candidates how they thought the recession had affected the lives of ordinary Americans. Bush came across looking uninterested in people and their problems. Indeed, he later stated that what he had been thinking as he looked at his watch was, "Only ten more minutes of this crap."

In the unofficial debate of 2015, Netanyahu won thanks to a picture. In the realm of television, size does matter. Since 1999, Netanyahu has refused to participate in direct debates against his rivals. Why? Because of the visuals. Branding himself as belonging to a different league, he doesn't want to be seen sitting next to his rivals as equals in a studio. Netanyahu was therefore interviewed from his office, and his picture was projected onto the huge video wall of the news studio. The director seated his rival, Herzog, at the table, with Netanyahu appearing behind him. When the camera showed a wide shot of the studio to include both candidates, viewers saw the diminutive Herzog forced to look behind himself in order to see Netanyahu – turning half away from the camera and the audience at home as he did so – while Netanyahu loomed large, his picture filling the entire screen. The director effectively determined the outcome.

■■■

For four years I presented a television show called "Beyond Words," analyzing body language and political rhetoric. It isn't easy to discern lies on the basis of body language, and I like to keep people's expectations realistic by joking, "What body language tells you that a politician is lying?" The answer: "He's moving his lips."

Studies have shown that there are in fact ways of detecting deception in a person's body language. (This is one of the elements that makes a polygraph effective.) What we look out for is incongruity. This term explains the results of the debate in 1996. According to Dr. Tsfira Grebelsky-Lichtman of the Hebrew University, there was a very specific aspect of body language that caused Netanyahu to win over viewers in his debate against Peres. Grebelsky-Lichtman's research examined every sentence that each of the candidates uttered, and monitored what his body language and facial expressions were saying at the same time. She discovered that in Peres's case there was incongruity between the words and the picture. When he spoke about hope for peace, his face was angry; when he promised economic growth, there was no smile; when he promised to protect the unity of Jerusalem, he recoiled; when he committed himself to acting against terror, his arms remained folded. What he was saying and what his body was projecting didn't match up.

Netanyahu maintained maximum congruity between his words and his body language. He moved and gestured exactly as he had rehearsed in his nearby hotel over several days. When he promised to fight terror, his hand closed in an adamant fist; when he blamed Peres, he wagged an accusatory finger; when he spoke of Jerusalem, he stood up straight; when he admitted to cheating on his wife, he lowered his voice as though confessing. Throughout, his hand gestures emphasized his conviction in what he was saying. And this visual argument won.

Just as his victory could be attributed to the visuals and his body language, the same could be said of his defeat. At the end of his first term, in a TV debate in 1999, he tried – as always – to talk in pictures. At one climactic moment he pulled out two large charts from under his seat with statistical data showing the improvement in the economic situation. The gimmick boomeranged: it was deemed a violation of the prohibition against election propaganda, and the host, Nissim Mishal, threatened to end the debate unless the pictures were removed. Mishal was shouting at the Prime Minister on live TV, while Netanyahu insisted on displaying his charts.

Yitzhak Mordechai, the Center Party leader sitting opposite him, joined the fray: "Listen to him, Bibi; listen to him," he rebuked the Prime Minister. The scene lasted for more than a minute – an eternity in television terms. Netanyahu looked desperate and confused; in the end he put down the pictures, in angry submission, defeated by the presenter and by his rival.

Once again, non-verbal communication had won the day. This time Netanyahu was defeated. The voters had watched the Prime Minister writhe uncomfortably in his seat, perspiring, his eyes darting back and forth, arguing. This time the incongruity lay with Netanyahu himself, who tried to project victory and the success of his first term in office, while at the same time projecting non-verbal defeat. Mordechai, his former Minister of Defense, now-turned bitter rival, addressed the Prime Minister again and again with contempt, accused him of being untrustworthy, and repeated over and over, "Bibi, look me in the eyes!"

Again and again, as Mordechai attacked, the camera showed close-ups of Netanyahu's face, looking downward.

The Dr. Fox Effect

Michael Fox sat tensely, adjusting his large and uncomfortable glasses and trying to calm himself with another sip of water. Then he got up and paced backwards and forwards in the small room. The lecturers around him tried to encourage him, but he recalls feeling great apprehension up to the very last minute. He was about to be invited on stage to deliver an important lecture to dozens of psychiatrists, psychologists and health experts who were gathered for a teacher training conference in continuing education, in the auditorium of the School of Medicine at the University of Southern California. Fox wasn't accustomed to feeling stage fright. Standing in front of cameras and an audience came very naturally to him, but right now he was very nervous. Taking a deep breath and whispering "I hope they won't recognize me," he walked into the hall holding the pages of a lecture that he had been given that same morning.

"We're happy to be hosting here today Dr. Myron Fox, an alumnus of the Albert Einstein College of Medicine," one of the participants presented him. He went on to describe Fox's medical credentials, and concluded, "He will be talking about Mathematical Game Theory as Applied to Physician Education." Fox walked to the podium.

Of course, he had not the slightest clue about either medicine or game theory. He hadn't seen an equation - much less solved one – since high school, where he had been a poor student. Fox, an actor, (not to be confused with Michael J. Fox,) had been chosen to deliver the lecture to the participants. Mathematical Game Theory as Applied to Physician Education is a non-existent topic. The actor was instructed to "present his topic and conduct his question and answer period with an excessive use of double talk, neologisms, non sequiturs, and contradictory statements. All this was to be interspersed with parenthetical humor and meaningless references to unrelated topics."

Fortunately, despite his fears, no one among the medical professionals recognized Dr. Myron L. Fox in his respectable suit as the inspector from Batman or the other roles that he had played. They laughed in the right places; many scribbled comments and notes as he was talking. Fox, encouraged by his success, began to feel more natural and relaxed on stage, and gave a dazzling performance. The video of the lecture is available for viewing on the internet. Fox's body language is most impressive and looks quite natural. The researchers' question, however, concerned not Michael Fox's acting ability, but rather the opinion of the audience. After the lecture, a satisfaction questionnaire was distributed so participants could offer feedback about the quality of the speaker's presentation.

Dozens of psychiatrists, psychologists, and social workers training to be more effective educators of other health professionals, along with a group of educators enrolled in a graduate level course, fell for the ruse, awarding significantly more favorable than unfavorable responses on the questionnaire. The hypothesis for the study had been that "given a sufficiently impressive lecture paradigm, an experienced group of educators participating in a new learning situation can feel satisfied that they have learned despite irrelevant, conflicting, and meaningless content conveyed by the lecturer." Students can effectively be "seduced" into an illusion of having learned if the lecturer simulates a style of authority and wit. The conclusion drawn by the authors of the study was that "there is much more to teaching than making students happy."

The experiment was conducted in 1973 and has since been repeated many times, including in 2012 at the School of Education at Hebrew University. The results showed that even in 2012, Michael Fox would have been able to trick his audience and sell them charisma and body language.

***

Even Netanyahu's political detractors wouldn't call him an empty suit. They would acknowledge that his messages are clear, well-reasoned, and have a firm ideological and rational basis. He proposes content that is clear and coherent, even where it might be argued that he is distorting the truth, mistaken, or politically motivated. Nevertheless, we must ask: Is Netanyahu rated in the same way that Dr. Fox was rated? In other words, to what extent does the non-verbal form in which he wraps his arguments, cause most of the public to agree with him?

It seems that part of what convinces us of his arguments is indeed the way in which he presents them. The same arguments, without the accompanying gestures and techniques, are less persuasive. An arresting bodily gesture can add weight to a weak argument. Moshe Sneh, a Haganah commander and politician who belonged to the Israeli Communist Party, wrote in the margin of the page of one of his speeches: "Weak argument – raise voice here."

The conventional wisdom among researchers of political communications is that the non-verbal channel is more important than the words themselves. The statement, "Netanyahu has done it again," can express jealousy, admiration, wonderment, or frustration, depending entirely on the intonation. How something is said is at least as important as what is said.

The Sound of Silence

Non-verbal messages are conveyed via voice, bodily gestures, posture, appearance, and more. Of all these different dimensions, Netanyahu's greatest non-verbal quality seems to be his voice.

Lilyan Wilder, who coached Netanyahu as a young diplomat in the US, wrote a book offering *7 Steps to Fearless Speaking*. She writes, "The first step toward fearless speaking … is to learn to produce a strong, relaxed voice that is easy to listen to, lively, and compelling." Netanyahu is in completely control of his voice; he maintains it and protects it. His voice is his weapon.

Our impression of a speaker's voice is a composite of seven different categories: diction, accent, fluency, pitch, tone, pace, and power. Benny Gantz, in a pre-election interview, came across as stammering when he repeated the first syllable of the interviewer's name over and over, in an attempt to interrupt her words that reached him via earphones while he was in the United States and with a fraction of a second's delay. Netanyahu's campaign exploited this moment as the raw material for videos that showed Gantz continuing his repetition, in a loop. Hundreds of thousands of voters watched these videos. The interview damaged Gantz's image.

Netanyahu's vocal qualities include refined Hebrew, fluency, and a range and versatility that extend from quiet intimacy or storytelling to booming enthusiasm. His clear, purposeful diction projects authority and accuracy.

Perhaps the most valuable aspect of his voice is his silence. For Bibi, the pauses between words and between sentences give him time to breath and project confidence. For his listeners, the dramatic pauses intensify his message. Spectrograms of his speeches show many areas where there is no movement.

Netanyahu also speaks slowly. His sedate pace leaves time for hand gestures that exemplify and emphasize his words. He calibrates the pace, tone and pauses of each sentence individually. How does he do it? One might say that his written notes do it for him.

∎∎∎

The handwritten instructions I found in the drafts of different speeches include requests to increase the font size, to keep the number of sentences on a page down, and "No page turn in mid-sentence." In some speeches – those that are of particular importance to him – he writes at the bottom of each page the first word on the page that follows. Here and there he writes himself a reminder: "Word for word."

Like a TV presenter, Netanyahu marks for himself in pen the key words, pauses, and desired rate of speech. Underlining reminds him to add emphasis through intonation; an arch over a word-pair indicates quick reading, and every period is a chance to take a breath. News headlines are circled. All this allows Netanyahu to create better eye contact with the cameras and with the audience. He looks at the sparse words on the page, straightens his neck and chest, recites the sentence while looking at the audience, and keeps looking at them and at the camera for another second or two. Only then do his eyes turn back to the page to read the next sentence.

Most of his speeches are read from notes, but while his eyes are on the page, he isn't speaking. He talks only when he is looking at the camera and at the audience.

Thus, the power of Netanyahu's delivery starts with the format of his notes. At every stage of his speech, he is seeing just one sentence; every sentence has its place, with a pause before and after.

When the print is sufficiently large, there is no need to lower the head in order to read, and there is more freedom to gesticulate and to pause. Since every speech consists of tens or even hundreds of pages, with a sentence or two on each page, Netanyahu has developed

We wish him continued success in this task. Nothing is more rewarding than the ability to stop bloodshed and bring peace.

I am sure his success will embolden /inspire our efforts to bring peace to our region.

The pending agreements with the Palestinians, are the ones who will benefit from a swift conclusion. Dahaniya airport and the Karni industrial park. And there is a tremendous amount of beneficial work on regional projects which the multilateral committees can do. In this, Europe can play a vital role to advance the peace process.

the knack of turning pages quickly and inconspicuously. One of his technical speaking skills is simply the ability to turn the page while keeping his eyes on the audience.

At a cabinet meeting, while he arranged his pile of papers on the table, the cameras zoomed in on the top page, which featured just one sentence: "Next week, I will deliver a major diplomatic speech in which I will present to the citizens of Israel our principles for achieving peace and security." Between one and four words to a line. In total, sixteen Hebrew words on the page. A page from a speech given at the UN, likewise caught on camera, showed just seven words. Sometimes there is just one word on a line: "Jerusalem". New line: "Complete". New line: "United". Last line: "Never to be divided." Applause.

Spread Open Equals Safe

As he stood by the President of Israel receiving – for the sixth time – the mandate to form a government, Netanyahu's gaze was lowered and his shoulders drooped. He knew that his chances of success were slim in view of the refusal by Blue and White to join. In an attempt to entice Gantz, he described at length the security threats facing the country, and then his proposed solution, in the form of a unity government with "broad shoulders for decision-making."

Broad shoulders are important not only for a government, but also for anyone who wants to lead. Physical bearing is an important area of non-verbal communications, and shoulders serve an especially important function: in evolutionary terms, shoulders signified physical strength and the ability to lead and take on major tasks. It is for this reason that in almost every country in the world, military officers wear rank insignia on their shoulders.

Bibi has broad shoulders. He also knows how to square them,

holding them open and pulled backward, stretching his chest and setting his head firm and upright on his neck. These are clues that tell us something about a person and his measure of self-confidence – and, accordingly, about the confidence others have in him.

Systematic observation of troops of monkeys showed that the alpha male takes up the greatest amount of physical space. His chest is puffed up, his arms are spread wide, and he stands taller than the rest. When a new alpha male takes over, within a short time he adopts the posture of his predecessor – the leadership posture.

A leader has to look like a leader. A peacock struts to show off its assets to a peahen; a cat arches its back to scare away rivals; boxers bare their chests to their opponents. Men in suits display similar behavior. Sitting at the cabinet table for his weekly "photo-op", Bibi always sits straight and tall, his body squared and his hands on the table rather than under it, taking care that whoever sits next to him doesn't look taller (where necessary, he has his chair slightly raised). Only after Netanyahu takes his seat are the photographers who snapped him walking into the room permitted to enter. Sitting down isn't photogenic.

■■■

Dr. Jessica Tracy of the University of British Columbia investigated the degree to which posture would determine a female candidate's chances of being chosen to manage a bank. Some participants in her experiment were given an excellent resume for a female candidate, including a good excellent training background, extensive experience, and manifest suitability for the job. Other participants were given a mediocre resume, indicating a lesser degree of suitability. After this, they were shown a video purportedly showing part of a job interview with the candidate.

The woman in the video was an actress. Some of the participants watched her talk as she sat proudly (upright, chin up, open body posture) while others watched her delivering exactly the same responses, but sitting in a posture that conveyed shame (shrinking, sagging).

The results of the study, published in the *APS Observer*, suggested that while the two groups of participants judged the candidate's intelligence mainly on the basis of her resume (with their ratings differing accordingly), when it came to the question of whether or not to hire her, the resume seemed to have no influence on the decision. When the candidate's posture displayed confidence and pride during the interview, the chances of the participants deciding to employ her were much better, even among those who had received a mediocre resume.

Netanyahu's presence in space, even at his age, is that of an alpha male. He always appears in control, with his shoulders squared and open. He almost never appears on camera drooping, leaning backwards, casual, hesitant or thoughtful. He is always the leader. Ready for whatever awaits him.

Yitzhak Rabin allowed himself to display bewilderment, and a more complex set of emotions, the likes of which are not usually observed in the leaders we are used to seeing on the screen. The restraint reflected in the body language of public figures such as Angela Merkel, Mahatma Gandhi, Bill Gates and others is becoming increasingly rare in an age where TV charisma and presence are de rigueur.

On stage in front of a live audience, too, Netanyahu uses space to project authority, even when seemingly stuck behind a bullet-proof barrier or confined to the podium at the Knesset. He doesn't stand in a single spot, focused on his notes – a pose that characterizes many speakers – but stands and moves comfortably, in control of the space. In the eye of the camera, the modest speakers' podium is a whole world. The way in which Netanyahu dominates this small space, rather than shrinking behind it, gives the viewer an impression of control. Where the nature of the occasion is less formal he even permits himself to use the entire breadth of the stage, returning to stand at the center and add an appropriate gesture of his arm when delivering a key line.

Similarly, Netanyahu makes sure to stand at the center of photographs with foreign leaders, and of course to walk at the head of his entourage.

■■■

Why is man the only creature in the world that shakes hands? Sociologists and biologists suggest that this habit developed as a way of signaling to whoever is in front of us that we are not carrying weapons, or hiding a knife or other threat in our hand. It is a carryover from ancient times when war was a way of life. Non-verbal communication letting others know that we can be trusted is distributed over many moments in our lives, and it is integrated as part of the message that politicians convey to their audience, signaling that we are partners.

Leaders address their audience with open arms as a way of creating closeness and projecting openness and honesty. Arm movements at the sides of the body signal trust in the other party, with no need to defend one's sensitive regions. The abdomen is one such region. Since man stands upright, unlike most animals his abdomen doesn't face the ground. When exposed to an external threat, our arms close in for protection. A leader who displays an open body to the cameras and addresses his audience with open arms, projects confidence. There are very few photos of Netanyahu with his arms crossed; they are always aligned with his shoulders.

Planning a Walk

"I want to see a map," he announced abruptly, shocking those around him. Many weeks of preparations had been focused on this moment. It seemed that everything was now ready and every detail had been taken into consideration – until, with three minutes to go, the Prime Minister gave his startling instruction. All the senior staff members were gathered in the small, well-guarded prefab structure. Everyone else was standing in the neighboring rooms, listening attentively to their walkie-talkies and waiting for the action to begin. In the control room, the tension was growing as the seconds dragged on and the green light had yet to appear. One of the officials yelled, "Get a map over here!" But to everyone's mortification, there was not a single map of the target to be had.

Two minutes to countdown. There was no choice but to take a paper and felt-tip and start drawing the exact route. One of the staff members sketched while Netanyahu watched, asked questions, nodded, followed the trail on the paper with his finger, and imagined how exactly it would look.

This wasn't about a Mossad operation. It wasn't a matter of IDF soldiers or Shin Bet members off on a mission. It concerned the approximately twenty-meter path that Netanyahu himself would be walking: the path from the door of the studio to the chair he would be sitting in. And this wasn't the CNN studio at a time of national emergency, nor even an election debate. The studio in question was set up for the *State of the Nation* satire show. But before every appearance, just as before any General Staff Reconnaissance Unit operation, Netanyahu studies the route before setting out on the mission. He seemed to know that the video of him entering the studio would rack up more views (around a half a million) than the show itself.

"Where do I come in from? Who opens this door? What's the

distance between me and the audience? Please sketch the location of the cameras; where is the camera that I should wave to? Where are the soldiers standing? Where should I shake hands with people? And where is Lior [Shlein, presenter] actually sitting? Remind me again what their names are – here is where Guri is sitting; here's Einav, okay, here's Orna, fine, and here I am ... Okay, I got it. Give me a second to look at it again. From here to here, and here's the camera, right? Okay. I understand. And where are the kids? One moment; what about the chair? Did you take care of what I asked?" Netanyahu, who suffers from back pain, had requested a chair that would not cause him discomfort. Only after some delay, and once he had a sound grasp of the route, did he emerge and head for the studio. The IDF orchestra had sent soldiers to announce the Prime Minister's entrance into the studio with a trumpet fanfare. "Ladies and gentlemen – Prime Minister Benjamin Netanyahu," announced Shlein, and the door opened. The camera dwelled for a moment on the uniformed soldiers, and then focused on the leader. In coordination with the Prime Minister's spokesman, two rows of young children had been stationed at the studio door, dressed in white shirts, to wave miniature Israeli flags "up, way up" as per the director's instructions, as Netanyahu walked between them. The technical director chose to show how the Prime Minister affectionately rumpled the hair of one of the children, waved at exactly the right camera, and strode towards the seat reserved for him in a manner that conveyed that he knew where he was coming from, where he was headed, and what his aim was. A perfect entrance.

■■■

Leaders have a different style of walking than regular citizens. A team of researchers at Queens University analyzed footage of several dozen leaders walking, and found that their gait correlated perfectly with their status.

People who are confident walk with their shoulders squared, their heads held higher and their arms moving more quickly, taking bigger steps, and their elbows are slightly further from their hips in comparison to people who lack confidence or who have a lower social status.

What does Netanyahu's stride towards the cabinet meeting every Sunday morning project in comparison with other ministers who climb the same steps and cover the same route? It matches what the researchers found among people of higher leadership status.

Netanyahu walks at the head of whatever entourage is accompanying him. The command "After me" is not just an IDF norm whereby commanders set a proper example for their soldiers, but also a sound strategy for a leader who wants to appear unassailable in the media. To engineer the perfect frame with no distractions, staff from his spokesman's office take care that the corridor is empty before Netanyahu appears. Netanyahu also insists that his military secretary, in IDF uniform, walk at his side. All of this creates the non-verbal message that viewers see on the Sunday evening news.

The way a leader walks is important. Putin, for example, was known for his purposeful stride, like the KGB officer he had been in the past, as displayed in a great many videos available on the internet. President Obama was known for hopping up onto stage like a rock star. Trump walked slowly, enjoying every moment. We might also mention the stumbling of candidates who didn't make it to the White House, like John McCain and Hillary Clinton.

A leader's walk is broadcast to millions. During these moments the viewers are listening to the correspondent, but watching the leader. Politicians know this and remain conscious of it. Netanyahu is the last to enter a room and the first to leave.

The new trend in the media prefers airing summaries and analyses by correspondents over the actual speeches by leaders. Analyzing the coverage of four US presidential elections on the main broadcast networks, communications researchers at Indiana University referred to footage in which a candidate is shown but not heard speaking as an "image bite." They discovered that over the years, campaigns had come to feature more and more image bites, and less sound bites. This leads to a reality in which the "visual argument" conveyed by the candidate is actually more important than the verbal message. The medium is the message; in the screen age, the picture is the message. Posture has political ramifications, and territory doesn't only mean land.

Handiwork

One of the people I have worked with in recent years is a senior figure from the Left side of the Israeli political map. Unfortunately, before we met, he was advised by one of his fellow party members: "Whenever you talk about Yitzhak Rabin, point humbly towards your chest." And so he did. When I practiced speeches and interviews with him, the gesture seemed forced. I asked him about it, and he explained: "It's a subconscious message that I'm conveying to voters. I'm talking about Rabin, but I'm signaling with my hand, without them noticing, that I am like Rabin." No matter how hard I tried, I couldn't get him to part with this habit.

The biggest mistake concerning hand gestures seems to be their application in an unnatural manner. Netanyahu, who has practiced extensively, has managed to make his gestures natural – or, at least, appear natural. While his body language seems transparent and effortless, the truth is that it takes effort and rehearsal for him no less than for his rivals or would-be successors and close attention to the stage directions he writes for himself in the margins of his speech notes).

One sometimes gets the impression that politicians are all clones of each other. This is not the result of them all training with the same media mentors. Rather, there are solid findings concerning gestures regarded as effective and persuasive, and for this reason gesticulation is employed by a variety of speakers.

Dr. Linda Talley has developed a unique leader development system based on empirical nonverbal behavior research data. In one series of experiments, she instructed an actor to present a text on camera accompanied by different gestures, and found that the audience's attitude towards the actor and the points he was making was directly related to his non-verbal behavior.

A study by body-language expert Vanessa Van Edwards monitored the number of hand movements in the first minute of hundreds of TED Talks, and found that the most popular viral lectures included almost twice as many hand gestures than the average. A series of studies by Prof. Markus Koppensteiner of Vienna University produced some surprising discoveries, the most significant being that people judge the qualities of a leader based on hand and arm gestures. Koppensteiner showed viewers footage of people speaking, without sound, and asked them to describe their qualities. The viewers were able to accurately estimate the seniority and status of the speaker based on his hand movements, and also identified qualities such as extroversion, amiability, and openness.

Like most politicians around the world, Israeli government ministers and their leader are well aware of the conclusions arising from these and other studies, and they plan their movements, adopt effective gesticulations, and undergo media simulations and rehearsals. As the service provider chosen by the Prime Minister's Office to offer media training, I am able to say – without disclosing the identity of my clients – that more than a third of the ministers in Israel's 34th government, from 2015 to 2019, underwent personal training with me in how to appear on camera. And what troubles many of them (and almost anyone who addresses an audience) is the question of

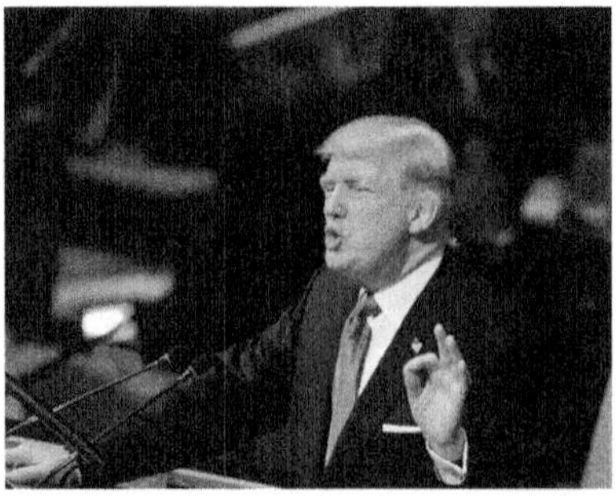

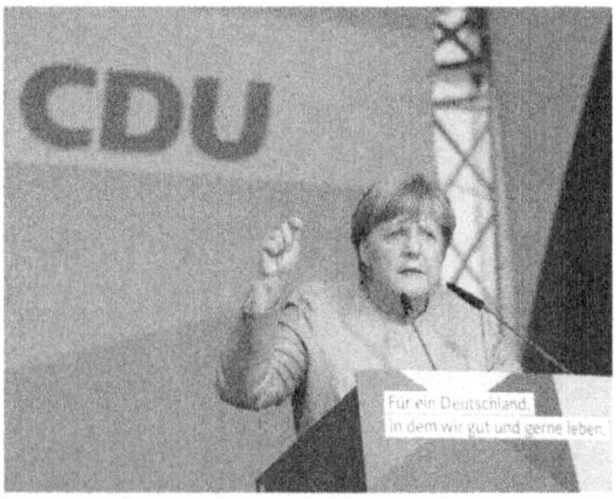
CDU
Für ein Deutschland,
in dem wir gut und gerne leben.

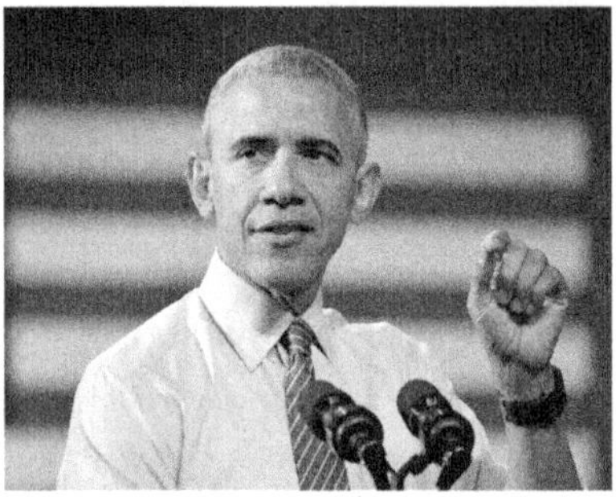

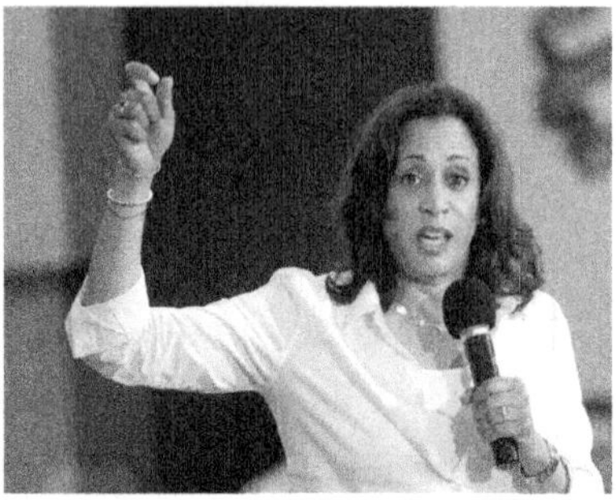

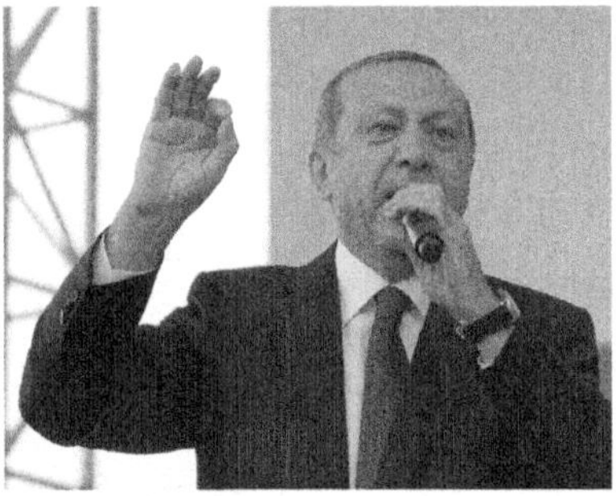

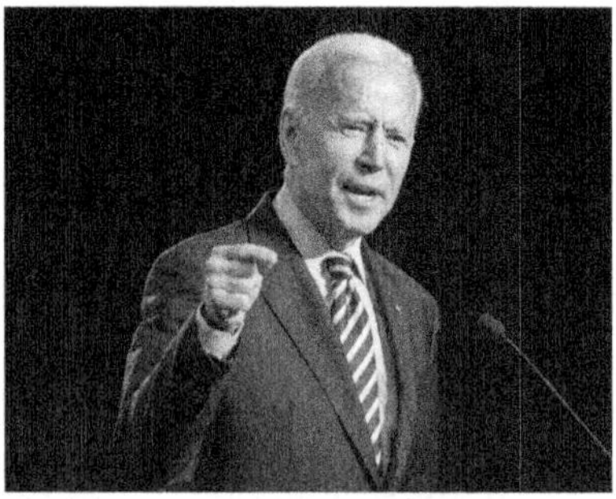

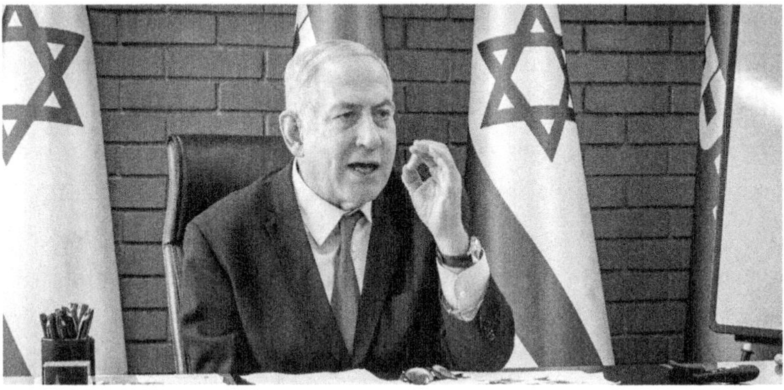

what to do with one's hands.

In this context Netanyahu – and many other public figures who have followed his example – has identified the critical importance of the bodily gestures with which a politician makes his point.

∎∎∎

Researchers at New York University Movement Lab decided to let computers and robots analyze the body language and charisma of leaders. Cameras were set up to monitor and characterize the hand movements of US President Obama and his rival in the 2012 elections, Mitt Romney. Every movement of the hand and the fingers was recorded and categorized. After dozens of speeches and interviews were filmed, it turned out that every leader has his or her own non-verbal signature; in other words, typical hand movements that repeat themselves throughout a speech. The computers were even able to identify what sort of speech was associated with some or other gesture. It was found that Romney, for example, nodded every time he was trying to persuade. (Netanyahu does the same. And when he talks about broad agreement with what he is saying, or logic that is widely shared, he spreads his arms as though for an embrace.) The most interesting gesture, identified by the computers as Obama's most frequent movement, was also one of the most three most frequent gestures in Romney's speeches, and Trump has also used it again and again. It has come to be known as the "politician's point," owing to its ubiquitous use among politicians throughout the world.

Netanyahu's version of it looks like this: the tips of the thumb and index finger are lightly touching, as though holding a tiny imaginary point between them, and creating a sort of circle. The hand is brought downwards as Netanyahu delivers his polished, firm punch line. The other three fingers might be curled and clenched or relaxed with space between them.

In the case of Obama – a gifted speaker in his own right – the computers found that he executed the gesture in the same way that one would press on a remote control to open a car or switch channels on TV. The thumb presses down on the button, as it were, while the harm drops downward for emphasis. Trump's signature "politician's point" is the OK sign, formed by connecting thethumbandindex fingerinto a circle. There are variations on this theme: some politicians prefer to turn the gesture towards the audience. Others turn it downward, towards the desk. Some touch two fingers to the thumb. Bill Clinton's signature gesture was the "Clinton thumb," whereby the thumb leans against the thumb-side portion of the index finger, which is part of a closed fist. Common to all of them is the touching of the thumb to the index finger in a gesture reflecting precision and emphasis. What is this movement supposed to mean? Why is it so popular? And why has it been adopted by Netanyahu and other world leaders?

The computers concluded that this gesture serves to create a sense of power. It is a softer and less threatening substitute for a fist, used by leaders to convey a firm, determined message. The "politician's point" is meant to project precision, persuasion, and absolute resoluteness. This determination aids in persuading the audience, especially at climactic moments of the speech and punch lines.

■■■

The non-verbal politician's point was part of a crisis that arose between Netanyahu and US President Obama. Following a tense telephone conversation between the two leaders, the White House released a photograph of Obama during the call.

Two non-verbal elements that converged in this single photo caused a furor in the Prime Minister's Office, where it was claimed that its publication humiliated Netanyahu. The first element was Obama's feet resting on the desk, a sign of disrespect. The second was his use of the politician's point, the symbol of adamant resolve. The release of the photo showing these two elements together, along with the backward-lean, expressing emotional distance, was regarded by Netanyahu as a deliberate snub and display of contempt by a figure of authority, a show of condescending distaste towards an underling, instead of a respectful conversation between two heads of state. The White House claimed that the selection of the photograph had been coincidental. It is difficult to believe that carelessness could have played a role, considering the extremely tense relations between the two leaders.

The politician's point aims to imbue spoken words with an authoritative air and extra emphasis, and as such it belongs to the family of validating gestures. These occupy an important place in body language, and they are the most common gestures in Netanyahu's non-verbal vocabulary. They are sometimes referred to as emphasizing gestures. They are different from illustrative gestures, which are demonstrated in pantomime-like fashion.

Netanyahu's most common gesture – his non-verbal signature – is his index finger pointed for emphasis. When he reaches the main point, he clenches his other fingers and bashes his index finger down like a nail into the podium, driving home his uncompromising message.

■■■

Secret #9: **Body Language Talks** Netanyahu's body language includes emphatic and resolute gestures, open posture, a purposeful gait, use of space, and control of his voice along with silences. By using non-verbal means, he adds weight and validity to his words and projects self-confidence and leadership. Along with what he says, the way in which he says it, and the way he walks, talks, and moves, are all part of his charisma.

10.
MEASURING VOTES IN CENTIMETERS
BIO-POLITICS

The Prime Minister's Office was holding a convention on economic development in the Arab sector, and Minister of Finance Yair Lapid approached the podium to speak. Behind the podium, ostensibly hidden from sight, a small plastic stool stood waiting to boost his height by a few extra centimeters. A camera happened to be located at just the right angle and Lapid became a laughing stock on the social networks.

Lapid is of average height, just 5'7". A leader of stature is expected to be taller.

In photographs of the quartet of leaders of the Blue and White party, Lapid stood next to Ashkenazi, and not between Gantz and Ya'alon, who are considerably taller than he is. Lapid once wrote that in Knesset photographs he likes to stand next to an MK who is shorter than he is.

Gantz is taller than Netanyahu. His advisors believed that his appearance – and especially his height advantage – is important and should be emphasized. One video showed the difficulty experienced by a tall leader facing microphones placed on the podium for speakers of average height. Adhering to his advisors' instructions, Gantz himself made mention in his speech of the fact that the microphones were too low and that this disturbed him. While obviously meant to be a spontaneous comment, it was clear that he was reading it from the teleprompter.

His campaign advisors worked assiduously behind the scenes to make sure that the media took proper notice of this issue. *Haaretz* obliged: "His impressive height – 1.95m (almost 6'4"), towering over regular politicians – is hard to ignore." All the papers cited his exact height. What they were reporting was, in fact, fake news.

■■■

Stand-up artist Hanoch Daum recounts once joking with Gantz about his height. Gantz told him that actually he is only 1.91m tall, but "for some reason the media gave him another 4 centimeters" or 1-1/2 inches.

The media didn't give him 4 extra centimeters; his own campaign staff did. The measurement 1.95m was emphasized in the party's ads, it appeared in videos, and was also repeated by his spokesmen in official announcements to the press and on the party's website.

Admittedly, there are bigger lies than this one in politics, but the seemingly unimportant discrepancy of four centimeters illustrates the way in which, by using non-verbal messages, photographs, and images, politicians try to create mental pictures that will exert subconscious and non-rational influences on voters' decisions.

■■■

An officer in Napoleon's army who once commented on the commander's short stature was told, "You're a head taller than me, but that head can come off." Height shouldn't be a consideration when it comes to leadership, so why did Gantz's advisors think that extra centimeters would bring extra mandates? Why the attempt to embellish his height? Why did Lapid use a stool? Can anyone doubt the greatness of Ben-Gurion, who was by all accounts short?

Statistics show that height is actually more important than ideology in determining the outcome of elections. In eighteen out of twenty-four presidential election campaigns in the US, the taller candidate won. Extra height confers extra value in many areas of life, from dating sites to economic markets. Research conducted at the University of Florida found that tall people earn more, and that most CEOs are taller than their subordinates. At Princeton it was found that tall people climb the corporate ladder faster, and a review of the 500 largest companies in the US, as ranked by *Forbes*, showed that the directors of more than half of them measured 1.80m (5'9") or more. Only three percent of them were less than 1.70m (about 5'6") tall. Netanyahu stands at 1.84m or just over 6 feet tall. This detail is important because of its halo effect.

The Halo Effect

The halo effect – a term borrowed from social psychology – refers to our tendency to allow our impression of a single characteristic of a person or entity to influence our overall judgment of that person or entity.

The halo effect is especially apparent when it comes to attractive external appearance. When someone is tall and attractive, we tend to view him or her as possessing a string of other positive qualities, too. When participants in a study were shown photographs of different people and asked to estimate their intelligence, those who were more attractive were also thought to be smarter. Aristotle summed it up when he said, "Personal beauty is a greater recommendation than any letter of reference."

Pleasing physical features are even more important as a political asset than height. Studies focusing on election victories by the more attractive candidates have proven this in almost every country and in every election campaign that has been analyzed.

Professor Yariv Tsfati of Haifa University conducted a comprehensive study that found that MKs who are considered attractive are interviewed by the Israeli press far more often than their "plain" colleagues. When American researchers repeated the experiments on Congressmen, they found that the US media, too, (TV more than radio,) prefer to listen to someone who looks good.

In his youth, Netanyahu was good looking. (There are those who consider him handsome even today.) When he first appeared on the public stage, German-born Israeli actress Hanna Maron declared, "This gorgeous man frightens me." Today, decades later, an astronomical budget and extraordinary efforts are invested in Netanyahu's hairstyle, make-up, and photographs. Looking good is a smart move.

■■■

The halo effect troubles a great many political scientists: is our judgment really so shallow? Biologists explain that from an evolutionary point of view, height and attractiveness brought better chances in finding a mate and in the battle of survival. With this in mind, the carryover into the political realm makes a certain amount of sense.

The University of Arizona researched election counties in which the health situation was poor, and found that in these areas particularly, candidates who were more handsome were more popular. Their study argued that voting for the more attractive candidate was the evolutionary product of the human desire to keep away from disease, mutations, and health risks.

Beauty, reflecting symmetry without anomaly, is an indication of good health and the absence of genetic defects. Height symbolizes strength and resilience. A deep voice hints to confidence. In pre-historic times, the tribe would choose someone strong as their leader, to hunt animals and bring food. Those who were healthy and strong were eligible mates who would pass their genes on to the next generation.

This subject has developed into a new area of research known as bio-politics: a merging of biology and politics. Studies in this area reveal how a candidate's biological attributes influence political prospects and voting trends. It is for this reason that Benny Gantz's height is important, that Lapid and Netanyahu's good looks are essential assets, and that Herzog's high-pitched voice is a disastrous liability. This is the biology of politics.

How Many Votes is a Voice Worth?

Researchers in the fields of politics and biology at Duke University and the University of Miami cooperated in a study that set out to discover how a winning leader sounds. They recorded women and men saying exactly the same sentence: "I call upon you to vote for me in November." Every recording was digitally manipulated to create versions in which the voice was pitched higher or lower. The results showed very clearly that both women and men said that they preferred voting for someone with a lower-pitched voice.

Faithful to their disciplines, the researchers argued that political behavior cannot be severed from the biological behavior of animals. Baboons express their virility in acoustic form; cats, songbirds, peacocks – the list of examples goes on and on, and man is part of this larger picture. Voice is a parameter for selection.

One study sought to award a numerical political value to the depth of a candidate's voice. A comparison was carried out between pairs of candidates competing for political positions in several different states and counties in the US. The comparison compared the pitch of their voices and their results in the elections. Their findings indicated that a deep voice increases a candidate's chance of election by 13%.

An article published by researchers at McMaster University in Canada used recordings of nine US presidents as the basis for a study about the voice qualities required of a leader. They manipulated the recordings and played them to the participants. What they discovered was that by making the voice an octave lower, they would raise the number of supporters. When the participants were told that a war was brewing and they had to choose a leader for the country, there was a clear preference for leaders with deep voices.

A deep voice is persuasive and conveys confidence. Male and female politicians alike dream about having a deep voice. Britain's Iron Lady, Margaret Thatcher, underwent voice training to achieve a lower pitch. So did Isaac Herzog, who wanted his voice to sound fuller, deeper, and more authoritative in dealing with Netanyahu.

Netanyahu has an ideal voice – a baritone that can, with a slight effort, become a deep bass. His voice is much deeper than the rivals he has faced over the years – Barak, Sharon, Livni, Yachimovich, Gabbay, Herzog and others. Lapid is his closest rival in this sphere, but even Lapid sometimes whispers, or gets caught up in the heat of a debate, causing his pitch to climb a few notches. Gantz was warned of this by his advisors; still, he forgot to take deep breaths in his first jittery public appearances, and his voice started climbing. Breathing is the key to voice control. Stress causes the voice to climb. In short, it helps a political candidate to be tall, attractive, and have a deep, authoritative voice.

Cognitive Miserliness

As we have seen, various indicators that have nothing to do with positions, policies or values influence election results: the candidate's height, voice, build, and more. The best predictor of all is his or her face. Even a quick glance is enough to help voters make up their minds.

Success has a face. It turns out that we choose leaders in much the same way that we browse through dating apps, with a 'yes' or 'no' forming in our minds in a fraction of a second. How long does it take us to identify the face of a good leader? The blink of an eye. We are favorably impressed by a square chin and firm, authoritative facial contours, and then we find logical justifications for our preferences.

The reasons for this go far back in time. The evolutionary process has taught us that the battle of survival requires that we save our strength and conserve efforts – including in the cognitive sphere. Psychologists describe the human mind as a "cognitive miser." People have no time or desire to invest the effort required to discern nuances and the fine print. Instead, we have become accustomed, since the dawn of evolution, to draw conclusions very quickly based on very limited information. Social psychologist Nalini Ambady speaks of "thin slice judgments." Her research shows how exposure to certain visual information for fractions of a second (i.e., in thin slices,) gives us what we need to draw generally sound (although sometimes mistaken) conclusions.

Malcolm Gladwell, in his book *Blink: The Power of Thinking Without Thinking*, explores how our subconscious brain scans features such as tone of voice, skin color, facial structure, accent, gait, or wardrobe choices almost instantaneously, and leads us to far-reaching conclusions, some of which we are not even aware of. In the Israeli context, Professor Ifat Maoz found that students' support for a peace agreement with the Palestinians depended on the face of the leader who would sign it.

A study conducted at a French university got children to participate in a game in which they were shown photographs of politicians unfamiliar to them and asked to choose a captain for their ship. The children's choices turned out to be an accurate indicator of which political candidates would later be elected to parliament. The study was published under the title, "Election predictions? Child's Play."

Professor Alexander Todorov of Princeton University discovered that exposure of less than a second to photographs of candidates was enough of a basis to predict the winner in around 70% of senatorial races in 2006. In his laboratory for face recognition, composites were created to depict different "ideal" faces of leaders. Todorov found that people preferred a dominant, well-defined and masculine face for a leader during war-time, and a softer, rounder, trustworthy-looking face for times of peace. There were also conspicuous differences between conservative and liberal voters. Conservatives preferred a "tougher" look, with a square chin and high forehead, while liberals tended towards more "feminine," rounded features, which are also regarded as inspiring trust.

Netanyahu is fortunate to have a facial structure that serves him well as a leader, especially for a country facing multiple, ongoing security threats.

A Real Man

"She's not up to the job; it's just too big for her," muttered the advisor, sitting in the back seat on the drive from the Knesset to Likud headquarters. "But how do we explain that to the public?" he asked, with the frustration that is familiar to any campaign manager at the slogan-hunting stage. "It's simply too big for her," he repeated again slowly, a smile starting to light up his face. "It's too big for her!" Netanyahu didn't like it. "It's great," the advisor insisted, and tried to get the Prime Minister's bodyguard on his side, with no success. When they reached the party headquarters and sat with the rest of the team, there were others who were hesitant. "It's too vulgar," someone commented. "More than anything else it'll make us look like chauvinists," was the ad manager's response. One or two of them deliberated a little longer; someone else chose not to comment. "Okay, we'll check it out," Netanyahu finally agreed. "Give the talk program a yes. Yossi will go."

Yossi Levy, spokesman for Likud chairman Netanyahu at the time, was sent to the studio try out the slogan as a trial balloon. On the air he debated with the manager of Tzipi Livni's campaign. The moment the campaign manager heard Levy argue, "It's too big for her," he objected: "That's chauvinistic. You're only saying that because she's a woman." "Absolutely not; that has nothing to do with it," Netanyahu's spokesman responded indignantly. "Even if it was a man with no experience, we would say that it's too big for him. It's got nothing to do with gender." Netanyahu watched the two of them on the screen, scrunched up his face at Livni's campaign manager, who had once been his own spokesman and was now doing all he could to obstruct his re-election, and resolved the question: "Go for it."

Within less than a week, dozens of billboards with the Likud symbol were spread on Israel's main highways, with a most unflattering shot of Livni, taken from an angle that made her look small, and the inscription in huge lettering: "It's too big for her." Obviously, the furious critics who denounced the campaign for its chauvinism only broadened its exposure and framed the media discourse around the question of Livni's suitability to make decisions and to answer the red phone.

Floating the gender issue serves the male rival even if he is accused of chauvinism. Livni's weakness was juxtaposed with the power of the man running against her. "A real man" is how Bibi's fans refer to him. From his point of view, this is worth emphasizing and exploiting.

■■■

Leadership = masculinity. This disturbing equation is the conclusion arising from the accumulated non-verbal elements that have been shown to be associated with leadership. We have discussed some of these above: voice, shoulders, height, taking up space – all these collectively sketch the ideal leader as a masculine figure.

The differences in body structure between the sexes also generally makes men physically stronger than women. Throughout the development of human culture this element undoubtedly played a significant role in the identity of the leader of a tribe, a village, and an army on the battlefield. Researchers of evolutionary psychology believe that the same considerations determine elections even in the modern age. A Prime Minister is perceived as an alpha male. There is a connection between physical power and political power. In the battle for survival, the strong win out.

In her book *Body Politics: Power, Sex, and Nonverbal Communication*, Nancy Henley shows how covert non-verbal communication in the social sphere – almost imperceptible signs, mostly in the realm of body language – serves and perpetuates male power. She points to the identification that is automatically made between feminine body language and submission, subservience, deprecation. The unstated, in-built contradiction, as it were, between femininity and leadership. The leader is necessarily the man.

The small, silent signs in human communication add up to a loud, constant message that reminds human beings again and again that the relations between men and women match the relations between those in power and those who are powerless. The body language inculcated by patriarchal culture causes women to smile more than men do, to take up less physical space, to perform less arm gestures, to sit in a more defensive and confining position, to speak less than their male colleagues in mixed meetings and classrooms (in contrast with the popular image of women as chatterboxes), and to be the last to offer their opinions and ideas. Men speak first. A man stands at the center and walks in the middle, in the lead; a woman walks at the side and slightly behind. In addition, a woman's personal space – smaller to start off with – is more often invaded against her will in the form of affectionate gestures that display male dominance. A man generally gives himself broader license to touch a woman than the other way around. The body tells a political story in which men have far more power than women. Body language serves male supremacy.

Physical power is seemingly less important than it was in the past. In our times greater importance is attached to economic power (women earn less), knowledge (women were long denied equal opportunities in education), or political power (women's suffrage, with the right to vote and to stand as candidates, was a hard-fought battle). In most places it is still men who hold the power. The correlation of all the reasons discussed above preserves masculinity as an inherent element in the perception of leadership, influencing voters even today.

All roads lead to the man. In Israel, language is also part of the same trend: in Hebrew, signs and official forms are formulated in the masculine. The culture points in that direction, as does language, the environment, evolution, anatomy, history, politics, statistics, advertisements, tradition, the militarism of Israeli society, and the country's security agenda.

Males are the majority in the army, in politics, in business, and also on screen. This creates a public consciousness. They are also more visible in reality. One example of a non-verbal environmental message is the pedestrian traffic light, which shows a male figure.

(Notably, the only road sign that makes room for a female figure is the sign for a pedestrian crossing, which shows a woman holding onto the hand of a little girl.)

Men are leaders of the pack - men who look like men, behave like men, talk like men, and make decisions like men. Even today, this is the covert criterion for getting votes, and Netanyahu's appearance and image are assets in this regard.

In the 2019 elections, Minister of Culture and Sport Miri Regev was not invited to appear in a Likud campaign photo even though she placed higher on the party list than those who were invited. In a private conversation Regev revealed the excuses Netanyahu had offered when she protested. He claimed that in-depth surveys had shown that the public at large tended to vote for Ashkenazi males and it was for this reason that she, as a Mizrahi woman, had not appeared in the photo.

■■■

In the 2021 elections, at the age of seventy-two, suffering from back pains and various health issues requiring increasing medical treatments, Netanyahu managed to conceal all of this and still maintain his image as Mr. Security. Well aware of the elements of the formula that occupies the public consciousness (male-strong-healthy-security), he had his publicity photos designed accordingly. Although he has put on a fair amount of weight over the years, he hides this fact behind his desk and in well-cut suits, taking care that photographs include the top half of his body and at an angle that doesn't reveal his double chin or a side view of his girth. He is shown wearing a black wind jacket, rather than in a suit and tie, to make him look younger. He cannot allow himself to look weak.

■■■

Along with emphasis on the leader's masculine qualities, the feminine weaknesses of the other side need to be highlighted.

Following an interview with former Chief of Staff Moshe ("Bogie") Ya'alon broadcast on Army Radio, the Likud issued the following response: "Bogie Ya'alon, who has exchanged a series of parties and positions, is the feminine version of Tzipi Livni." Fickleness is a misogynic stereotype attributed to women.

Benny Gantz was labeled with a different feminine stereotype: mental instability. The messages conveyed by Likud ministers and the videos released in the last two weeks of the 2019 campaign focused on insinuations and allegations that included the expressions "half-baked" and "gone off the rails." One official Likud response stated explicitly, "Gantz is paranoid and unstable." For one of the campaign videos casting Gantz in a negative light, Netanyahu's campaign managers used music from the movie *Psycho*. Other videos focused on Gantz's supposedly glazed eyes.

The pitting of masculine against feminine is a phenomenon that crosses cultural boundaries. Some pundits pointed out the unmistakable similarity between Trump's campaign against Clinton (accusing her of being not in her right mind, physically weak, and having the Russians hack her emails), and Netanyahu's campaign against Gantz (highlighting the hacking of his phone by the Iranians, and labelling him as not mentally fit). One of Netanyahu's tweets read, "It's too big for him."

■■■

Netanyahu's "It's too big for her" campaign against Livni in 2009 was labelled by Livni's party as "swinish chauvinism." Livni maintains that Netanyahu was not the only Israeli politician who tried to prove his masculinity by highlighting her feminine "weakness." Avi Gabbay, chairman of the Labor party, announced the end of the Zionist Union partnership between his party and Livni's on live TV with no advance warning, thereby publicly humiliating her. Livni was livid, and referred to his conduct as an attempt to look like a "real man" at her expense.

In a sort of aside, during the buildup to elections, Livni commented about Netanyahu that he was "impotent; a failure when it comes to performance." When a woman claims that the Prime Minister is unfit for his job because he is "impotent," she is in fact saying that he lacks the virility needed to lead, and thereby reinforces the unspoken and largely subconscious convention that a Prime Minister has to be a man. Someone who is impotent can't be the alpha male of the tribe; he won't survive the processes of natural selection and won't be able to produce healthy, strong progeny. Surely, the message suggests, now isn't a good time to elect an impotent Prime Minister as the leader of our tribe.

Politics is still controlled by men whose masculinity is evident. Predatory men. President Bush, Sr. was accused of sexual harassment by seven women. One would not be sued for slander for calling Trump a serial philanderer who harassed a number of women. Netanyahu himself was unfaithful to each of his three wives. And let's not forget Putin, who was filmed shirtless on horseback, setting off on a hunt. He has also been photographed with tigers, or practicing judo.

Netanyahu has established his ownership of the role of Prime Minister as a predatory male.

When Bibi Took a Bullet

"I have to be there," Yoni Netanyahu insisted. "I have more experience than you do; they need me there." "But they're my soldiers," replied Bibi, not giving an inch. The two brothers were arguing in the hangar for airplanes awaiting repairs, at the far end of the terminal at Ben Gurion Airport; brother vs. brother; officer vs. officer. Both full of adrenaline, both fired up for battle.

"I'm more senior," Lieut.-Col. Netanyahu pointed out to his brother, a first lieutenant. "No way," Bibi insisted, "they're my soldiers." "Then we'll both go." "And if something happens? Who will be with Mom and Dad?" Bibi asked. The response he got from Yoni is not fit for print. The bothers had no choice but to approach Ehud Barak, who was leading the operation, to decide the matter. "Bibi will get on the plane. Yoni stays at the terminal," Barak decreed. And, seeing that Yoni was about to argue, he added, "It's final."

Bibi quickly put on the white overalls so he could hurry back to join the other commandos, not looking back at his brother. A moment later the group climbed aboard the open vehicle that would drive them, disguised as technicians, to the Sabena plane that had been hijacked by terrorists. According to intelligence information, explosives had already been placed at various points in the plane, ready to blow it up together with the hostages.

A representative of the Red Cross approached the vehicle. "Hide your weapons," Barak instructed the soldiers. Netanyahu pushed the small pistol he was holding to his back, inserting it under his belt. The Red Cross functionary went from one to the next, patting their technician tags and their legs to check that they weren't armed. When he reached Bibi, his hands felt something protruding at the back. "What is this?" he asked in English. The entire operation could have failed because of Bibi's pistol, which almost gave the ruse away. But Bibi and Barak improvised answers that satisfied the Swiss representative. The group of technicians received his approval to approach the hijacked plane.

Bibi and his team, standing on the left wing of the plane, were waiting as agreed for Barak's whistle – their cue to break in and to rescue the hostages. Suddenly one of Bibi's soldiers whispered to him,

"Sir, I need to go to the toilet." "Now?" Bibi asked, dumbfounded. "Yes, I just flew here, and the toilets on the plane were occupied all the way; I can't hold on any more." "Bladder or bowel?" Netanyahu asked his subordinate. "Bowel," came the reply. "Wait here." Bibi slid carefully off the wing and passed under the plane's belly to where Barak was stationed. He explained the urgent situation and asked to delay the whistle for a moment. "Toilet?!" Barak exclaimed. "Bladder or bowel?" he asked his subordinate. "Bowel," Netanyahu replied.

The urgent call of nature was answered under the plane, and the soldier climbed back onto the wing behind Netanyahu. A few seconds later, Barak blew his whistle. It took Netanyahu's team a few seconds to realize that the operation had begun, because the whistle had not been very loud, but as soon as the first shots were fired, they pushed open the door of the plan and burst in. The first thing they encountered was the body of a female hostage. Bibi charged forward along the aisle between the seats.

"Here's the terrorist; here's the terrorist!" the passengers shouted, pointed to a red-headed woman who was trying to pass herself off as a regular passenger, sitting among the hostages. First Lieutenant Netanyahu ran towards her and grabbed her hair. The wig came off in his hand. He lunged again, grabbed her real hair, held tight and shouted in English, "Where are the bombs? Where are the bombs?" while at the same time checking that she was not armed. Behind him, Marco, another soldier in the unit, came running up the aisle, shouting, "Bibi, let me!" He quickly struck the terrorist with the grip of the gun, to make her talk. The gun went off. "I felt acute pain in my arm," Bibi recounted. "Then they took me off the plan and lay me on the terminal floor."

A red stain spread slowly on the white overall. Thus ended the Sabena operation, from the perspective of the future Prime Minister.

Lying under the plane, slightly dazed, Netanyahu saw a figure running towards him in a panic. It was Yoni, rushing over, aghast.

The fright on the face of the older brother dissipated when he saw the crimson sleeve and understood immediately that it was a light wound. Smilingly, he said, "I told you I should have gone!"

■■■

"The Likud is family …" Gideon Sa'ar tried to talk, but was interrupted by catcalls. "The Likud is family …" he tried again. Someone in the audience, outraged by Sa'ar's challenge to Netanyahu for the party chairmanship, yelled, "And one doesn't betray family!"

"Keep it all in the family. Even in politics." That's the message cognitive linguist and philosopher George Lakoff has for politicians around the world who seek to influence the masses. Lakoff is known mainly for his innovative thesis that people's thinking and conduct are significantly influenced by conceptual metaphors. His study of metaphors led him to conclude that a person perceives the state in terms of the primal worlds of the body and the family, and he chooses his leaders accordingly.

The state is a body. The heart, if we are speaking of Israel, is Jerusalem. The economy is the body's state of health; the brain is represented by the heads of state and their advisors. Society is perceived as a human body, with the Prime Minister at the head.

At a different level of consciousness, the state is a family, as reflected in many commonly used metaphors. Israel is part of the "family of nations," there are "founding fathers," soldiers are "our sons," and citizens often call each other "bro." There are "neighboring countries," and the main aim is to "protect our home."

Why is this important? Because, according to Lakoff, as well as a long list of psychologists, Freudians, and adherents of Embodied Cognition theory, the real (albeit covert) dilemma entailed in voting is that one has to choose between the father figure or the mother figure.

This political question relates to the nature of the family in which the voter grew up. It also speaks to the extent to which his background is religious or traditional, since even higher than the head of the family or the Prime Minister we find the representation of the heavenly Parent. Indeed, analyzing voting patterns in the US, Lakoff concluded that the difference between fundamentalist Christianity and progressive Christianity boils down to the central metaphor for God: a disciplinary parent (heavenly reward, punishment for sinning) or a nurturing one (unconditional love, making room for the individual, empathy). This, to his view, explains why fundamentalist Christians tend towards the political Right. The same might be said with regard to the Israeli context.

According to the theory of embodied cognition, then, the state is unconsciously perceived by the voter as a sort of family, and a citizen votes in accordance with the sort of home and family that raised him. Someone who grew up in a traditional environment with a rigid hierarchy, votes for the "authoritative father" model. A voter who grew up in a liberal environment that glorifies individual rights and freedoms will prefer the "nurturing mother" model. In other words, Lakoff argues that the conservative Right votes for a leader and party which, in its eyes, represent the father figure, while the liberal Left votes for a leader and party that represent, for them, the mother figure.

As a symbol of the "Mother of the West" we might propose Angela Merkel, with Putin as the paternal counterpart. Hillary vs. Trump; Theresa May vs. Boris Johnson; Livni-Herzog-Yachimovich vs. Netanyahu. Mother vs. Father.

On his visits to the Machane Yehuda fresh produce market in the capital, Netanyahu receives a royal welcome. Bibi the King; only Bibi. The reason for the profound identification that his followers feel with him goes back to early biological and tribal roots. Bibi is the head. He is the father. There is none like him; no one can take his place. The vote comes from a primal place, from somewhere inside the body, as it were. In the political and limbic systems alike, logic plays a marginal role.

"It's all in the family" is Lakoff's way of explaining the support for Trump and for Netanyahu. The voters are the children. They always will be. There's no need for rational justification. Biology precedes politics. Like a mother who will give up her life to protect her offspring; like a son who will fight to the death for his father. Bibi is the father.

I was a Little Boy, and Hungry

There was only one speech that Bibi has ever delivered in which he broke into tears. It was during the eulogy he delivered for his father, when he read out, in a trembling, choked voice the following passage, recalling his earliest childhood memory:

> "The three of us kids were with you in the hotel. A heavy snowstorm was going on outside; I was a little boy. A little boy who was hungry. You said to Mom, 'I'm not going to let the kid go to bed hungry,' and you went out into the blizzard. A while later you came back, drenched and frozen to the bone, holding a tray of warm food that you had brought for me, your little boy. But there were much greater storms - not just in our private lives, but in our national life …
>
> "There were terrible storms that overtook the Jewish People over the 102 years that you lived – and you, Dad, never once hesitated to go out into the storm and to contribute

to the defense of our nation, with your profound thinking and incisive writing. Two years ago, on your 100th birthday, I had the rare privilege that few sons enjoy of telling you, Dad, while you were still alive, how much I love you. How much I admire you."

■■■

Netanyahu is the father of the family that is gathered together in the Jewish villa in the jungle. He speaks a fluent and eloquent English to the terrorist animals of prey; he is strong, decisive, and masculine; and has what it takes to save us from the metaphoric or real holocaust that hovers over Jerusalem, which is "the heart of all of us." There are those who, molded by a compassionate mother, vote with the hope for goodness and justice. Others, with an eye on looming threats and brewing trouble, feel safer relying on an all-powerful father.

■■■

Secret #10: **Bio-Politics Wins Out** Biological, cognitive and evolutionary mechanisms that exert subconscious influences on the public's vote, point to Netanyahu - his height, his appearance, his voice, his facial contours. That's what a leader looks like. An alpha male. A man ready to take on the world. The father of the nation.

THE LAST SECRET

Israel's finest public diplomacy machine comes with very specific user instructions. As one would expect from high-quality public relations, the instructions are concise and clear. A classified document that has never yet been published sets out the essence of Netanyahu's entire diplomatic strategy. This is the outline that he created for himself:

Micro:

1. Present Israel's positions in a positive light
2. Note violations of agreement, crimes, and hostility on the part of the Arabs, without cutting off dialogue
3. Disprove the arguments of the other side, the enemy, and the hostile media, and respond to libels

Macro:

1. Create support and positive interest towards Israel

"All on one page," he instructed his secretary. When he received the printed page he looked proudly at the four-point formula he had created, including the juxtaposition of the enemy and the media, and the highlighting of the positive on our side and the negative on theirs. After further thought he picked up his pen and added a handwritten reminder to himself in the margin, as an addendum to presenting Israel's positions in a positive light, "Responses to events," lest he forget that current events also deserve comment. Netanyahu doesn't shoot from the hip. He doesn't improvise. When he makes an appearance, it is guided by strategy and tactics. Micro and macro. The brief, clear formula page is in front of him, dictating what he should say. He has everything planned in advanced. Systematic, organized.

When Netanyahu Fell

The echoes of the fireworks died down. It was late at night; Netanyahu sat in the living room in his official residence, watching the screen, making no effort to hide his disappointment at the missed opportunity. "It should have been different," he banged angrily on the table as he watched himself speaking at the torch-lighting ceremony marking Israel's 70th Independence Day. More effort had been invested in this speech than in any other he had given in his life, and he was extremely upset that his appearance had not made the desired impression. "Okay, I heard you already," muttered someone standing nearby, trying to convey that he was being too hard on himself.

Learning lessons from past speeches and appearances is a habit that Netanyahu adopted early on. Rolando Eisen, his boss at the Rim furniture company in Boston during the 70s, told *Time* magazine, "His first appearances on television weren't good. Bibi used to watch the recordings over and over again in order to improve."

In this instance, there was no second chance. His speech at the torch-lighting ceremony, on live TV and watched by the entire country, had been preceded by a well-publicized crisis vis-à-vis Chairman of the Knesset Edelstein, who had threatened to boycott the event if Netanyahu spoke there, in contravention of protocol. Netanyahu insisted on speaking, and eventually a compromise was hammered out whereby the speech was defined as mere greetings, and limited to five minutes. In actuality, it lasted three times that long. One of the reasons for this was over-excitement. Netanyahu was so hyped about the event that he spoke too slowly and didn't keep to the time that he had set for himself. Appearing before the Israeli public on this occasion seemed to him like the pinnacle of his life's achievements. When he was invited to the podium he walked slowly, feeling the entire weight of history on his shoulders. When he started speaking, his words, too, came slowly. He kept his eyes almost glued to his notes, lest he mix up the words he had worked on so hard, and those close to him noted that his voice trembled slightly. It took him two or three minutes to warm up and to overcome the tension, but even after he started feeling more comfortable, he still had trouble. He was speaking at a podium that had been placed a great distance from the audience, and the lighting was blinding. He couldn't see the cameras or the eyes of the people around him, and he wasn't at his best.

"It's too pompous," he raged at himself as he watched the speech, sensing that the heavy ceremonial pathos that he had worked on for weeks hadn't sat well with the atmosphere of celebration and fireworks. "I should have told a different story," he mumbled in frustration when he saw how an experience he had recounted (watching a group of tourists react with wonder upon seeing the Menorah [candelabrum] from the Temple carved into the Arch of Titus) had not moved the audience. The media, as usual, weren't complimentary, and the headline focused on the fact that the Prime Minister had exceeded his time allotment.

Netanyahu is a professional, and therefore he reaps great success. But his greatest success lies in his failures – or, more precisely, his ability to learn from them and emerge stronger and better.

■■■

One sunny day, the Prime Minister visited a Navy base. After a tour of one of the large missile boats and a submarine, Netanyahu, wearing a military lifejacket, climbed down the rope ladder to the small dinghy that would carry him back to shore. As he transitioned from one vessel to the other, his elegant black leather shoe missed its footing on the ladder and he started to fall. The alertness and quick response of his bodyguard saved him from falling into the water. The bodyguard grabbed his back, and the two of them somehow made a muddled landing in the rubber dinghy. For a moment the fall had looked dangerous, (not to mention the media fallout that would have accompanied a photograph of Netanyahu falling into the sea in his suit,) but he got up, stood up straight, and continued with the tour.

This wasn't the first time he had experienced such a fall. As a soldier, serving in the General Staff Reconnaissance Unit in the 70s, he had fallen from a rubber dinghy into the waters of the Suez Canal with all his heavy equipment on him. Another soldier managed with great difficulty to pull him to safety, dragging Netanyahu by his hair.

Netanyahu's approach to life mirrors his dealing with these episodes. He falls and gets up again. He has experienced tremendous failures and made comebacks. He looks his failures in the eye, scrutinizes his appearances for mistakes and room for improvement, analyzes, learns lessons, and heads back to the microphones.

The man prepared himself for years to become Prime Minister. Classified documents dating back to the 80s show slogans that he formulated while serving in New York: "For the sake of our children's security – a strong leader." Netanyahu is continually learning and constantly preparing; even after decades in politics he devotes considerable time and effort to rehearsing, polishing his speeches and improving his appearances in front of audiences and cameras. He views the media and politics as a profession, and uses established methods to create influence.

His spine is firm but flexible. He plucks up the courage to change his style of media engagement in accordance with the needs of the hour and technological and political developments, always remaining attentive to public opinion. Every fall or crisis is, for him, an opportunity to relaunch. Sometime he even generates the crisis deliberately, but he has weathered many genuine storms.

In contrast to his popular image as a "magician" or "invincible," he has in fact suffered significant losses and painful falls.

In 1996, he achieved the impossible and won the election, beating Peres by a razor thin margin of a few thousand votes. In 1999, after a turbulent term in office characterized by mistakes and conflicts, he lost badly to Ehud Barak, who received 56% of the vote. The Likud crashed. He erred when he refused to take on leadership of the country in 2001 without the Knesset dispersing, thereby losing an opportunity to return to the Prime Minister's Office. In 2002, he lost the Likud primaries to Arik Sharon, and failed in his late attempt to stop Sharon from carrying out the Disengagement in 2005. In 2006, he brought the Likud to a nadir of twelve seats, and in 2009 received one seat less than Tzipi Livni and her Kadima party. In 2019, the Likud under his leadership was on par with Blue and White, headed by Gantz, and he became the first Prime Minister in Israel's history to fail in his attempt to form a government through coalition negotiations. Despite the good showing in the elections, he was forced to lead the country to another set of elections. Which brought another failure. The magic never dissipated, because there was never any magic. His method has been consistent all along. It hasn't always been successful, but he has always kept trying – even when all seemed lost.

The Image is Coming Apart

Netanyahu is a man of opposites. He belongs to the upper class, but speaks in the name of the masses; an outsider who acts from the heart of the establishment, an underdog who holds great power. He is greatly admired, but alone. A Mr. Security who feels persecuted. A proud Jew who fears annihilation. A secular Ashkenazi from Rehavia who fights against the elites. Faithful to history while distorting reality. A leader of the Right who has voiced and implemented policy of Left. A man who hates the media and is enslaved to it, controls it and is controlled by it, hounds it and is hounded by it. He detests the Left, yet begs its representatives to join his government. He lacks close friends, but has the people on his side. He saves his people, sowing division and generating conflict. He is strong and fearless, weak and picked-on.

The image he has built up is starting to crack under the pressure of these disparities and seemingly impossible contrasts. He has described chiefs of staff with whom he had together protected Israel's security as security threats; he has accused people whom he appointed and who decided to indict him as aiding and abetting a coup; he has presented the media as the enemy while striking deals with them; he has called the leftists traitors and then tried to woo them into his government. It's all starting to come apart. One spin follows another. The warning of impending disaster has become routine. The public has become accustomed to it, and tired of it.

As the façade starts to crack, the secrets that Netanyahu didn't want us to see are starting to show themselves. From investigations to exhaustion. He falls and gets up again, crashes and rises, fails and returns. He knows no rest; every crisis is an opportunity, and every end is a beginning. He works hard, and isn't ready to stop.

The gap between the image and reality is widening. The façade isn't a good fit for the real world any more. Perhaps, as it goes with heroes, it's a matter of hubris. Some of his confidants say that with age he has softened. One sees this in discussions behind closed doors, but not on the screen.

He never gives up. Every time he loses, falls, fails, he recovers, rises, survives. He isn't a magician, he's a professional. He works on every word and every gesture, fully in touch with the deeper currents running through Israeli society. He doesn't go easy on himself. He believes that his gift of the gab will get him through this time too. Letting go isn't an option.

The harder falls are leaving longer-lasting scars and bruises. One sees that it's getting difficult for him. It's difficult to watch, too. But he's still getting up, falling, still going. The ravages of time are starting to show on the façade. Still, he has to keep going, carrying all of history on his back, the entire nation on his shoulders. Will this journey have a happy ending? Will history smile on him? He is convinced that it depends on himself alone – but he, too, knows that his power comes from the public that stands by, watching him in awe.

His former friend, Attorney General Avichai Mandenblit, makes another dent in Netanyahu's façade by issuing a severe indictment. The schism amongst the nation is also widening. Netanyahu truly believes that he is irreplaceable, and that he has to continue. He owes it to himself and to the nation. He is ready to give up everything for it. He papers over the crack, has another round of makeup applied, and sets off again. The cameras are rolling.

His hat holds no rabbits. He works hard, planning and calculating every move, and adjusting to reality. He moves forward, slips down, catches himself, and then sets his sights on a new horizon.

He is suspended between heaven and earth by a thin wire of support, his loyalists on one side, his detractors on the other. All gazing at up at him, hoping.

It's a matter of continuing onward or falling. There's no other option. He concentrates, formulates another sentence, plans another move. Stubbornly he presses on, ready to meet the next challenge. The sun is setting, the shadows are lengthening, but Netanyahu is still full of confidence, sure of himself and sure that the nation is with him. He is the nation. There are more threats to be dealt with, more miles to conquer. He is certain that he can. Who, if not himself? He falls, tumbles, immediately steadies himself, grasping at the words that will help him out of the crevice. He fights with the sheer force of his rhetoric for his place in the book of chronicles. He stays true to his path. He will continue to the end, whatever the end may bring. He is systematic, professional, a believer. He is prudent and prepared. Ultimately, the real secret is that there are no secrets at all.

ACKNOWLEDGEMENTS

My thanks and appreciation to the editor-in-chief of non-fiction books at Kinneret Zmora Dvir Publishing House, Shmuel Rosner, and the publication directors. To editor Rami Rutholz for his speedy, dedicated and professional work. To Orna Bachar, Yael Naamani, Sarit Rosenberg, Imri Zertal, Efrat Gever, Ravit Ben-Ari and Rama Ashuah.

A great thank you to those who made the book accessible to the English-speaking public: Kaeren Fish, who approached the translation with dedication and professionalism, and the eBook-Pro team headed by Benny Carmi and including Kim Ben-Porat, Amitay Rotman, Nave Carmi and Sara Davis

I owe a great debt of gratitude to Israel State Archives - an invaluable resource that I recommend warmly to the public at large. Special thanks to Li-Or Squire and Itamar Yoeli. The Archive is a model of innovation and efficiency in the public sector, and the documents it holds opened a new window for me onto Netanyahu's world.

Thanks to the Government Press Office and its director, Nitzan Chen, under whose directorship the GPO has become one of the most efficient and best evolving bodies in the sphere of media and press in Israel.

My grateful appreciation to the many friends who read the manuscript and offered comments.

Thanks to all those who cannot be named here, who shared with me goings-on in the Prime Minister's Office.

Thank you to all of my family for their listening, their advice, and their restraint. To my mother, my sister, my brother.

Special, warmest thanks to my father, Rabbi Prof. Yigal Shafran. For everything.

The book is dedicated with boundless love to my daughters, Shaharit, Shaked, and Ruth.

Printed in Great Britain
by Amazon

84519631R00183